BAPTISTS IN EARLY NORTH AMERICA SERIES

Volume V

General Editor

William H. Brackney

Welsh Neck, South Carolina

BAPTISTS IN EARLY NORTH AMERICA SERIES

General Editor

William H. Brackney

Volume I
SWANSEA, MASSACHUSETTS
Ed. William H. Brackney with Charles K. Hartman

Volume II
FIRST BAPTIST, PROVIDENCE
Ed. J. Stanley Lemons

Volume III
NEWPORT, RHODE ISLAND, SEVENTH DAY BAPTISTS
Ed. Janet Thorngate

Volume IV
FIRST BAPTIST CHURCH, BOSTON, MASSACHUSETTS
Ed. Thomas McKibbens

BAPTISTS IN EARLY NORTH AMERICA SERIES

Volume V

General Editor

William H. Brackney

Welsh Neck, South Carolina

John Barrington ed.

MERCER UNIVERSITY PRESS | MACON, GEORGIA
WITH THE WILLIAM CAREY CENTRE AT CAREY THEOLOGICAL COLLEGE
2018

MUP/ H956

© 2019 by Mercer University Press
Published by Mercer University Press
1501 Mercer University Drive
Macon, Georgia 31207
All rights reserved

9 8 7 6 5 4 3 2 1

Books published by Mercer University Press are printed on acid-free paper
that meets the requirements of the American National Standard for
Information Sciences—Permanence of Paper for Printed Library Materials.

Printed and bound in the United States.

ISBN   978-0-88146-677-5

Cataloging-in-Publication Data is available from the Library of Congress

Contents

PREFACE TO VOLUME V

The Baptist experience in early North America displays rich ethnic diversity. Among those groups to join the Baptist stream in the colonial period were English, Scottish, Welsh, and Germans. Of these four, the Welsh formed congregations eventually in New England, the Middle Colonies, and the South. The two leading congregations that spread their influence broadly were the Welsh Tract in Delaware (1703) and the Welsh Neck Baptist Church in South Carolina (1738). The latter is derived from the former.

In this fifth volume in the *Baptists in Early North America Series*, following First Baptist Swansea, Massachusetts, First Baptist, Providence, Rhode Island, the Newport, Rhode Island Seventh Day Baptists, and First Baptist, Boston, Massachusetts, we present the Welsh Neck Baptist Church in South Carolina, the first southern congregation to appear in the Series.

The editor and historical analyst of this volume is John P. T. Barrington of Greer, South Carolina. Dr. Barrington is an accomplished American historian in the Department of History at Furman University in Greenville, South Carolina, where he was chair of the Department from 2008-2015. He is eminently qualified to bring forth this volume, having received degrees from St. John's College, Oxford University (B.A.), and the College of William and Mary (Ph.D.). He has previously taught at Skidmore College, the College of William and Mary, and since 1996, Furman University. The author of numerous papers and articles as a specialist in colonial America and the 18th century British Empire, Prof. Barrington has received a Mellon Foundation Grant and recognition as a Commonwealth Fellow in the Virginia Council of Higher Education.

Dr. Barrington has meticulously researched the original records of the congregation from 1738-1798, plus the papers of Edmund Botsford and related archival materials. In this volume, the reader will be introduced to an unusual congregation that enjoyed the ministry of nationally-reputed Baptist ministers like Elhanan Winchester, Evan Pugh, and Edmund Botsford, as well as the influence of the pre-eminent Baptist clergyman of the state, Richard Furman. There are important religious and cultural issues contained in the record, including the interplay of a black slave section of the congregation swept in by the forces of revivalism, then integrated within the white congregation, the travail of a church during the Revolution, the role of women, and issues of theology such as a universalist tendency becoming evident during the pastorate of Elhanan Winchester. Dr. Barrington quite adeptly analyzes the Baptist and larger theological nuances, African religious backgrounds, and the social context of the region. For those tracing the Welsh pilgrimage in America, this volume details the church's genetic origin in the Rhydwilym Church in Llandysilio, Carmarthenshire, Wales, through emigration to the Welsh Tract in Delaware, its separate intergenerational establishment as a mission of the Church in Delaware to Carolina, and its chain of Welsh descendent pastors.

Included in the volume are a wealth of historical notes, a comprehensive bibliography, and an exhaustive index, of inestimable value to genealogists.

We are appreciative to the Special Collections and Archives Department of James B. Duke Library of Furman University for preserving this piece of religious Americana, and to our distinguished historian and editor, Dr. John Barrington.

We are profoundly grateful for the participation and funding of the William Carey Centre at Carey Theological College in Vancouver, British Columbia, in publishing this volume. President Colin Godwin and the Board of Administration have led in establishing Carey as a premier multicultural theological school in the Baptist tradition. It is indeed fitting that they identify with the narrative of the Welsh Neck, South Carolina, Church as the oldest multi-ethnic, multi-racial Baptist congregation in colonial North America.

The Editors

ACKNOWLEDGMENTS

This project would have been impossible without the highly capable assistance of Su Min (Jasmine) Hwang, an undergraduate History Major at Furman University. Jasmine carefully transcribed the Welsh Neck Church Book and identified entries that related to African American members of the church. Her work on this document was efficient and painstaking, and it provided me with an important and reliable starting point for exploring the eighteenth-century history of Welsh Neck. Both Jasmine and I owe thanks to the Waco and Elaine Childers Fund, which provided Jasmine with the resources that enabled her to spend a summer working on this project.

My profound thanks are also due to the staff in Special Collections and Archives at Furman University's James B. Duke Library. Jeffrey Makala and Julia Cowart were always eager to make materials available and to suggest relevant supporting documents. I appreciate their patience with my sometimes erratic schedule. I would also like to acknowledge the work of a past Special Collections Librarian, Glen Clayton, who spent years compiling, organizing, and safeguarding the South Carolina Baptist Historical Collection at Furman – an extraordinarily rich collection, full of potential for many further projects. Dr. Clayton's notes on the Botsford papers, along with his typed transcriptions of one Botsford-Furman letter and of Botsford's "On Slavery," made my work a great deal easier.

I am particularly grateful to Dr. William Brackney, the editor of this series, for giving me the chance to undertake this project, and for offering speedy, helpful, and encouraging guidance throughout. His patience with my sporadic progress was remarkable and is deeply appreciated.

Last, but not least, I would like to thank my wife, Anne, whose experience in historical editing made her a valuable resource on many occasions, and whose willingness to listen to my discussions of Welsh Neck minutiae went beyond the call of duty.

Part I

The History of the Welsh Neck Church, 1738-1798

The Welsh Neck Church Book

The document that provides the central focus for this volume is the Welsh Neck Church Book, the most important record left by one of the most influential Baptist Churches in eighteenth-century South Carolina. The part of the Church Book included here relates to the years 1738-1798, when the church was located at Welsh Neck, on the eastern side of the Great Pee Dee River, not quite twenty miles south of the North Carolina border. The original Church Book from this period has not survived; fortunately, its contents were transcribed at some point after the congregation moved across the river to Society Hill at the start of the nineteenth century. At the time of this transcription, the original Church Book had already deteriorated: records of the church's first two decades (1738-1758) were largely unrecoverable, and the detailed record starts in 1759. The transcriber provided useful notes about changes in handwriting, as well as occasional commentary on the events recorded, but the majority of the transcription is simply a reproduction of what could still be deciphered from the original documents.

The Church Book records the appointment (or "calling") and the departure of ministers, decisions about doctrine and practice, including two full covenants (drawn up in 1760 and 1785), as well as important details about church members. Baptisms and the receptions of members from other churches, along with deaths, "dismissions," suspensions, and excommunications constitute the majority of the entries.[1] There are also lists of church members at various points in the church's history: at its founding in 1738; in 1759, when the Rev. Nicholas Bedgegood became pastor; and at various points in the 1770s, during the momentous pastorate of the Rev. Elhanan Winchester. The original Church Book was generally kept by the minister. The energy and detail of the record varies over time, as does the content: the Rev. Edmund Botsford, for example, focused less than his predecessors on details about the admission and departure of members, and more on issues concerned with church property.

---

[1] Letters of "dismission" stated that a departing member was an upstanding individual, in full communion with the church. These letters were essentially good references, allowing those who carried them to join Regular Baptist churches elsewhere. In turn, Welsh Neck received new members who carried letters of dismission from other Regular Baptist congregations.

Although the Church Book is a spare and even "dry-to-read" document at first glance, it can be used in conjunction with other primary sources and with the secondary literature on eighteenth-century South Carolina to reconstruct a multi-faceted history. A handful of these other primary sources—letters, an essay on slavery, and an allegorical autobiography, all by Edmund Botsford—are reproduced in this volume. The history of Welsh Neck is primarily important for what it reveals about the evolution of a Regular Baptist congregation on the southern frontier: about its beliefs and practices, as well as the challenges it faced in keeping its identity intact amidst the tumultuous changes of the eighteenth century. Perhaps the most intriguing aspects of Welsh Neck's story are the conversion and incorporation into the church of enslaved African Americans, and the role of Welsh Neck in the emergence of the Universalist movement in the United States. The Church Book and related documents reveal the interaction of ordinary individuals with the great events and developments of the age.

A. The Colonial Period, 1738-1775

The Founding

Welsh Neck Baptist Church was constituted in January 1738 by a group of migrants from a region known as Welsh Tract, in Newcastle County, Delaware.[2] Thirteen of the fifteen men who founded the Welsh Neck Church were "dismissed" by the Welsh Tract Baptist Church in 1735, 1737, and 1738; their wives were not named in the Welsh Neck record, but, on the basis of surnames, it seems likely that all or most were among the emigrants listed by Welsh Tract.[3] The other two men who founded Welsh Neck certainly or possibly had connections with the Welsh Tract congregation. Thomas Evans, Jr. was the son of a Welsh Tract migrant, and the other, Griffith Jones, may have been related to another member of the Welsh Tract group. Two others dismissed by the Welsh

---

[2] William H. Brackney, *Baptists in North America* (Oxford; Malden, MA: Blackwell, 2006), 16-17.

[3] The surviving transcription of the original Welsh Neck Church Book lists the names of the male founders and simply states "and wife" after each one. According to Morgan Edwards, two of the male founders, Thomas and David Harry, were not married. Edwards saw the original records when he visited Welsh Neck in 1772, and his statement therefore carries some weight. It seems very possible that the transcriber added "and wife" to all the men as a careless reflex. There were thus either twenty-eight or thirty founding members, depending on which version one accepts. Welsh Neck Church Book (hereafter, WNCB), 1; Morgan Edwards, "Materials towards a History of the Baptists in the Province of South-Carolina," (Manuscript at Furman University, 1772), 4, 17; Leah Townsend, *South Carolina Baptists, 1670-1805* (Florence, SC: Florence Printing, 1935), 62-63.

Tract Church in 1741, Walter and Rachel Downs, were not founders, but later joined the Welsh Neck Church. From its start, the church was a group of individuals who already knew each other; the move to the Pee Dee was very much a community migration. The leader of the migration was James James, a wealthy member of the Delaware church, but he died soon after he arrived in South Carolina; he never received a land grant in the region.[4] Three of his sons, Philip, Abel, and Daniel, were among the founding members, and the Welsh Neck area was originally called "James Neck." The church was initially referred to simply as the "Pee Dee Church," but later came to be known as the "Welch Neck Church."[5]

The individuals who became members of the Welsh Neck Church were accompanied by other migrants from the Welsh Tract region of Delaware. Some of these fellow migrants would have been family members or neighbors who had not felt called to join the church, either at Welsh Tract or at Welsh Neck. Others were Welsh Tract Church members who settled elsewhere along the Pee Dee: the Welsh Tract Church dismissed fifty-one members to "our christian friends on peedee in South Carolina" over the years 1735, 1737, 1738, 1739, and 1741.[6] Only twenty-eight of these, at the highest estimate, founded or later joined the Welsh Neck Church. Morgan Edwards (1722-1795), an eighteenth-century historian of the Baptists in America, stated that James James and his fellow-migrants first settled at Catfish before moving fifty miles up the Pee Dee to the region that came to be called Welsh Neck.[7] During the two to three years that lapsed between the first wave of migrants and the founding of the Welsh Neck Church, it seems likely that the migrants explored the potential of the area and

---

[4] The transcriber wrote James James into the Church Book and then erased it. There is no way of knowing what conflicting records or oral testimony caused the original mistake and its subsequent correction, but the erasure means that, in a quite fitting manner, James James's ghost presides over the record of the Church's founding. WNCB, 1.

[5] Edwards, "Baptists in South-Carolina," 4, 16, 17; Townsend, *South Carolina Baptists*, 61; Wood Furman, *A History of the Charleston Association of Baptist Churches in the State of South Carolina; with an Appendix containing the principal circular letters to the churches.* (Charleston, SC: J. Hoff, 1811), 6, 7.

[6] *Records of the Welsh Tract Baptist Meeting, 1701-1828,* (Wilmington, DE: The Historical Society of Delaware, 1904), Part I, 83-86. In 1735, the dismissed members were vaguely recommended "to ye church of Christ in Charles Town or elsewhere in South Carolina, or they might constitute themselves into a church." By 1741 the dismissal was more precise: "to our sister church on the Pee Dee river in South Carolina."

[7] Townsend denies Edwards' claim that the migrants first settled at Catfish before moving to Welsh Neck on the grounds that the later Welsh Neck Church members did not take out land grants at Catfish. Townsend, *South Carolina Baptists,* 61; but there were migrants from Welsh Tract who did not become part of Welsh Neck. These may well have settled at Catfish, providing the basis for Edwards' account. (See note 19 below for biographical information on Edwards.)

that different individuals settled in different places. A dispersed settlement of this type would explain an important aspect of Welsh Neck's impact on the region: Welsh Neck gradually established outlying branches along the Pee Dee and in neighboring districts, several of which were later constituted as independent churches. Like the Charleston church in the Lowcountry, Welsh Neck became the hub of a Baptist network in the northeastern part of the colony. There are few details about the establishment of this network: Welsh Neck's daughter churches at Catfish, Beauty Spot, Marrs Bluff, Cashaway, and Lynches Creek were constituted during the first two decades of Welsh Neck's existence, a period barely covered by the Church Book.[8] These new foundations may not have come about because Welsh Neck members moved elsewhere, but rather through a process whereby Welsh Neck reconnected with former relatives and neighbors who had settled at a variety of locations during the original migration.

The Welsh and Delaware Valley Background

The Welsh and Welsh-American migrants to the Pee Dee came from a region of Delaware with a marked Cambrian presence. William Penn had established a strong connection between Wales and his two American colonies of Pennsylvania and Delaware right from the start of his proprietorship. Penn was himself of Welsh stock, and he used his connections to advertise his colonies among Welsh Quakers, who were among the very first to petition him for land grants. Welsh Baptists soon joined the migration, for many of the same reasons as the Quakers did: they were interested in finding not only a place where they would enjoy economic opportunity and freedom of worship, but also a home from home where they could be largely self-governing and preserve their language and customs. In fact, Penn was reported to have promised that he would create specific areas within his colonies where Welsh would be the official language of the courts and government.[9] Welsh migrants made up the most numerous ethnic group of settlers during Pennsylvania's first two decades. The Welsh were perhaps one third of the total population of Pennsylvania in 1700; their descendants numbered some 12,000 on the eve of the Revolution. The Welsh in general were seen as very industrious. They were better educated than the average migrant: an unusual proportion of the doctors in early Pennsylvania were Welshmen. The Revolutionary leader, John Dickinson of Delaware (1732-1808) and the influential financier, Nicholas Biddle of Pennsylvania (1786-1844),

---

[8] Townsend, *South Carolina Baptists,* 78-106.
[9] Boyd Stanley Schlenther, "'The English is Swallowing up Their Language': Welsh Ethnic Ambivalence in Colonial Pennsylvania and the Experience of David Evans," *Pennsylvania Magazine of History and Biography,* Vol. 114, No. 2 (April 1990), 201.

were perhaps the best-known descendants of this Welsh migration to Penn's colonies.[10]

After the Quakers, the Baptists were the second most important denomination among the Welsh migrants.[11] Baptists settled with other Welshmen in Pennsylvania's Welsh Tract, west of the Schuylkill River in Montgomery County; they also settled north of Philadelphia at Gwynedd, and to the west, in the Great Valley of Chester County. The direct antecedents of the Welsh Neck Church in South Carolina arrived in Pennsylvania in 1701 from Rhydwilym, on the border of Pembrokeshire and Carmarthen. They settled northeast of Philadelphia, in Bucks Country, where the Cold Spring Baptist Church and its successor, the Pennepack or Lower Dublin Church, had already been founded, in 1684 and 1688 respectively, by Irish, English, and New England immigrants.[12] The new Welsh migrants worshiped with the existing Baptist community, but disagreements over the laying-on of hands prevented joint communion. Desiring a community and a church more suited to their culture and beliefs, the Welsh newcomers joined other Welsh migrants in 1703 and purchased a tract of land in Pencader Hundred in Newcastle County, in Penn's other proprietary colony of Delaware.[13] The Rhydwilym and other Baptists in the Delaware Welsh Tract founded a church soon afterwards.

One important contribution of the Welsh Tract Church towards the development of the Baptist faith in America was its involvement, along with four other churches, in founding the Philadelphia Association in 1707, one of the first organizations in the western hemisphere that sought to forge stronger connections among individual Baptist churches. As it grew, the Association mostly admitted churches in Pennsylvania, New Jersey, and Delaware; Welsh communities dominated its membership, keeping it firmly in the Regular, Calvinist camp. Welsh Baptists had a marked tendency towards creating larger associations that would support individual congregations, and this "Welsh Baptist associational principle was at the forefront of English and North American Baptist experience."[14] The Philadelphia Association later became the model for the

---

[10] Wayland F. Dunaway, "Early Welsh Settlers of Pennsylvania," *Pennsylvania History: A Journal of Mid-Atlantic Studies*, Vol. 12, No. 4 (October 1945), 251-254, 263-267.

[11] Ibid., 267.

[12] Ibid., 260-262; Brackney, *Baptists in North America*, 15-17.

[13] *Welsh Tract Baptist Meeting*, I, 7-8. The Welsh Baptists believed firmly that the laying-on of hands should take place after the baptism of every new member; their co-religionists believed that each new member could decide for him or herself.

[14] Five Baptist churches in Wales had formed a larger association as early as the 1660s, well in advance of any equivalent in England, and Welsh migrants were instrumental in creating an association among Six Principle Baptists in New England during the 1670s. William H. Brackney with Charles K. Hartman, *Baptists in Early North Amer-*

Charleston Association, co-founded by the Welsh Neck Church in 1751. The Philadelphia Association (like its Charleston offspring) held annual meetings, asked for reports on its member churches, answered queries, and helped supply vacancies in pastorates, but it had no authority over individual member churches.[15]

The Welsh migrants in Pennsylvania and Delaware were part of a larger diaspora that took Welsh natives away from their homeland in search of economic opportunity. These migrants were proud of their heritage and culture. In Penn's colonies, they hoped to maintain their language and traditions by creating largely autonomous communities on the American frontier. Their efforts were regarded by Welsh patriots in Britain as an important part of the movement to keep Cambrian culture alive: Jeremy Owen, a Welsh migrant to London, portrayed the American settlements as an integral part of modern Wales.[16] Philadelphia briefly became a minor center for Welsh-language publications during the 1720s and 1730s.[17] A common boast of Welsh scholars was that their language was among the most ancient in the world, going back to the scattering of mankind after the fall of the Tower of Babel, when Gomer, son of Noah's son Japheth, had founded his own people: the Welsh translation of the Old Testament was often said to be the closest of all translations to the original Hebrew.[18] Morgan Edwards, the historian of the Baptists in America mentioned above, lent his authority to this claim for the Welsh Old Testament; as a scholar with good knowledge of Greek and Hebrew, his repeated assertion that the Welsh version captured the idiom of the Hebrew text almost exactly was taken seriously by the Baptist community on both sides of the Atlantic.[19] Members of the Welsh dias-

---

ica: Swansea, Massachusetts. (Macon, GA: Mercer University Press, 2013), xciv-xcv. The Philadelphia Association was the first among Regular Baptists in North America.

[15] Furman, *Charleston Association,* 8; Jessica Lee Flinchum, "Reluctant Revolutionaries: The Philadelphia Baptist Association and the American Revolution," *Pennsylvania History: A Journal of Mid-Atlantic Studies,* 74/2 (Spring 2007): 175-177.

[16] Sarah Prescott, "'What Foes more dang'rous than too strong Allies?': Anglo-Welsh Relations in Eighteenth-Century London," *Huntington Library Quarterly,* 69/4 (December 2006): 539-542.

[17] Schlenther, "Welsh Ethnic Ambivalence," 225-226.

[18] Prescott, "Anglo-Welsh Relations in London," 542-545.

[19] John Rippon, *The Baptist Annual Register For 1794, 1795, 1796-7. Including Sketches of the State of Religion among Different Denominations of Good Men at Home and Abroad,* (London: Dilly, Button, and Thomas), 309, 311-313. Morgan Edwards (1722-1795) was born at Trevithin, Monmouthshire, Wales. Educated at the Bristol (England) Baptist College, he became the pastor of the First Baptist Church of Philadelphia from 1761-1771. He was a strong supporter of the Philadelphia Association, of Rhode Island College, and of closer union among American Baptists. He traveled throughout the colonies, collecting materials for histories of the Baptists in each province, some of which he published. He visited the Welsh Neck Church as part of his research tour in

pora in England and America recalled, in poetry and literature, their ancestors' resistance to the Anglo-Saxon invaders, and celebrated the 1 March feast day of Wales's patron saint, David.[20] Preaching in the Welsh language continued in some Welsh Baptist churches in Pennsylvania until the end of the colonial period.[21]

One of the most interesting Americanizations of Welsh nationalism, and one that attracted attention among Welsh Baptists in America, was the story of Prince Madoc. A poem published in 1734 by "Philo-Cambrensis" in the *American Weekly Mercury* in Philadelphia told of a Welsh migration to America, around the year 1170, led by Madoc, a son of the heroic king, Owain Gwynedd. It was said that, somewhere out West, there were still white-skinned Indians, descendants of these medieval migrants, who continued to speak Welsh. The legend of Madoc can be traced back to Elizabethan times, but it gained new currency in the eighteenth century; western expansion of the British colonies produced repeated speculations about the whereabouts and nature of these occidental Welshmen. Believers in the Madoc story wondered whether the "Welsh Indians" still practiced Christianity, and perhaps possessed copies of the Welsh Bible.[22] Among the late eighteenth-century tales of searches for Welsh Indians was one published by the Rev. David Jones in the widely-read *Baptist Register*, to which a number of Welsh Neck Church members subscribed. Jones wrote that John Evans of Wales had obtained permission from President Washington in 1793 to search beyond the Mississippi for the Welsh Indians. Unfortunately, Jones had heard nothing from Evans, whom, he feared, had met a cruel end at the hands of Spaniards or hostile natives.[23] However far-fetched these ideas may seem, Welsh migrants and their descendants in America found ways of updating their heritage so that it remained relevant to their new home on this side of the Atlantic.

Yet, despite much evidence of enduring Welsh identity, Welsh communities outside Wales faced pressures to conform to the dominant, Anglophone culture. The hopes for autonomous Welsh communities in Pennsylvania died when Penn decided to create a system of county government that placed Welsh Quakers and Baptists alike under outside authority, even in local matters. Land grants in Welsh areas were given to non-Welshmen, so that, even in Pennsylvania's Welsh Tract, ethnic Cambrians found themselves far outnumbered by other

---

1772. William H. Brackney, *Historical Dictionary of the Baptists* (Lanham, MD: Scarecrow Press, 2009), 197-198.

[20] Prescott, "Anglo-Welsh Relations in London," 542-551.

[21] Dunaway, "Welsh Settlers," 262-263, 267.

[22] Derrick Spradlin, "'God ne'er bring to pass such things for nought': Empire and Prince Madoc of Wales in Eighteenth-Century America," *Early American Literature,* 44/1 (2009): 39-41, 48-50, 54-55, 57-58.

[23] Rippon, *Baptist Register, 1794-1797,* 132-133.

groups at the end of the colonial period.[24] On top of the usual pressures for minorities to acculturate, Welsh patriots' stress on Welsh distinctiveness was undermined by a peculiar temptation. The Act of Union of 1707 had created a new, supra-national identity for members of the United Kingdom: Englishmen, Scots, and Welshmen were now all "Britons."[25] Champions of Welsh identity were torn between stressing the ancient separateness of Wales or celebrating its contributions to the new union. Welsh patriots could point out that the Hanoverian monarchy had Welsh blood in its veins (through Tudor ancestors), and that the Reformation had been a joint achievement of the Welsh and English; Protestantism was a central element of the new British identity.[26] The very name of the nation, "Britain," carried resonances of ancient Britons, the ancestors of the Welsh, and of the Brythonic (Welsh) tongue. Even the Prince Madoc legend had an important British dimension: eighteenth-century versions of the story stressed that Madoc's discovery and colonization gave the British Empire a superior claim to the New World over Spain's.[27] Assimilation to the dominant Anglophone identity, since it brought as much cultural pride as cultural loss, was too tempting. By mid-century, the Welsh enclaves in Pennsylvania and Delaware had adopted English as their primary tongue. The Welsh generally proved less tenacious of their language and culture than their German neighbors.[28]

This process of Anglicization can be tentatively traced in the story of the Welsh Tract and Welsh Neck Churches. When the Welshmen from Rhydwilym first arrived in America, they worshiped at times with non-Welsh Baptists at Pennepack, but more often met for weekly services and monthly meetings in private homes; aside from their concerns about differences over the laying–on of hands, these meetings allowed them to worship in the Welsh language.[29] When they moved to Newcastle County in 1703, they purchased lands in an area set aside by William Penn specifically for Welsh migrants, the 30,000-acre Welsh Tract, deeded to David Evans and William Davis at the start of the eighteenth century. In this Welsh enclave, they continued to use their native tongue. The importance they placed on the Welsh language was demonstrated when the Welsh Tract Church adopted a confession of faith in 1716. The church adhered to the Second London Confession of 1677, formally adopted by a large assembly of representatives from Baptist churches in England and Wales in 1689. The Welsh Tract Church added a few additional articles, including one that support-

---

[24] Dunaway, "Welsh Settlers," 258-260, 263-264, 269.

[25] Linda Colley, *Britons: Forging the Nation, 1707-1837* (New Haven, CT: Yale University Press, 1992), 17-18.

[26] Prescott, "Anglo-Welsh Relations in London," 537-539.

[27] Spradlin, "Prince Madoc of Wales," 39-40, 43-45.

[28] Schlenther, "Welsh Ethnic Ambivalence," 225-226.

[29] Brackney, *Baptists in North America,* 16; *Welsh Tract Baptist Meeting*, I, 8.

ed their firm belief in the laying-on of hands. As was customary, all the members of the Welsh Tract Church signed this confession of faith to indicate their adherence to its provisions. The version they signed was a Welsh translation made by the Rev. Abel Morgan of Philadelphia.[30] The church members may have signed a Welsh translation instead of the English original because some were literate in Welsh, but not English, or they may simply have wished to make so important a statement about their beliefs in a language that they cherished deeply. In either case, the continuing importance of Welsh in this church is evident; one historian of this congregation claims that preaching in Welsh continued until 1800.[31]

When members of this congregation moved to the Pee Dee in the 1730s, they continued to have some respect for and knowledge of the Welsh language, since they brought with them an alphabetical concordance of the Scriptures in Welsh, compiled by Abel Morgan.[32] However, it proved harder to sustain their Welsh identity in their new home. The Welsh Tract in Delaware had been set aside for Welsh migrants, and the Baptists there had many Welsh neighbors of various denominations, reinforced by a strong Welsh presence in the Pennsylvania counties to their north. The Pee Dee region was settled from the start by a variety of ethnic groups, and the Welsh there were a tiny minority. While the name "Welsh Tract" in Delaware indicated a Welsh norm, the name "Welsh Neck" that was eventually attached to the church on the Pee Dee indicated a group that stood out because of its idiosyncrasies. The loss of the Welsh Neck Church Book's first two decades makes it hard to discover how much Welsh language and identity survived during the earliest years. Two of the first four ministers, Philip James and Joshua Edwards, were strongly Welsh; Philip James was born at Pennepack in 1701 to a family that was probably part of the Rhydwilim migration; Joshua Edwards was born in Pembrokeshire, Wales, and migrated via Pennsylvania to South Carolina. It is not clear whether John Brown or Robert Williams, both born in America, were markedly Welsh. By 1759, when the church members chose the Englishman Nicholas Bedgegood for their pastor, they were clearly no longer concerned about having a Welsh-speaking minister. Evan Pugh was probably second generation Welsh-American, but there is no evidence that he spoke Welsh; moreover, the church rapidly dismissed

---

[30] *Welsh Tract Baptist Meeting,* I, 3, 18-23.

[31] *Ibid.,* 4.

[32] Townsend, *South Carolina Baptists,* 63; Schlenther, "Welsh Ethnic Ambivalence," 225-226. The original publication information is: Abel Morgan, *Cyd-Gordiad Egwyddorawl o'r Scrythurau: Neu Daflen Lythyrennol o'r Prif Eirau Yn y Bibl Sanctaidd.* (Philadelphia, PA: Samuel Keimer & Dafydd Harry, 1730). Charles Evans, *American Bibliography: a chronological dictionary of all books, pamphlets, and periodical publications printed in the Unites States of America from the genesis of printing in 1639 down to and including the year 1820* (New York: P. Smith, 1941-1959), #3323.

him, the most Welsh of its post-1759 ministers. Elhanan Winchester had Welsh ancestry, but his links with Wales were distant. Edmund Botsford was an Englishman, with no known Welsh connections whatsoever. While the Welsh Tract Church apparently continued some Welsh-language worship until 1800, its daughter church on the Pee Dee seems to have lost most of its Welsh heritage some decades earlier.

The Carolina Context

What brought Welsh and Welsh-American migrants from Delaware to the distant colony of South Carolina? The immediate impetus was a new policy of generous land grants on the South Carolina frontier, stemming from a growing sense of insecurity among the white residents of the coastal region. The mastery of rice cultivation at the turn of the eighteenth century had led to an exponential rise in the population of enslaved Africans, whose labor and skills were essential for this lucrative crop. By 1708, enslaved Africans and Native Americans had become a majority of the population; by the 1720s, slaves, mostly African, were sixty-five percent of the colony's population, and they outnumbered whites by three or even four to one in some parishes.[33] Fear of slave revolts made the white minority feel increasingly insecure. Tensions with the neighboring Spanish Empire added significantly to these fears. Spanish officials in San Agustín could easily exploit the racial imbalance in South Carolina by inciting revolts, possibly in conjunction with a Spanish invasion.[34] In order to make white South Carolinians secure against such a prospect, South Carolina strove throughout the 1730s to buffer its rice-growing region with communities of white farmers who would grow crops on a small scale, without slave labor. One result of this policy was the new colony of Georgia, where slavery was initially banned and the size of land grants was limited in order to encourage yeomen farmers rather than large planters. The same policy led Governor Robert Johnson of South Carolina to establish a series of townships in the interior to attract white settlement: New Windsor, Orangeburg, Amelia, Saxe Gotha, Fredericksburg, and Queensborough were created in the mid-1730s. The last of these townships was along the Great Pee Dee River. Slavery was not banned in these interior regions, but land grants were limited in size to encourage smallholders. Immigrants were given fifty acres per head as well as tools. The South Carolina government advertised the new opportunities among Protestant populations in the Rhineland, Switzerland,

---

[33] Louis B. Wright, *South Carolina: A Bicentennial History* (New York: W.W. Norton, 1976), 59; Peter Wood, *Black Majority: Negroes in South Carolina from 1670 through the Stono Rebellion* (New York: Norton, 1974), 142-150.

[34] When long-simmering tensions over British smuggling led to war in 1739, these fears proved well-grounded, and a major uprising, incited by Spain, took place on the Stono River in September of that year. Wood, *Black Majority*, 308-323.

and the British Isles. The new settlements filled with Germans, Swiss Huguenots, Ulster Protestants, and the Welsh. The South Carolina backcountry became
unusually diverse; the promise of land and of freedom of worship for all
Protestants, along with the targeted recruitment of immigrants from outside England, made the South Carolina interior resemble the Delaware Valley colonies in
many respects.[35] The leap from the Delaware Valley to the Pee Dee was therefore less strange than it might at first appear.

The migrants who came from to the Pee Dee grew a variety of crops. A
few began to produce indigo, a crop that gained ground in South Carolina from
the 1740s, requiring considerable investment and a specialized labor force. Most
Pee Dee farmers were smallholders, owning 100-200 acres and producing
wheat, corn, tobacco, oats, barley, rye, hemp, madder (a dye), or fruit using their
own and their family's labor. The farms generally remained small, in part because of taxation policy: all land in the colony was taxed by the acre, so acquir-
ing large tracts would have resulted in a huge tax bill. Only with a sufficient
labor force could large farms have been made economically viable, and yet
white labor was scarce, and enslaved labor expensive. A part of the crops raised
on these small farms was transported to the coast, a slow journey of two to three
weeks by wagon. Upriver, cattle were raised and then driven to the Lowcountry:
the members of the Welsh Neck Church would have seen regular cattle drives
through their community. Crops and cattle were exchanged in Charleston and
elsewhere along the coast for imported manufactured goods. There was no urban
center in the region during the first decades of settlement. By the 1760s,
Cheraw, about twelve miles north of Welsh Neck, had become a center for exchange, with a store maintained by Christopher Gadsden, the future revolutionary radical.[36]

An important incentive—indeed, a necessary condition—behind the Baptist migration from Welsh Tract to Welsh Neck was religious toleration. The
Carolina colony had been one of the earliest to grant its inhabitants broad rights
regarding worship. The *Fundamental Constitutions* of 1669, drawn up by Anthony Ashley Cooper and John Locke, granted toleration to all Christians, Jews,
and "heathens," a right revised to exclude Roman Catholics after the Glorious
Revolution of 1688-1689.[37] Although the Church of England was given a privi-
leged position as the established church, with a taxpayer-supported clergy, the
toleration for all non-Anglican Protestants was significant: unlike other colonies,

---

[35] Wright, *South Carolina,* 49-50, 57-59, 84-88; Richard Maxwell Brown, *The
South Carolina Regulators* (Cambridge, MA: Harvard University Press, 1963), 2-3;
Townsend, *South Carolina Baptists,* 61.

[36] Wright, *South Carolina,* 88; Brown, *Regulators,* 14-19, 24-27, 139-140.

[37] John Frederick Woolverton, *Colonial Anglicanism in North America* (Detroit,
MI: Wayne State University Press, 1984), 157.

such as Massachusetts and Virginia, there was no law punishing those who re-fused to baptize their children.[38] Dissenters enjoyed not only freedom of wor-ship, but the right to hold public office, a right that survived an Anglican attack in 1704; in fact, seven of the first thirteen governors of the Carolina colony were Dissenters.[39] The Church of England establishment remained weak and under-manned, especially outside the coastal region; the colony was divided into par-ishes in 1706 and the Society for the Propagation of the Gospel (SPG) provided a handful of ministers in an attempt to staff these, but there were no Anglican churches or clergy in the Pee Dee when the Welsh Baptists arrived.[40] Early in South Carolina's history, toleration of Dissenters attracted a considerable num-ber of Huguenots, who were about one-eighth of the white population in 1695. Presbyterians from Scotland and Ulster, along with a variety of German Protestants also entered the colony.[41] By the time the Welsh Baptists arrived on the Pee Dee in the late 1730s, only about 45% of South Carolina's white popula-tion belonged, even nominally, to the Church of England; the majority of the whites were Dissenters.[42] The Pee Dee Baptists had little to fear from the weak church establishment. In fact, Morgan Edwards argued that South Carolina Bap-tists had suffered more from the hostility of the Presbyterians than from any other sect.[43]

South Carolina's toleration had attracted a small number of Baptists almost from the beginning. Among early Baptist immigrants, the most significant was the Rev. William Screven (1629-1713) of Maine, who arrived with a group of followers in 1696. Screven had converted to the Baptist faith in 1681 and as a result had faced harassment, including a period in jail, from the Congregational-ist establishment in Massachusetts. He and his followers founded a church near Charleston that was the antecedent of First Baptist, Charleston and of congrega-tions on the Ashley and Stono Rivers, on Edisto and James Islands, and at Eu-

---

[38] Townsend, *South Carolina Baptists,* 2-3.

[39] A Church of England majority and a sympathetic governor excluded Dissenters from public office in 1704, but the Whig administration in London persuaded Queen Anne to veto the measure. Woolverton, *Colonial Anglicanism,* 156-158.

[40] Samuel Thomas, a missionary from the Church of England's Society for the Propagation of the Gospel, complained at the start of the eighteenth century that there were more Dissenting than Anglican ministers in South Carolina. Even in its most ag-gressive phase, between 1704 and 1714, the Church of England was far from dominant; it was in many ways attempting to catch up with the lead already established by Dissenters in the colony. *Ibid.,* 155-156.

[41] Wright, *South Carolina,* 50-51, 55.

[42] William Howland Kenney III, "Alexander Garden and George Whitefield: The Significance of Revivalism in South Carolina, 1738-1741" *The South Carolina Historical Magazine,* Vol. 71 (1970), 709.

[43] Edwards, "Baptists in South-Carolina," 26-31.

haws.[44] Therefore, when the Welsh Baptists arrived on the Pee Dee, they entered a colony with a small, but well-established Baptist presence. Although during its first decade the Welsh Neck Church often looked northwards towards the Delaware Valley and the Philadelphia Association for fellowship and advice, by the mid-1740s it began to establish closer ties with the Baptists in the Lowcountry. The founding of the Charleston Association in 1751 by the Charleston, Welsh Neck, and Ashley River Churches represented a marked reorientation of Welsh Neck towards the Baptist community along the coast.

The Pastorate of Philip James

The first minister at Welsh Neck was Philip James, son of James James, the leader of the first wave of Welsh Tract migrants. Philip James was born at Pennepek, Pennsylvania in 1701. He married Elizabeth Thomas, and they had three sons, Daniel, James, and Philip.[45] He was part of the original group of migrants, and he received land grants of 100 and 250 acres in 1740, purchasing another 100 acres in 1751.[46] Although he seems to have served as Welsh Neck's *de facto* minister from its founding, Philip James was not formally ordained until 4 April 1743 when the Rev. Isaac Chanler of Ashley River and the Rev. Thomas Simmons of Charleston visited Welsh Neck and performed the ceremony.[47] Chanler preached the ordination sermon: "The Qualifications *for* and Duty *in* studying rightly to divine the Word of Truth."[48] The choice of Chanler and Simmons for this function was significant. George Whitefield's preaching in South Carolina during his three visits in 1739, 1740, and 1741 had caused deep divisions in the colony. One aspect of these divisions concerned theology: Whitefield was an uncompromising enemy of Arminian tendencies in the Church of England, and he had engaged in an extensive controversy, in sermons, in pamphlets, and in the press, with Alexander Garden, the commissary or representative of the Bishop of London in the colony, and therefore the highest official of the established church.[49] Chanler had publicly and energetically support-

---

[44] Townsend, *South Carolina Baptists,* 3-12, 36; Brackney, *Dictionary of the Baptists,* 509-510.

[45] Edwards, "Baptists in South Carolina," 19-20.

[46] Townsend, *South Carolina Baptists,* 63.

[47] Edwards, "Baptists in South Carolina," 4; Furman, *Charleston Association,* 70.

[48] Townsend, *South Carolina Baptists,* 64.

[49] George Whitefield, *A Letter from the Rev. Mr. Whitefield from Georgia, to a Friend in London, shewing the Fundamental Error of a Book Entitled the Whole Duty of Man.* (Charles-Town, SC: Peter Timothy, 1740); Whitefield, *Three Letters from the Rev. Mr. G. Whitefield* (Philadelphia, PA: B. Franklin, 1740); Alexander Garden, *Regeneration and the Testimony of the Spirit. Being the Substance of Two Sermons lately Preached in the Parish Church of St. Philip's, Charles-Town, in South-Carolina. Occasioned by some erroneous Notions of certain Men who call themselves Methodists.* (Charles-Town,

ed Whitefield's anti-Arminianism, having been involved in a similar controversy within the Charleston Baptist Church during the 1730s. Simmons, pastor at Charleston during the Whitefield controversy, had been more mixed in his support of the revivalist, but his virtually moribund church had been revitalized by Whitefield's preaching.[50] Given the bitterness of the recent controversies between the Calvinists and Arminians within the Baptist and other Christian communities in South Carolina, it seems very likely that Welsh Neck's choice of Chanler and Simmons for this ordination represented a conscious affirmation of its Calvinistic, Regular Baptist allegiance.

The public dispute between Whitefield and his Arminian opponents took place against the background of the scientific and philosophical Enlightenment, which rejected the idea that supernatural forces of any kind intervened in the human and natural worlds. Exponents of "rational" religion, such as Garden, attacked the belief that those saved by God could discern His spirit at work in their souls. Such beliefs were superstitious "enthusiasm," lacking "any rational or objective Evidence, or clear and efficient Proof."[51] The brief references in the Welsh Neck Church Book to prospective church members who "gave in their experiences" of God's grace and who were then admitted to the church through baptism were examples of the "enthusiasm" lambasted by Garden. The members of the Welsh Neck Church retained elements of a pre-Enlightenment worldview, believing that they lived in a world permeated by miracles, by God's active intervention. A story that Morgan Edwards related about Philip James brings this mentality to life. Not long before James's death on 31 January 1753, he lost a favorite child.[52] While mourning that child, he collapsed and was taken for dead, and his body was stretched out on the bed beside his deceased offspring. An hour later, he awoke and related a vision: his soul had left his body and a man in black had taken hold of him. Chiding him for wishing to die, the man had led James towards the sun, so that James became frightened; at that point, a "bright

---

SC: Peter Timothy, 1740; Boston, MA: Thomas Fleet, 1741); Kenney, "Garden and Whitefield," 1-16.

[50] Edwards, "Baptists in South- Carolina," 5-9; Isaac Chanler, *New Converts Exhorted to Cleave to the Lord. A Sermon on Acts xi.23. Preach'd July 30, 1740 at a Wednesday Evening-Lecture in Charlestown. Set up at the Motion and by the Desire of the Rev. Mr. Whitefield; with a brief Introduction relating to the Character of that excellent Man.* (Boston: D. Fowle, 1740); Joe M. King, *A History of South Carolina Baptists* (Columbia, SC: R.L. Bryan, 1964), 15-17.

[51] John P. Barrington, "Suppressing the Great Awakening: Alexander Garden's Use of Anti-Popery against George Whitefield," *The Proceedings of the South Carolina Historical Association* (2003), 6-8; Garden, *Regeneration and the Testimony of the Spirit*, 1.

[52] Edwards gives this date for Philip James's death ("Baptists in South-Carolina," 18); Townsend records it as 31 January 1754 (*South Carolina Baptists*, 63-64); Furman states it as 1753 in one reference and as 1755 in another (*Charleston Association*, 7, 70).

figure" had interposed and pushed away the man in black. James was then led to a company of angels that surrounded the soul of his child, now fully grown. James's conductor promised that he would soon join that company, but for now he was returned to his body on the bed. When he awoke, James was able to assure those around him that the dead child was heaven-bound and enjoyed more happiness in each moment than the sum of all the misery and pain he had experienced on earth. In order to "prove" the truth of this account, his wife, Elizabeth, and the others who were gathered in the room signed a written statement saying they had heard this narrative from the minister's lips.[53] The solemn attestation of this vision in a quasi-legal document is as striking as the vision itself; it reveals the seriousness with which members of the Welsh Neck Church regarded the interaction of the supernatural with this world. The story is a reminder that there was an extraordinary drama of divine intervention, salvation, and damnation taking place behind the Church Book's spare record.

Philip James's ordination in 1743 was closely followed in 1744 by the building of the first church at Welsh Neck. Until that time, the congregation had met in the home of John Jones.[54] The new church building stood on land owned by founding member Daniel Devonald, who in 1768 donated this two-acre plot to the church.[55] James was buried in the church-yard next to this old church.[56] His widow, Elizabeth, remarried (a Mr. Simonson, not a church member) sometime between 1759 and 1761. She was suspended from Welsh Neck on 1 August 1761 for abusive language, but restored on 6 September.[57] She was suspended again on 4 June 1763 for living apart from her husband, and again restored on 1 September 1764. She died, still a church member, on 20 April 1778. Two of the three sons of the Rev. Philip and Elizabeth James, Daniel and Philip, are not recorded as members of the church; the James James who was suspended for beating a neighbor on 5 April 1760 (and restored 31 January the following year) may have been the third son.[58] Daniel and Philip, Jr. may have moved away

---

[53] Edwards, "Baptists in South-Carolina," 19-20. Philip James was not the only Welsh Neck pastor to have a heavenly vision; Edmund Botsford also experienced the supernatural in a dream as a young boy (see below). Philip Mulkey, a Separate Baptist who on occasion ministered to Welsh Neck (WNCB, 16) encountered, while he was awake (though possibly inebriated), a "hideous specter" when he returned home from playing the fiddle at a dance. This meeting with the specter, whom Mulkey took to be the Devil, began the long and complex process of Mulkey's conversion. In another incident, several members of the Lynches-Creek Church, a daughter church of Welsh Neck constituted in 1755, heard the preaching of a disembodied voice in the woods near their homes from 5-7 February 1772. Edwards, "Baptists in South-Carolina," 35, 48.

[54] Townsend, *South Carolina Baptists,* 63-64, 73-75.

[55] WNCB, 15.

[56] Townsend, *South Carolina Baptists,* 64.

[57] WNCB, 9, 11, 23.

[58] Ibid., 4, 7.

from the area as young adults; but the experience of the James family serves as a reminder that, although there were many family connections among members of the Welsh Neck congregation, there was no guarantee that children would follow their parents into the community of the elect.

Philip James died in 1753 or possibly later; however, he probably retired as pastor in 1750, since he is said to have been succeeded briefly by John Brown, whose pastorate ended in 1751.[59]

John Brown

John Brown was born near Burlington, New Jersey on 14 August or 20 August 1714.[60] He was raised in Frankford, Pennsylvania, about six miles from Philadelphia. He migrated to the Pee Dee region in 1737. There is no evidence that he was connected with the migrants from Welsh Tract, and certainly he was not a founding member of the church. He joined Welsh Neck at some time between its founding and the mid-1740s. Even while Philip James was serving as pastor, Brown regularly preached to the congregation. It was a normal practice for multiple individuals to serve simultaneously as preachers in Baptist churches of this region.[61]

While Philip James was still alive, Brown was involved in a dispute over the compulsory laying-on of hands. This particular issue was an important one for many members of Welsh Neck; decades earlier, the Welsh migrants from Rhydwilym had refused to join in communion with the Pennepack church because of differences over this question, and the Welsh Tract church had added to their 1716 confession of faith a clause requiring the laying-on of hands at every baptism. Now, in 1746, Welsh Tract's daughter church at Welsh Neck was again engaged in this controversy. A copy of John Gill's commentary on the New Testament arrived in the area, and Brown used it as an authority for opposing the compulsory laying-on of hands.[62] He and his supporters were prepared to allow this practice to those who wished it, but also to allow those who were opposed to opt out. Brown seems to have won this debate, since Welsh Neck adopted the following resolution: "Agreed, that those who may desire to have hands laid on them shall be indulged; and that those who are against it shall be received into

---

[59] Edwards, "Baptists in South-Carolina," 19-20; Townsend, *South Carolina Baptists,* 63-64; Furman, *Charleston Association,* 7, 70.

[60] Edwards gives the date as 14 August; Furman as 20 August. "Baptists in South-Carolina," 21; *Charleston Association,* 70.

[61] Edwards, "Baptists in South-Carolina," 21; Townsend, *South Carolina Baptists,* 63.

[62] John Gill (1697-1771) was an English theologian whose commentaries and other works became the standard authority for Baptists who adhered to a strict Calvinist position. Brackney, *Dictionary of the Baptists,* 251.

communion without it."[63] Given the insistence on the laying-on of hands by the Welsh Tract Church, it is possible that this controversy represented a split between the Welsh Tract migrants and new members who, like Brown, came from different backgrounds.[64]

The following year, another controversy erupted when Brown preached a sermon that speculated on the nature of the first resurrection, the Last Judgment, and the degrees of glory in heaven. Some of his views offended certain members of the congregation. The matter was appealed to the Philadelphia Association, which decided that Welsh Neck was making much ado about nothing.[65] It is significant that the distant Philadelphia Association was seen as the best authority to turn to in the midst of a disagreement. The Delaware Valley roots of so many of the church members, plus the lack of an alternative in North America, explain this appeal. Welsh Neck's role in the founding of the Charleston Association four years after this controversy is not surprising. While much credit for creating the second Regular Baptist association in America must go to the Rev. Oliver Hart of Charleston, Welsh Neck's familiarity with the benefits of a larger association made the Pee Dee church quick to endorse Hart's initiative.[66]

Brown was ordained on 7 May 1750. He must have begun his pastorate shortly after his ordination, presumably taking over from the respected but aging Philip James.[67] Brown was one of Welsh Neck's two ministerial representatives at the founding of the Charleston Association on 21 October 1751.[68] The other representative was Brown's successor, Joshua Edwards. Edwards seems to have begun his six-year pastorate soon after his ordination in July 1751, so that Brown's ministry was a brief one.[69] Brown helped to constitute the Cashaway Church on 28 September 1756, and he may have been dismissed to Cashaway at that time, though he did not initially serve as its minister. When Joshua Edwards

---

[63] Edwards, "Baptists in South-Carolina," 18.

[64] After this 1746 controversy and the new policy making laying-on of hands optional, the practice seems to have suffered a decline. By the time Morgan Edwards visited in 1772, it had fallen entirely out of use at Welsh Neck. "Baptists in South-Carolina," 17.

[65] Ibid., 18.

[66] Furman attributed the founding of the Charleston Association almost entirely to Oliver Hart, who had recently migrated from the Delaware Valley area and "had seen, in the Philadelphia Association, the happy consequences of union and stated intercourse among Churches maintaining the same faith and order." *Charleston Association,* 8. Yet many of the Welsh Neck members had similarly witnessed the benefits of such a "union" when they had been members of Welsh Tract, and they had recently benefited from the Philadelphia Association's guidance even in their new South Carolina home.

[67] *Ibid.,* 7, 70; Edwards, "Baptists in South-Carolina," 21.

[68] Furman, *Charleston Association,* 8-9.

[69] Edwards, "Baptists in South-Carolina," 21; Townsend suggests that Brown's controversial views about the first resurrection and Last Judgment may have prevented him serving long as pastor. *South Carolina Baptists,* 64.

was forced to step down as Cashaway's pastor because of his excessive drinking, Brown temporarily stepped in, and he was involved with other ministers in helping Cashaway to arrive at a decision regarding Edwards.[70] Brown's beliefs continued to stir controversy; one member of Cashaway, John Jamison, accused Brown in September 1760 of preaching false doctrine, though Jamison failed to provide specific examples. The Cashaway Church decided in Brown's favor and suspended Jamison for casting aspersions;[71] but Brown's pastorate may have ended soon afterwards.[72] Certainly, Evan Pugh was performing many ministerial functions at Cashaway from 1764, and he received a formal call to be its minister in 1766. Brown was not in the care of any church when Morgan Edwards visited the Pee Dee area in 1772; he was recorded in the 1790 census as living in Cheraw and owning nine slaves. He married Sarah Newbery and had seven children.[73]

Joshua Edwards

Joshua Edwards was born in Pembrokeshire, Wales, on 11 February 1704. He emigrated to the Welsh Tract of Pennsylania, where he was baptized in 1721. He moved to South Carolina in 1749 and was ordained at the Welsh Neck Church on 15 July 1751.[74] Along with John Brown, he represented Welsh Neck at the founding of the Charleston Association in October of that year.[75] He took over as pastor at Welsh Neck at some point during 1751. He helped to constitute the Lynches Creek Church in 1755 and the Cashaway Church on 28 September 1756.[76] He was dismissed to the latter, where he served as pastor for three years. His pastorate ended on Thursday, 25 December 1759 when he confessed to "being overtaken and intoxicated with liquor." Cashaway therefore "concluded to suspend him from all his ministerial affairs, [and] from Communion in the Church until the matter is properly settled, and ... that it may be done in the best matter, we are to wait until the [arrival of the] ministers of the Welsh Neck ... and their advice to be taken for procedure." Bedgegood, then the pastor at Welsh

---

[70] "Cashaway Church Book" (Microfilm copy at Furman University, Special Collections), 28 September 1756, 23 February 1760, 29 March 1760.

[71] Ibid., 26 September 1760.

[72] Edwards states that Brown's pastorate ended in 1760. "Baptists in South-Carolina," 36-38.

[73] Ibid., 21; Townsend, South Carolina Baptists, 64.

[74] Rippon, Baptist Register, 1794-1797, 500; Furman, Charleston Association, 9, 70-71; Edwards, "Baptists in South-Carolina," 21-22. Townsend gives the ordination date as May 1752 (South Carolina Baptists, 64), but since Edwards was included with the ministers rather than messengers on the list of signatories of the Charleston Association's founding charter (October 1751), Edwards must have been ordained at the earlier date.

[75] Furman, Charleston Association, 8.

[76] "Cashaway Church Book," 28 September 1756.

Neck, referred the matter to the Charleston Association, which seems to have recommended a formal hearing, over which Bedgegood and the Rev. John Stephens presided. Edwards' repentance at the December 1760 hearing was judged insincere. The stand-off between Cashaway and Edwards continued until he was threatened with excommunication in August 1761. He was readmitted to membership but not restored to his pastoral office, and he soon left to become pastor of Catfish, a post he held until 1768. Thereafter he did not serve any church; he died 22 August 1784, leaving behind eighty grandchildren and great-grandchildren.[77]

Edwards married twice and had twelve children;[78] at least two of these became members of Welsh Neck. One son, also Joshua, followed in his father's footsteps by being suspended on 6 September 1761 for excessive drinking, as well as for "in an illegal manner taking some negroes into his possession."[79] Joshua Jr. was restored to church membership after repentance on 1 June 1765.[80] Another son, Abel, had a far more distinguished career. He was dismissed from Cashaway to Welsh Neck in 1761, during the final stages of Cashaway's controversy with his father. He became a trustee of Welsh Neck in 1768 and a deacon in 1777.[81] He died in 1793, aged fifty-four. His obituary appeared in the *Baptist Register*, bringing his "esteemed and highly useful" diaconate to the attention of a wide readership on both sides of the Atlantic.[82]

Robert Williams

When Joshua Edwards left for Cashaway in 1756, he was succeeded as pastor by the Rev. Robert Williams. Williams had been born in Northampton, North Carolina, near the Virginia border, on 20 December 1717. He moved to the Pee Dee in 1745 and was ordained at Welsh Neck on 30 September 1752 by Philip James and John Brown. He did not remain pastor for long. [83] The Welsh Neck Church Book's detailed record opens in early 1759, in the midst of a controversy between Williams and his congregation. Unfortunately, there is no information about what caused the rift. The Church Book simply states that "Mr

---

[77] Ibid., 25 December 1759, 7 April 1760, 5 May 1760, 8 December 1760, 22 August 1761, 27 September 1761; Rippon, *Baptist Register, 1794-1797,* 500; Furman, *Charleston Association,* 70-71; Edwards, "Baptists in South- Carolina," 31-32.

[78] Edwards, "Baptists in South-Carolina," 21-22.

[79] WNCB, 9.

[80] Ibid., 12.

[81] Ibid., 9, 15, 21.

[82] Rippon, *Baptist Register, 1794-1797,* 500-502; Furman, *Charleston Association,* 70-71.

[83] Edwards, "Baptists in South-Carolina," 22.

Williams could not give proper attendance to his office," and so the members gave a call to the Rev. Bedgegood on 5 April 1759. Later information demonstrates that at some point before this date Williams had applied for, and obtained, a letter of dismission. He was still in the Welsh Neck area on 9 August 1759, when he asked to be excused from the quarterly communion: the Church heard that behind this request lay some bitter allegations that Welsh Neck was not an authentic Church of Christ. In October 1759 and January 1760 the Church sent two letters of admonition, asking him to appear and to justify his attacks. He refused to receive their letters or acknowledge their authority, and so was suspended on 2 February 1760. Further admonitions followed; his wife, also, was understood to be rejecting the legitimacy of the Church. She, too, refused to accept any letters or to comply with other disciplinary measures. On 5 January 1761, the Church's patience was exhausted, and both Robert and Anne were excommunicated. Williams then went to the Charleston Association's annual meeting in the fall of 1761 and convinced them that he was ready to make amends for his part in the quarrel; the Association sent a "letter of advice" to Welsh Neck, asking the Church to reinstate Williams, along with a letter, signed by Williams in front of the Association, expressing repentance for his faults. The members considered the Association's request, and concluded that if Williams would commune with them, they would restore him. When he failed to appear at the February communion service, the Church decided to continue his excommunication. As far as the members were concerned, that was the end of the matter.[84] Williams' appeal to the Association illustrates well the relationship between the Association and its constituent member churches: the Association could advise, but not compel action by Welsh Neck. Welsh Neck took the Association's advice seriously, but ultimately made its own decision about its former minister.

Williams seems to have continued to live somewhere in the vicinity of Welsh Neck, for when he died on 8 April 1768, the Rev. Pugh, then at Cashaway, delivered the funeral sermon, stressing that Williams was remarkably kind to the poor and afflicted. Williams and his wife were not listed as members of Cashaway on the list of those who signed that church's covenant in 1767 or who joined thereafter.[85] It would have been problematic for Cashaway, given its close links to Welsh Neck, to accept as members a couple who had been excommunicated. Pugh's willingness to deliver the funeral sermon may indicate the respect that many outside Welsh Neck had for the Williamses; it may also be significant that Pugh had been unceremoniously ejected as minister of Welsh Neck just

---

[84] WNCB, 3, 4, 5, 7, 10. Townsend incorrectly states that the Association succeeded in adjusting the quarrel between Williams and the Welsh Neck Church. *South Carolina Baptists*, 64-65.

[85] "Cashaway Church Book," 1767 list. Edwards, "Baptists in South-Carolina," 22.

over a year earlier, perhaps giving him sympathy with another pastor who had fallen out with the Welsh Neck congregation.[86] Robert and Anne Williams (née Bunn) had six children. One of their grandsons, David Rogerson Williams, became governor of South Carolina from 1814 until 1816.[87]

Nicholas Bedgegood

Nicholas Bedgegood served as pastor of Welsh Neck from 1759-1763 and from 1767-1774. The Bedgegood years saw the drafting of a formal covenant for Welsh Neck and the building of a new meeting house. His long tenure represented a period of relative stability for a church that had hitherto experienced a high turnover in its pastors and an ugly dispute with its most recent minister, Robert Williams. However, the Bedgegood period was also marked by controversy. The discovery that he was a bigamist led to his temporary replacement by the Rev. Evan Pugh; Pugh's failure to satisfy the church's needs led to Bedgegood's recall, a testimony to the gentlemanly and scholarly qualities that made Bedgegood popular, despite the scandal over his double marriage. During his first term as pastor, the Church Book was kept very diligently, providing a detailed picture of church life.

Bedgegood had been born at Thornbury, in Gloucestershire, England on 30 January 1731 (N.S.). He was raised in the Church of England and received more formal education than any other minister of the early Welsh Neck Church. His training included the classical languages and three years studying law in Bristol. At an early age, he married his first wife, Mary Weston; she refused to accompany him when he emigrated to America in 1751. In his new home, he began to think seriously about sin and salvation after hearing George Whitefield preach, and he became Whitefield's agent at the Bethesda Orphan House near Savannah, Georgia. When he read a sermon by Isaac Watts (1674-1748) in support of infant baptism, he decided that if Watts' arguments were "the best that could be said on the subject," then infant baptism was unsupported by Scripture. He was rebaptized by Oliver Hart on 19 July 1757 and ordained by him in February 1759.[88]

---

[86] WNCB, 14.

[87] Furman, *Charleston Association,* 75.

[88] Oliver Hart, "Diary," ed. Loulie Latimer Owens (Typescript in Furman University Special Collections), 4 records the ordination of a "Nicholas Bridgegood" on 26 February 1759; Morgan Edwards gives 1 February 1759 as the ordination date. "Baptists in South-Carolina," 23. Hart's "Diary" is a transcription of a transcription of the original; Edwards gathered his information directly from Bedgegood himself. Edwards' date is more likely to be accurate.

Bedgegood was not only well-educated, but had a gentlemanly demeanor that set him apart from others in the Baptist Church of that period.[89] These accomplishments contrasted with those of Oliver Hart, who had received "no more than a plain English education," though Hart was eager to make up for his deficiencies through private study. A faction of the wealthier members of the Charleston congregation attempted to replace Hart with Bedgegood, with the latter's compliance. When their attempt failed, many of Bedgegood's supporters withdrew from the church.[90] In the wake of this dispute, Bedgegood left Charleston in April 1759 to be pastor of the Welsh Neck church for one year. His personality and talents evidently pleased his new congregation, which renewed its call permanently on 8 March 1760.[91]

The Welsh Neck Covenant of 1760

On 2 August 1760 the pastor and members of the Welsh Neck church signed a covenant, which was reproduced in full in the Church Book. This signing was described as a "renewal" of the church members' commitments to each other, and certainly at least one earlier covenant existed.[92] The 1760 document was probably a reformulation of earlier agreements, with more defined, though probably not radically different, provisions. Leah Townsend, comparing the Welsh Neck covenant to covenants drawn up by other Baptist churches in South Carolina, concludes that it was relatively well-written, as might be expected of a scholarly pastor such as Bedgegood, and that it was of average length. Unlike other covenants, it dealt in detail with the issue of educating children in Christian knowledge and behavior, while saying nothing about the conduct of church meetings, about members' commercial activities, or about providing support for indigent church members.[93] It is tempting to wonder whether Bedgegood's influence explains the unusual provisions about bringing up children, given his previous work for Whitefield's orphanage in Georgia. The covenant covered doctrine, worship, and relations among members, defining the church's theoretical stance on each area of religious life. It was an important document that was supposed to inform the behavior of church members on a regular basis: a resolu-

---

[89] Elhanan Winchester described Bedgegood as "a good scholar, and a sound divine, an eloquent preacher and a polite gentleman." WNCB, 16. Furman stated that "Mr. Bedgegood was a classical scholar, and an accomplished speaker." *Charleston Association,* 75-76.

[90] Furman, *Charleston Association,* 76-77.

[91] WNCB, 3, 4; Edwards, "Baptists in South-Carolina," 22-24; Townsend, *South Carolina Baptists,* 281-284.

[92] The Church Book recorded a resolution to read an earlier covenant once a quarter. WNCB, 3.

[93] Townsend, *South Carolina Baptists,* 286-290.

tion of 2 September 1759 had called for an earlier version of the covenant to be read once a quarter at church meetings, "in order that by the divine blessing, the members may be animated in the discharge of the several duties incumbent upon them."[94] The Church Book provides the modern historian with some sense of how the covenant's goals were realized in practice.

Relatively little space in the covenant was taken up with the definition of doctrine.[95] Its brief references to doctrine indicate the strict Calvinism of the church, typical of Regular Baptists: the covenant portrays members as "desiring by the Grace of God to live & die in the faith of God's elect, constantly and steadily adhering to the glorious doctrines of Free Grace, and the plain scriptural administration of the words and ordinances."[96] The relatively brief coverage of doctrinal issues probably indicates that such matters could be taken for granted, rather than that they were unimportant. Under Bedgegood, the church made a couple of specific decisions about how it would apply its Calvinistic beliefs. On 4 April 1761, the church unanimously decided that Christians of other denominations who had been baptized as infants by "sprinkling" and who wished to join Welsh Neck, but did not wish to be rebaptized by immersion, would be admitted without a second baptism. This significant departure from a practice that normally distinguished Baptists from other sects was adopted because two Presbyterians, Alexander McIntosh and Roderick McIver, sought admittance to Welsh Neck.[97] McIver left Welsh Neck at some unrecorded point, but McIntosh

---

[94] WNCB, 3.

[95] By contrast, the Covenant adopted in 1767 by the Cashaway Church, an offshoot of Welsh Neck, dedicated eleven of its twenty articles to a careful definition of the Church's strict Calvinist doctrine, with entire paragraphs defining specific aspects of faith, such as the election of a "certain" number of men "before the world began," the imputation of Adam's sin to all, Christ's "special and particular" redemption of the elect only, man's utter incapability of doing good, and the "Resurrection of both the just and the unjust" at the Last Judgment. "Cashaway Church Book," 20 June 1767.

[96] WNCB, 6. Townsend describes this covenant as "heavily Calvinistic," influenced by the London Confession of 1689, which was adopted by the Philadelphia Association in 1742 (*South Carolina Baptists,* 286-290). Yet elsewhere, inconsistently, she states that "[t]he facts support the tradition still extant in the Peedee that the Welsh Neck Church in its earlier days was more Arminian than Calvinistic in its beliefs and practices." *South Carolina Baptists*, 76. The 1760 covenant drafted by Bedgegood, the care taken to procure a minister with strict Calvinist credentials when Winchester was called, and the revised covenant of 1785 drafted by Botsford all support the conclusion that the Welsh Neck church adhered to the strict Calvinism of the Regular Baptists throughout the eighteenth century.

[97] The Presbyterians were a dominant sect during the 1750s, when the South Carolina backcountry first began to be settled in earnest, but the lack of qualified Presbyterian ministers meant that Baptist churches began to take over as the most vital centers of religious life (Brown, *Regulators*, 20-22).

became a prominent member whose slaves later became the core group of the African American church. Did this waiving of the requirement for adult baptism by immersion indicate a "broad and tolerant spirit" at Welsh Neck?[98] This decision did suggest a certain flexibility, but the language of the church's resolution on this point makes it very clear that Welsh Neck members thought baptism by "sprinkling" wrong, and wished to impose strict limits on exceptions to adult baptism by immersion: the validity of infant baptism was accepted only for those "who were educated in the belief of Infant Baptism by sprinkling and as they labour under the prejudice of such an education can't see it their duty to submit to Immersion, having been already sprinkled." Even though Welsh Neck was willing to accommodate the "prejudice" of such applicants for admission, it was not willing to bend on the most fundamental point: they must "nevertheless satisfy the Church as to their real conversion," ie. by relating the experience of God's grace at work in their hearts. McIntosh and McIver both convinced the church of their experiences before they were admitted. The church's resolution on baptism made it clear that this choice was not open to those who had been brought up as Baptists: any who should "apostatize from the Truth in which they have been educated by getting themselves sprinkled, and refuse to submit to the mode of Immersion" would be denied membership, however clear their "account of a work of Grace on their hearts," for turning against immersion would render any such account "suspicious." The church thus provided a means for McIntosh and McIver to join while at the same time defining its principles unambiguously.[99] It should perhaps be noted that McIntosh, who owned 1,000 acres and over thirty slaves by the mid-1770s, was an extremely wealthy man by Pee Dee standards.[100] His social position was similar to that of Bedgegood's partisans during the controversy in Charleston.

The second area covered by the Welsh Neck covenant was the need for regular worship: "We promise to meet together every Lord's day and at all other opportunities as divine Providence shall permit; Keeping our places in the

---

[98] This judgment by Townsend has been picked up and repeated elsewhere. Townsend, *South Carolina Baptists,* 75-76; J. Glenn Clayton, "South Carolina Baptist Records," *The South Carolina Historical Magazine,* 85/4 (Oct. 1984): 319-320.

[99] WNCB, 8. Townsend incorrectly reports this decision on admitting those sprinkled, suggesting that it allowed anyone to avail themselves of this option, until the church later returned to a strict Baptist position. She also puts this decision forward as evidence of Welsh Neck's Arminian tendencies (*South Carolina Baptists,* 75-76). In fact, Welsh Neck never departed from the strict Baptist—and Calvinist—position on the fundamental issues: baptism by immersion was the only correct mode and, however they were baptized, members must have had an incontrovertible experience of the work of God on their hearts as adults.

[100] "Only a handful" of backcountry farmers owned more than twenty slaves (Brown, *Regulators,* 25, 140-141).

House of God as becometh Saints, 'not forsaking the assembling ourselves to-gether as the manner of some is.'"[101] However, the document said nothing about the details of church meetings. The Church Book reveals that first Sunday of each month was of particular importance, often a time for baptisms and for for-mal acts such as suspending, excommunicating, or restoring members to com-munion. The church decided, on 5 June 1762, that the day before the first Sun-day of the month would be the church's business meeting, when the experiences of prospective members were heard; similarly, complaints about members for "disorderly walking" were made at this meeting, and messengers or letters were dispatched to investigate or admonish the errant.[102] This decision seems to have confirmed a practice already in place. Once a quarter, the monthly Saturday and Sunday meetings assumed particular importance. The covenant provided that members should support the minister according to their ability; according to a resolution of 5 July 1760, the deacons made a collection for the support of the church at the quarterly business meeting, with each contributing "as God shall be pleased to influence the hearts of the members to give."[103] The quarterly business meeting on Saturday was then followed by quarterly communion on Sunday. The church decided on 1 August 1767 to have communion every two months, but by the time of Morgan Edwards' visit in 1772 the church had re-turned to quarterly communion, on the first Sundays of February, May, August, and November.[104] From 4 July 1761, communion was restricted to members of Welsh Neck, since allowing outsiders to commune was causing divisions in oth-er churches.[105] On 3 November 1770 communion was further restricted: no out-siders were allowed even to attend, except "such serious persons only, who par-ticularly desire to see it."[106] This provision suggests that non-members were not treating the occasion with the required solemnity. Monthly business meetings and quarterly communion were standard practices in South Carolina Baptist churches, though other churches sometimes held their business meetings on the Friday before the first Sunday.[107] In July 1760 Welsh Neck did resolve to set aside the first Friday of each month for public prayer regarding the "calamities" facing South Carolina, no doubt referring to the bloody Cherokee War that rav-aged the backcountry, caused a flood of refugees, and disrupted trade between 1760 and 1761.[108]

---

[101] WNCB, 6.
[102] Ibid., 11.
[103] Ibid., 5.
[104] Ibid., 14; Edwards, "Baptists in South-Carolina," 16.
[105] WNCB, 9.
[106] Ibid., 16.
[107] Townsend, *South Carolina Baptists,* 292-295.
[108] WNCB, 5; Brown, *Regulators,* 4-12.

The third and most important emphasis of the 1760 covenant was to create a community of believers who were both morally upright and bound together by mutual love. The first step towards such a community was ensuring that those who became members were truly chosen by God. The covenant was brief on this point: it simply instructed church members to pray "that our Church may flourish & many be added to it who shall be saved." Welsh Neck decided "who shall be saved" by asking prospective members to "give in their experiences" of God's grace working in their souls. Such experiences normally consisted of a profound sense of sinfulness and worthlessness followed by a conviction that, despite this worthlessness, God had determined to save this particular individual. At the beginning of Bedgegood's pastorate, such experiences of God's grace had to be related before the entire church, usually at the end of the Saturday business meeting at the start of each month.[109] These experiences were deeply personal, and it cannot always have been easy for shy folk to make these public relations. Therefore, on 2 May 1761, the church decided to provide an easier, though no less strict, means for prospective members to share their experiences: "As many difficulties attend persons, who apply for communion with us, [in] their relating their experience before the whole Congregation, it is concluded that such persons shall first apply and communicate the dealings of God with their souls, to the minister and such others of the members as the Church shall think proper; that they [ie. the minister and selected members] may relate it to the Church. Nevertheless such persons must appear before the Church to make a confession of their faith."[110] Evidence that each individual had been singled out for salvation was a vital precondition of membership; even in making accommodations for the bashful, this criterion had to be upheld.

Another means of receiving new members was by a formal letter of dismission issued by a church "of the same faith and order," to a Regular Baptist who had moved to the Pee Dee from elsewhere. These letters demonstrated that the individual in question was a member in good standing, that his/her theological beliefs were orthodox and behavior godly. Welsh Neck similarly issued letters of dismission to members who moved away. It took these letters very seriously, reissuing them to keep them current and recalling them if they decided that, after all, the departing member was not in good standing and would not reflect well on Welsh Neck if s/he applied for membership elsewhere.[111]

---

[109] Having prospective members relate their experiences after the monthly business meeting was standard practice in Regular Baptist churches. Townsend, *South Carolina Baptists,* 295-305.

[110] WNCB, 8.

[111] On 9 August 1759, the letter of dismission granted to the Rev. Williams was recalled when it was discovered he was charging the Welsh Neck church "with such crimes as to prevent his communion" (Ibid., 3). William Rowel and his wife were told to apply for a letter of dismission after it was learned they had moved to the Congarees (Ibid., 5).

Among those admitted to membership, a delicate balance had to be struck in their relations with each other. On the one hand, members were "to watch over the conversation of each other and not willfully to suffer sin upon one another without a gentle reproof." On the other hand, rebuking others' faults must always be done in a spirit of Christian charity, and members must "keep the unity of the spirit in the Bonds of peace; to bear with one another's infirmities, putting on bowels of Compassion as the elect of God, to forbear rash judging, evil surmises and reproachful or censorious Language."[112] The Church Book demonstrates the balance between discipline and loving forbearance set out in the covenant; it records an unceasing effort to call errant members to account, along with a sometimes quite extraordinary patience in convincing the guilty to return to the fold. The process generally started with a report of "disorderly walking" delivered at one of the monthly business meetings. Depending on the seriousness of the offense and the quality of the evidence, the church would either summon the accused to explain him/herself at the next meeting, or would proceed to immediate suspension. Suspension was a temporary excommunication from the church community. Messengers and sometimes letters were sent to those under suspicion or under suspension to inform them of the charges against them and to recommend repentance. In some cases, repeated messengers were sent to those sinners who failed to respond. The intended end of this process was that the accused would appear before the church, confess and express repentance for the fault, and be restored to communion. Only the truly stubborn were excommunicated, an extreme and unusual measure.[113] The elaborate process of disciplining and reconciling sinners demonstrated both the church's firm refusal to tolerate ungodly behavior and also its commitment to doing all that it could to bring its members back into the fold.

The patient determination to win its members back was not simply kindheartedness, but also part of the church's identity as a community of God's elect. New members were only admitted to the church after they had provided a

---

John Perkins was told to apply for a letter after he had moved away to another, unspecified, church (Ibid., 3).

[112] Ibid., 5-6.

[113] For example, Jacob D'Surrency was suspended for non-attendance at church in July 1759; three messengers were sent to him over the next two years, and he appeared before the church to express repentance in 1761, just in time to stave off full excommunication, though his suspension remained in place. Over the next four years further waywardness meant that five more messengers were sent to admonish him. He is not mentioned after October 1765; his eventual excommunication, death, or departure from the area may have occurred during the late 1760s or early 1770s when the Church Book was not being kept up (Ibid., 3, 4, 8, 9, 10, 11, 12). Another member who was suspended and restored more than once was Walter Downes, who received at least four messengers during Bedgegood's pastorate. Ibid., 3-15.

convincing account of an experience of God's saving grace. If that experience was real, then the individual was one of God's chosen. Even God's chosen might sin, but then God's grace should restore them to holy ways. If the church could not win them back, and had to proceed to the extreme measure of excommunication, then the church had been mistaken about that member's original relation of saving grace. If such mistakes occurred too often, then the crucial distinction between the elect and the damned was undermined. For the same reason, the church was careful to make sure that the repentance of sinners was sincere; hypocrisy might mislead the church about repentance just as it could with regard to the original experience of saving grace. In certain cases, the church refused to accept a statement of repentance or it asked the penitent to consider carefully whether s/he was truly sorry for the fault.[114] For example, on 2 August 1760, John Booth, who had been suspended for quarreling with a neighbor and for profanity, gave "a clear verbal account of his repentance" so that "the Church could not fairly reject him; but as some circumstances gave them occasion to be jealous over him, lest he was deceiving himself, they informed him of it, and left it to his own conscience to judge for himself whether it would be best to take his place, or to remain as he is till he has farther examined his heart. Upon which he concluded to delay for that purpose."[115] The church was anxious to restore sinning members and to vindicate its original judgment of their election, but repentance had to be as authentic as the original experience of God's grace. Disciplinary procedures were an important means of both purifying the church's membership and confirming its special spiritual status.

There were several specific faults for which members were admonished, suspended, or in extreme cases excommunicated. One was failure to attend worship without sufficient excuse, which was not only in itself a breach of the covenant, but often also a sign that the absentee was departing from godly behavior in other ways.[116] Drinking to excess or being "disguised with liquor" was a common charge; this was a pre-temperance age, and the Church Book always specified that it objected to drinking to excess, rather than to alcohol consump-

---

[114] For example, Jane Poland appeared and acknowledged her crimes, but failed to convince the church of her sincere repentance, so that she was suspended, though she was later restored to communion (Ibid., 8, 12); Samuel Reredon repented for his earlier "obscene conversation," but failed to satisfy the church of his sincerity (Ibid., 3).

[115] Ibid., 7. Booth was finally restored to communion on 4 April 1761 (Ibid., 8).

[116] Jacob D'Surrency was admonished for his absence from church in July 1759 and he soon afterwards was discovered to be guilty of a train of other faults, including drinking to excess and attending a horse race (Ibid., 3, 10). Walter Downes was similarly suspended for non-attendance, but was also found to have been idle, drinking to excess, contemning church authority, and other, unspecified offenses (Ibid., 3, 10).

tion *per se.*[117] Though a common failing, excessive drinking was nevertheless a serious one, and frequently led to suspension. If the guilty party failed to repent and reform, drunkenness could even contribute to excommunication.[118] Drunkenness, unlike most other offenses, only ever involved men; just one woman, Jane Poland, got in trouble for an alcohol-related offense, and that was for selling liquor at a horse race. Sexual offenses, though less common, also appear in the Church Book: Samuel Reredon was suspended for "obscene conversation" and the church refused to restore him because his repentance was unsatisfactory; David Baldy was similarly called before the church on reports of "guilty conversation with a woman," but was able to satisfy the church of his innocence. Even pre-marital sex was unacceptable: David and Martha Evans were forced to repent publicly for "criminal conversation before marriage."[119] Two women, Eleanor Evans and Elizabeth Simonson, were disciplined for living apart from their husbands. It is not entirely clear from the Church Book whether they were simply expected to return to their spouses or whether they needed to provide a satisfactory reason why they were living apart.[120] One common offense was using abusive language or spreading false reports against others; the church took seriously the language of its covenant, which forbade "rash judging, evil surmises and reproachful or censorious Language." The church also sent messengers to heal quarrels among members.[121]

Admonitions, suspensions, and excommunications were intended to keep the church community as morally pure as possible. There was, at least in the Church's first decades, another aspect to these punishments: humiliation in the face of society beyond the Church, or at least in the face of certain elements in that society. Many of those who were suspended or excommunicated had family members in the church or among those people who attended services and who might hope one day to experience God's saving grace and then become members.[122] Welsh Neck was a small community; those who fell afoul of the church

---

[117] Jacob D'Surrency, Walter Downes, Philip Douglass, William James, Jr., Philip Howel, James Harry, Joshua Edwards, David Evans, William James, William Jones, and William Thomas were all admonished, suspended, or excommunicated at least in part for excessive drinking (Ibid., 3, 5, 9, 10, 11, 12, 14).

[118] Philip Howel and William James were both excommunicated for excessive drinking, along with other sins (Ibid., 13).

[119] Ibid., 3, 10, 15. The reference to David and Martha Evans' "criminal conversation" makes it clear that "conversation" in these contexts meant more than talking. Mere bad language was referred to as "profanity" (Ibid., 4).

[120] Ibid., 5, 11.

[121] Ibid., 4, 9, 12, 14.

[122] For example, the 1775 list includes Anne and Paul Baldy, possibly relatives of David and Sarah, who were suspended during the 1760s for pre-marital sex and for other offenses; John Booth, who had to repent twice for quarreling and profanity before he was restored, may have been related to church members Rhoda and Sarah Booth; the latter

could not avoid regular contact with neighbors and relatives who regarded their disgrace as shameful. The messengers who were sent by the church to admonish the wayward were of course neighbors, too. Many of the behaviors that led to suspension or excommunication were not simply spiritual failings, but would have been regarded as moral breaches by society at large. In some cases, sinners probably sought reconciliation because of social pressure. The Welsh Neck Church was aware of this social dimension to suspension. On 6 September 1760 the church decided that if member had been publicly suspended, then his or her restoration should also be public.[123] It was clearly unfair not to repair a reputation damaged by temporary exclusion from communion. On 16 February 1765 the church adopted a different policy that seemed aimed at excluding the influence of the outside world from church decisions: the members decided that public suspension would no longer be practiced at Welsh Neck.[124] Whether this measure was adopted out of sensitivity to its members' feelings, out of a desire to prevent church discipline from becoming entangled with public gossip, or because of the scandal developing around the discovery of the Rev. Bedgegood's bigamy is unclear; but certainly it changed the dynamics behind suspension and restoration.

When church members were dealing with the world outside the church, they were not only mixing with neighbors and family members who respected Welsh Neck's values and reinforced the church's discipline. The Church Book also affords glimpses into a very different outside world: the rough and vibrant society of South Carolina's backcountry. Church was only one forum for community gathering, and it was not the most attended. Visitors to the backcountry during the 1760s and 1770s described militia musters and the convening of magistrates' courts, usually on Saturdays, when people from isolated farms and hamlets would converge on such population centers as there were for commerce and conviviality. Markets, shooting matches, horse races, dancing, drinking, lovemaking, and general rowdiness would accompany the official legal or military activities.[125] The Cashaway Church Book made it clear that even pious church members sometimes had to mix in these worldly gatherings in order to conduct

---

married into the Wilds family, and so was connected to a clan that supplied several members to the church, including a deacon, Abel; William Thomas, suspended for drink in 1765, was married to a church member, Mary, and may have been related to one or more of the other four Thomases who were church members. Not all those who shared a surname were necessarily related – Thomas, of course, was a common Welsh last name – but given the many clusters of homonymous individuals in the church, there must have been occasions where individuals under suspension faced embarrassment as they lived and socialized with those in good standing. Ibid., *passim*.

[123] Ibid., 7.
[124] Ibid., 12.
[125] Brown, *Regulators*, 23-24.

legitimate business.[126] When the Welsh Neck Church Book chided Jane Poland for selling liquor at a horse race, or James James for beating his neighbor, or Philip Howel for "unworthy conduct at a public sale," or David Evans for drinking to excess and "attempting to dance in public" (was he too drunk to stand up?), it becomes clear that the members of this serious and pious community sometimes interacted with a very different crowd in their lives outside church, and that they faced temptations that could be more compelling than their church membership.[127] Some historians have argued that Welsh Neck and other churches were the only important institutions imposing law and order in the back country, and that the example they set had a wide influence.[128] There were certainly instances of Baptist churches providing arbitration for disputes over property.[129] However, such interventions were infrequent, even among church members. Given the tiny proportion of the backcountry population that belonged to such churches, and the difficulties faced by Welsh Neck and no doubt other churches in keeping some of their own members in line, the claim that Baptist churches had a significant role in enforcing law and order seems somewhat extravagant. Among a certain, limited group, already inclined to certain moral norms, Baptist discipline may have helped sustain order. Among the more lawlessly or licentiously inclined, it seems unlikely that Welsh Neck or other churches had much influence. More believable is the assessment that the churches, like other representatives of hierarchy and order, had to fight hard to prevent the unruly culture of the backcountry from corrupting their congregations.[130]

---

[126] "No member of this church shall at any time without lawful call go to any horse race, shooting match, or public place of carnal mirth, or diversion whatsoever. And when lawfully called shall not stay longer there [than] to do his and their business and when any person shall have a call to any of the aforesaid places, they shall produce to the Church their reasons for going and the Church shall judge..." (Cashaway Church Book," 12 September 1759).

[127] WNCB, 4, 7, 10.

[128] Townsend, *South Carolina Baptists,* 293.

[129] For example, on 16 April 1768, Welsh Neck appointed Thomas James, Howel James, and Thomas Evans as arbitrators in a dispute between James James and Thomas Jones, and in 1770 the Cashaway Church settled a dispute between William Owens and "Big" Benjamin James over the sale of a mare. WNCB, 15; "Cashaway Church Book," June 1770.

[130] Note that there were four militia units of 1500 men each in the South Carolina backcountry in this period. Regular militia training provided a sense of disciplined group identity for many more settlers than churches did. Brown, *Regulators,* 23-24. In the late 1760s, military action rather than religious revivals brought law and order to the backcountry.

The Pugh Interlude

Bedgegood's first four years at Welsh Neck seem to have been energetic and successful. The Church Book reveals that monthly meetings were held regularly, discipline was enforced vigorously, and that Welsh Neck continued to participate in the Charleston Association, of which it was a founding member.[131] In fact, Welsh Neck briefly became the center in 1759 of a sub-Association, consisting of a number of North Carolina churches that had joined the Charleston Association, but which wished to meet at a more convenient location.[132] Bedgegood was asked to intervene during the awkward situation that developed at Cashaway in 1760 when its pastor, Joshua Edwards (formerly pastor at Welsh Neck), was discovered to have engaged in excessive drinking. Bedgegood became an intermediary between Cashaway and the Charleston Association, seeking the advice of other pastors, including Hart, before recommending specific action with regard to Edwards. In the midst of this crisis, Bedgegood helped to provide alternate leadership for the Cashaway church by ordaining Anthony Pouncey as deacon there.[133] Under Bedgegood's leadership, Welsh Neck even supplied new ministers for churches beyond South Carolina. Hezekiah Smith of New Jersey was ordained at Welsh Neck in 1763 and, after a period supplying Cashaway, went on to serve at Haverhill, Massachusetts.[134] Bedgegood started off as a well-respected pastor with a more than local standing among Regular Baptists.

The first clouds appeared in 1762, when differences between Welsh Neck and the Charleston Association emerged over the status of Welsh Neck's deposed pastor, the Rev. Williams. As described above, Welsh Neck did not follow the Association's advice to accept Williams back as a member of the church. The difference with the Association over Williams may explain the apparent failure by Welsh Neck to participate in the 1762 meeting of the Association. A far more serious crisis erupted the following year. After settling at Welsh Neck, Bedgegood married a local woman, Mary Morphy, by whom he eventually had two children. Then, probably in 1763, news arrived in South Carolina that Bedgegood's first wife, Mary Weston, was still alive in England. Bedgegood was summoned to explain himself before the Charleston Association. He claimed that he had had convincing information that his first wife, whom he had not seen since his emigration in 1751, was dead, so that he thought himself free to remarry. However, he refused to attend the formal enquiry ordered by Association, which then disowned him. Bedgegood's former stature meant that the

---

[131] See WNCB, 4, 7, 10 for the record of the messengers or letters sent in 1759, 1760, and 1761.

[132] Furman, *Charleston Association,* 13.

[133] "Cashaway Church Book," 26 July 1760.

[134] Furman, *Charleston Association,* 12, 71.

scandal damaged the reputation of the entire Association, and contributed to a religious decline over the next decade.[135] The Welsh Neck Church Book omits any mention of this embarrassing issue, but its detailed record-keeping suddenly faltered in the summer of 1763 and then went silent for over a year. There are many possible explanations for this sudden change, such as lost or damaged pages (although it seems likely that the transcriber, who recorded such information, would have noted this), but it may be that the hiatus is an eloquent indication of loss of confidence by the minister and of confusion in the church.[136] It is clear that by the beginning of 1765, if not before, the Rev. Pugh was keeping the Church Book, even though he had not yet been called to be pastor of the church.

It seems a reasonable assumption that Welsh Neck was ready to accept Bedgegood's claim that the bigamy was an honest mistake. Not only was the Church Book studiously silent about the issue, but the church was ready to issue letters of dismission for Bedgegood on 2 March 1765, on 4 October 1766, and again on 6 December 1766. The October 1766 letter was replicated in full in the Church Book, and it stated that Bedgegood "is now a member in full communion with us" and that during his time as a member and pastor of the church, "he was unusually beloved."[137] Yet, beloved or not, even accidental bigamy could not be simply ignored. There are only fragments of information available to support educated guesses about the discussions and disciplinary measures that took place over the period 1763-1766. The October 1766 letter of dismission stated that Bedgegood had served as minister for "four years and better"; since he began his pastorate in April 1759, it would seem that he ceased to act as pastor sometime over the summer of 1763, at the same time the record-keeping in the Church Book faltered. Was he suspended at some point, and forced to repent publicly before he was restored? Did the church's decision in February 1765 to end the practice of public suspension have any connection to the Bedgegood affair? If he did undergo some form of discipline, and succeeded in convincing the church that his crime had been a mistake and that his repentance was sincere, the church may have restored him to communion, while feeling that he could not resume his ministerial duties; Welsh Neck had taken action of this kind in September 1760 when one of the church's deacons, Philip Douglass, suspended for excessive drinking, repented before the congregation; he was restored to communion but not to his diaconal role.[138] Just as Bedgegood had been asked to preside over the enquiry into pastor Joshua Edwards at Cashaway in 1760, it seems that Oliver Hart came to Welsh Neck to help the church make its decision re-

---

[135] *Ibid.,* 16, 75-76; Townsend, *South Carolina Baptists,* 68-69n.
[136] WNCB, 11.
[137] Ibid., 12, 13.
[138] Ibid., 7.

garding Bedgegood. On 1 March 1765, Pugh wrote in his diary of going "a gun-ning" with Hart;[139] it was at the church meeting on the next day that Welsh Neck issued a formal letter of dismission for Bedgegood to the Charleston church.[140] Hart's intervention seems to have involved an invitation for Bedgegood to take refuge at Charleston, presumably to avoid the awkwardness of having a deposed minister in the congregation at Welsh Neck. However, if Bedgegood ever went to Charleston, he never became a regular member of the church there, since his next two letters of dismission the following year were both issued by Welsh Neck, and the 4 October letter described him as in "full communion" with the Welsh Neck Church.[141] It cannot have been any easier for Bedgegood to face the Charleston community under the shadow of his disgrace, given his popularity there six years earlier. Certainly Bedgegood was still at Welsh Neck (or back at Welsh Neck) and was even preaching there in January 1766; Pugh recorded him leaving the area on 19 January.[142]

Meanwhile, Welsh Neck was seeking a replacement pastor. In August 1765 the church issued a call to Hart, who was well-known and respected throughout South Carolina and who was familiar to the Welsh Neck congrega-tion from his visits in March and May of that year. Hart, not surprisingly, de-clined the call in December, preferring to stay at the more prestigious church in Charleston. Once Hart had turned down Welsh Neck's invitation, in January 1766 the church turned to Evan Pugh, who accepted the call.[143]

The Rev. Evan Pugh was born 2 April 1732 in Metachin, Pennsylvania, to Quaker parents. He converted to the Baptist faith in 1754, and John Gano pro-posed that he be the first beneficiary of the Charleston Association's education fund. Pugh received training from Hart and Francis Pelot; he preached before the Association in 1762, met with its members' approval, and was ordained the

---

[139] Evan Pugh, *Diaries, 1762-1801.* (Florence, SC: St. David's Society, 1993), 42.

[140] WNCB, 12.

[141] Ibid., 13; Pugh, *Diaries,* 59. Townsend suggests that Bedgegood's departure from Welsh Neck for Charleston in 1765 was part of a plan on his part to supplant Hart as pastor in the port city. This seems an unlikely explanation. Bedgegood's disgrace meant that he was in no position to make a bid for the Charleston pastorate at this stage; Town-send confuses the controversy between the Hart and Bedgegood factions in 1759 with the very different situation pertaining in 1765. Furthermore, Hart would hardly have traveled to Welsh Neck to preside over the dismissal of Bedgegood to Charleston, if Hart thought his former rival was attempting to unseat him.

[142] Pugh, *Diaries,* 52. The second letter of dismission for Bedgegood, issued on 4 October 1766, stated that he had been a member of Welsh Neck for six years and eight months. Since Bedgegood had joined the church in the spring of 1759, this statement reinforces the idea that he did not go to Charleston in 1765, but stayed on at Welsh Neck until January 1766. WNCB 3, 13.

[143] WNCB, 12.

following year.[144] By 1764 he was preaching at Cashaway and was also performing many pastoral functions at Welsh Neck after questions had arisen concerning Bedgegood's marriages; on 2 January 1765 he, rather than Bedgegood,
preached at the funeral of Jane McIntosh, wife of one of the most prominent
members of the church.[145] Throughout 1765 he served Welsh Neck by persuad-
ing miscreants to repent and he was sent to represent the church at the Charleston Association in October of that year, the first recorded participation of Welsh
Neck in the Association's annual meeting since 1761.[146] By the time he was
formally called to be the church's pastor, in January 1766, he had been serving
as *de facto* minister for over a year.

The curt but regular entries in Pugh's private diary show his routine while
he was minister at Welsh Neck. In addition to preaching at Saturday church
meetings and Sunday services, he visited the dying and their families, preached
at their funerals, less frequently performed weddings (usually at people's
homes), and on one occasion went to see a woman who was "out of her senses."
While serving at Welsh Neck, he often preached at Cashaway. As he traveled
around his parish and between the two churches, he regularly had to spend the
night with various church members. Many of his parishioners knew Pugh not
just as a preacher in the pulpit, but as someone who shared their meals and slept
in their homes, giving comfort and sharing celebrations.[147] His travels included a
trip to Charleston in October 1766, again to represent Welsh Neck at the annual
meeting of the Association.[148]

Yet, despite the arduous routine recorded in his diary, Pugh for some reason did not win the affections of his flock. On 6 December 1766, at a monthly
church meeting when Pugh was not present, Abel Wilds raised the question of
why the church was in a "declining state." The meeting reached "the unanimous
opinion, that it was owing to the general dislike of Mr. Pugh." The members
then discussed "whether it would be most for the glory of God for Mr. Pugh to
continue our minister or to remove to some other place." The decision "was a

---

[144] Furman, *South Carolina Association,* 10-11, 79-80. Edwards put his ordination
in 1764. "Baptists in South-Carolina," 36-38. Townsend states that Pugh's tombstone at
Black Creek Church records his birth in 1729. *South Carolina Baptists,* 68. Brown is
incorrect in stating (*Regulators,* 20-22) that Pugh arrived in South Carolina as part of the
wave of "New Light" Baptists headed by Philip Mulkey; Pugh was trained and ordained
by the Regular Baptists. Pugh did join Hart and other Regular Baptist leaders in attempting to establish some degree of union with Mulkey and the Separates, but the attempt
failed. Furman, *South Carolina Association*, 13-14.

[145] "Cashaway Church Book," 22 December 1764; Pugh, *Diaries,* 42.

[146] WNCB, 12. Pugh procured the repentance of Joshua Edwards and William
Thomas.

[147] Pugh, *Diaries,* 52-61.

[148] WNCB, 13.

matter of consequence [so] it was thought advisable to consider it with deliberation." Their deliberations lasted a week. On 13 December 1766 the church met with Pugh and terminated his pastorate. The Church Book labeled Pugh's departure a "resignation" and stated that he "acquiesced in their opinion." Pugh saw the matter differently; his diary entry on 13 December bluntly stated: "had a Church Meeting I am Dismiss'd from ye Church in ye Welch Neck." Unlike Bedgegood, who seems to have lingered in the parish for almost a year after he received his first letter of dismission, Pugh moved away suddenly—on the following Monday (15 December) he was "in ye Study searchg my papers & packg them up in order to move." Fortunately for Pugh, he had somewhere to go: less than two weeks later, on 27 December, he received a call from Cashaway. [149]

Why had the members of Welsh Neck taken a dislike to Pugh? Townsend suggests that Pugh's participation in the Regulator movement may have been the reason for his dismissal. [150] It is true that Pugh attended Regulator meetings, but his earliest recorded involvement was almost two years later, in August and September 1768. [151] In fact, the Regulator movement only got underway in the summer of 1767, after Pugh had left Welsh Neck. It is also the case that prominent members of the Welsh Neck church, including Alexander McIntosh and George Hicks, were local leaders of the Regulators, so Pugh's association with the movement would hardly have earned him the unanimous dislike of the Welsh Neck Church. [152] A better explanation might be Pugh's poor health; during 1766 he was frequently unwell. On 13 July of that year he was taken ill in the pulpit, and he spent the rest of that month and much of August at home, suffering from a fit of ague, incapable of performing his duties. [153] However, in another pastor, illness might have provoked compassion instead of impatience, and the explanation for Pugh's short tenure at Welsh Neck may simply be that there was an incompatibility of personality between Pugh and his parish; he seems to have been a reluctant choice in the first place, given that the church waited for a year and first tried to recruit Hart before they gave Pugh a call, even though he was actively ministering among them.

The timing of Welsh Neck's decision to dispense with his services is interesting. At the same meeting where Abel Wilds raised the question of why the church was in decline, the members also signed a third letter of dismission for

---

[149] Ibid., 14. It was Bedgegood who wrote the details of Pugh's dismissal into the Church Book some months after Pugh had left. Bedgegood did not supply any dates, and the transcriber guessed that these meetings took place at the beginning of 1767. Pugh's record of these events makes it clear that the preliminary discussion was on 6 December 1766 and the dismissal was on 13 December. *Diaries,* 61.

[150] Townsend, *South Carolina Baptists,* 68.

[151] Pugh, *Diaries,* 76, 77.

[152] Brown, *Regulators,* 54-58.

[153] Pugh, *Diaries,* 57-58.

Bedgegood, who had recently obtained a position at a church on James Island.[154] The discussion of this third letter may have led to a discussion about having Bedgegood back; if he was fit to serve as pastor on James Island, presumably he was fit to serve again at Welsh Neck. The availability of Bedgegood may have triggered the decision to clear the way for his return by dismissing Pugh. It seems very unlikely that Welsh Neck would have allowed Bedgegood back if he still had two living wives, however anxious they were to replace Pugh. Some change of circumstances must have taken place, such as trustworthy reports from England that Mary Weston, his first wife, really was dead. Certainly, the restored relationship between Welsh Neck and the Charleston Association continued unimpaired by Bedgegood's return: Welsh Neck sent a letter to the 1767 meeting and in December read a letter from the Association and the minutes of the annual meeting to the church members.[155] Whatever the exact situation may have been, it is clear that on the very day the church endorsed Bedgegood in a third letter of dismission, they began the discussions that led to Pugh's removal a week later.

Despite Pugh's short tenure as pastor at Welsh Neck Church, he continued to be a significant figure among the Regular Baptists of South Carolina. In June 1767, under his leadership, his new congregation at Cashaway drafted its covenant. Pugh delivered the official sermon—"Ministers, Fellow Workers in Christ"—at the Charleston Association's annual meeting in November 1767 and published it at the Association's request. By 1770 he owned 300 acres in the Cashaway area, and according to the 1790 census possessed 17 slaves. He may have owned as many as 1,000 acres by the time of his death.[156] Sometime before 1772 he had married Martha Magee and had three children. He seems to have borne no ill feelings towards Welsh Neck, and stepped in to help with preaching and baptisms during the hiatus between Bedgegood and Winchester and again during the Revolution.[157] He also at times served the church at Catfish.[158] He

---

[154] The James Island church was a branch of the Charleston church. Townsend, *South Carolina Baptists,* 68. Since Bedgegood was dismissed to any church of the same faith and order in the October 1766 letter, it seems unlikely that he was serving as minister to a particular church at that stage. The appointment to the St. James parish is therefore likely to have been very recent indeed when the December letter was issued.

[155] WNCB, 14.

[156] Brown, *Regulators*, 140-141.

[157] Pugh baptized fifteen new members of the Welsh Neck congregation between 1774 and 1775, after seven years under Bedgegood with no baptisms at all (WNCB, 16). During his August 1774 visit to Welsh Neck, he stayed with Abel Wilds, the man who had initiated the move to get rid of Pugh in 1766. Pugh, *Diaries,* 136-141. Either Pugh did not know about Wilds' role, or the two men had decided to forgive and forget.

[158] Edwards, "Baptists in South-Carolina," 31-32; "Cashaway Church Book," 20 June 1767 .

received an A.M. degree from Rhode Island College and served as a delegate to South Carolina's constitutional convention in 1790. He died, still a resident of the Pee Dee region, on 26 December 1802, "a man of genuine Piety, of sound judgment, of plain unaffected manners, and of a cheerful entertaining conversation."[159]

The Return of Bedgegood

With Pugh gone, the Welsh Neck congregation recalled Bedgegood on 7 March 1767; he quickly accepted the call and preached his first sermon at his old church on 12 April. As part of the attempt to revive religious life, messengers of care were sent to "several persons" in May; these were reconciled to the church in June.[160] However, despite an energetic start, Bedgegood's second term as pastor of Welsh Neck was generally marked by a lack of activity, and certainly by a lack of new members for the church. An entry in the Church Book, possibly by his successor, Elhanan Winchester, summed up his pastorate as follows:

> He was regarded a good scholar, and a sound divine, an eloquent preacher and a polite gentleman; and well beloved by his acquaintance: Yet notwithstanding all his abilities and endowments, he was never very successful, especially in the latter part of his life: none being baptized after his return.[161]

The difficult and embarrassing circumstances surrounding his bigamy may have reduced his stature and self-confidence, making energetic leadership difficult for Bedgegood during his second term as pastor. Further challenges arose from the disruption caused by the Regulator conflict, which erupted during the summer of 1767, months after his resumption of the Welsh Neck pastorate. The Regulator Movement was a response to a long-standing wave of crime and disorder in the interior of South Carolina. Migrants who were moving into the colony from the north, along the migration trail that led along the Appalachian Mountains from Pennsylvania to Georgia, were not only hard-working farming families in search of land, but also refugees from the law, husbands escaping wives, and debtors escaping creditors. Escaped slaves, both African and Indian, joined the ranks of the marginalized. The disruptions of the Cherokee War from 1760-1761 had given many rootless migrants an opportunity to live off plunder and rapine; when peace returned, they continued their lawless way of life, engaging in property theft and even in the abduction of young women. Gangs of outlaws, sometimes led by notorious families such as the Blacks, Moons, and

---

[159] Furman, *Charleston Association,* 79-80; Townsend, *South Carolina Baptists,* 68; Edwards, "Baptists in South-Carolina," 36-38.
[160] WNCB, 14.
[161] Ibid., 16.

Tyrells, could number as many as 200-300. Networks stretching along the frontier up into Virginia allowed these gangs to dispose of their ill-gotten gains in distant markets. The fear of murder, mutilation, and torture ensured that no-one stood up to these criminals. Legitimate traders profited by disposing of stolen property; informants, including wagon drivers, who were important in the exchange of goods between the interior and the coast, provided details about potential plunder.[162] Justices of the Peace, the only representatives of law and order in the interior, had limited jurisdiction and limited means of enforcing such jurisdiction as they had.[163] Isolated from the government in Charleston, many were bribed or intimidated into ignoring depredations. The few criminals who were apprehended had to be taken to Charleston for incarceration and trial, an expensive and laborious process that too often prevented justice from being done. Complaints to the authorities in Charleston, including requests for local jails and courts, had brought no response. During the summer of 1767 some of the leading men of the interior – large landowners, mill owners, and others who had the most to lose in the rising disorder – formed the Regulators, an unofficial militia that was determined to enforce law and order in the vacuum of authority in the interior.

The Pee Dee region was particularly plagued by criminal activity; the wealthy farmers who worked the rich land of the area were tempting prey. It is therefore not surprising that prominent members of the Welsh Neck and other Baptist churches in the region took a leading role in the Regulation.[164] Alexander McIntosh and George Hicks were two wealthy members of the Welsh Neck church who participated in this movement, and other members or relatives of members may have done so as well.[165] Experience as militia commanders made some of these men ready and able to assume leadership of Regulator units. The Regulation began as a series of local initiatives during the summer of 1767 and then evolved into a formal organization—which assumed the name "Regulator"—at a mass meeting in October of that year.[166] From December 1767 until March 1768 the Regulators across South Carolina energetically tracked down the criminals in their remote bases and even pursued them out of the colony, as far north as Virginia, to recover abducted women and stolen goods.[167] The

---

[162] Brown, *Regulators*, 27-37.

[163] Justices of the Peace could only decide civil cases concerning property valued at less than £20. More serious civil cases and all criminal cases had to be referred to Charleston. *Ibid.*, 13-14.

[164] *Ibid.*, 40.

[165] McIntosh and Hicks both owned upwards of 1,000 acres at the height of their wealth; McIntosh owned over thirty slaves during the 1770s; Hicks at one point owned forty-two. *Ibid.*, 140-141.

[166] *Ibid.*, 38-41.

[167] *Ibid.*, 45-46.

Regulators' energy emboldened resistance among many of those formerly intimidated by the outlaws. The criminals increasingly found it hard to operate within South Carolina. After initial reservations, the colonial government lent its support to the movement.[168]

As the Regulators asserted their power, some of the respectable inhabitants began to complain of abuses. In some cases, individual Regulators undoubtedly used the movement to pursue vendettas against personal enemies. A rather different and more interesting type of abuse was that the Regulators went beyond the apprehension and punishment of criminals and attempted to impose a new moral order on the interior. This new phase of the movement was initiated by a "Congress" held at the Congarees in June 1768; "several of the principal settlers ... men of property" from the Pee Dee attended. One goal of this Congress was the punishment of idleness and vagrancy. Since many landless males had joined outlaw gangs to live off plunder, or had engaged in pettier crimes such as stealing fruit and pilfering crops, the Regulators intended to force males without land to take up gainful employment or face physical punishment. While there were real dangers in the existence of a rural underclass that might well prefer theft to work, the landowners who headed the Regulator movement were also benefiting from solving a problem that had long held back their ability to develop their lands: it was easy to obtain large acreage, but almost impossible to find anyone to work it. Slaves were too costly for all but the very wealthiest, and white men would not work at a wage the landowners were ready to pay. The Regulators were beginning to turn their war against crime into an excuse to create a system of forced labor from which they would profit. Another sign that the Regulators were wealthy men or supportive of the wealthier class was that creditors, even from outside the colony, were invited to use the Regulators' power to seize those who owed them money. It was not only the protection and enhancement of property that interested the Regulators. "Loose" women were ducked and flogged for prostitution and even for having children out of wedlock, a widespread situation in a region with few churches. Unlicensed taverns, often the resort of the idle underclass, were closed.[169] Clearly, basic law and order was linked in the Regulators' minds with a moral order similar to the one enforced by Welsh Neck, Cashaway, and other churches. Leaders like McIntosh and Hicks were using their paramilitary organization to extend the discipline revealed in the Welsh Neck Church Book to the community at large. Evan Pugh, now pastor at Cashaway, was willing to attend Regulator meetings and lend his

---

[168] Governor Montagu issued a proclamation against the Regulators on 6 October 1767, but when 4,000 men signed a petition demanding local courts and jails and cheaper access to the law, he created an official force, the Rangers, which essentially legalized the movement. *Ibid.,* 41-45.

[169] *Ibid.,* 20-22, 46-52, 83-90, 135-136.

moral support to their activities.[170] The outside world that had tempted Walter Downes and Jane Poland and Jacob D'Surrency to sin was now experiencing retaliation from respectable members of the Baptist community.

The excesses of the Regulators sparked increasing opposition from locals and from the colonial authorities during the summer of 1768. In July, McIntosh and Hicks were among the Regulator leaders involved in open defiance of colonial authorities at Marrs Bluff, when the Regulators refused to release one of their prisoners, a militia captain named Joseph Holland, on the orders of South Carolina's Provost Marshall, Roger Pinckney.[171] Along with similar actions elsewhere, the Marrs Bluff confrontation led Lieutenant Governor Bull to issue a proclamation on 3 August 1768 suppressing the Regulators.[172] To enforce this order, the colonial government sanctioned a rival paramilitary organization, the Moderators, led by men of property but also enlisting many of the landless—and perhaps even some of the outlaws—who had faced the Regulators' wrath.[173] Even so, Regulator activity continued: Evan Pugh attended Regulator meetings as late as November 1769; Philip Pledger, a Pee Dee planter, led an expedition against the Driggers gang in September 1771, summarily hanging its leader.[174] Regulators finally ended their paramilitary activity when the colonial government responded to their demands for local courts and jails, so that law and order could be easily and cheaply enforced. The Circuit Court Act of 1769 established six circuit courts for South Carolina, each with a jail.[175] One of these was to be located in the Pee Dee valley; after some debate, the site chosen was Long Bluff, close to Welsh Neck. The colonial government spent £71,000 in South Carolina currency to build the courthouse and jail for the Pee Dee; the construction was supervised by a group of commissioners, including Welsh Neck parishioners and former Regulators, McIntosh and Hicks. Bedgegood preached at the opening of the new court house in 1772, a testimony to the status of the Welsh Neck Church in the community that was now the center of law and order for the ar-

---

[170] Pugh attended Regulator meetings in August and September 1768 and in November 1769. *Ibid.*, 102-103; Pugh, *Diaries*, 76-77.

[171] Brown, *Regulators*, 54-58. Another Regulator leader at this action, Philip Pledger, may have been related to the several Pledgers (Elizabeth, John, Joseph, Phebe, and Sarah), who were members of Welsh Neck.

[172] *Ibid.*, 58-60.

[173] *Ibid.*, 83-90.

[174] Winslow Driggers had served under Capt. Alexander McIntosh during the Cherokee War, and had chosen to continue his life of raiding and plunder in the Pee Dee region when peace came. *Ibid.*, 29, 102-103.

[175] An earlier Circuit Court Act of 1768 was disallowed by imperial authorities because it had made "good behavior" the basis for the judges' tenure, placing them effectively under control of the Assembly instead of the Crown (Ibid., 64-82).

ea.[176] Along with the institutions of law and order came representation in the Assembly: the Pee Dee region became part of the new parish and constituency of St. David's (perhaps a nod to its Welsh inhabitants?) in 1768. Once the courts were established, prominent local men, including McIntosh and Hicks, were generally chosen to serve on the grand jury; these Regulator leaders continued to enforce law and order, including anti-vagrancy laws, but now as part of the legal system.[177]

Despite the prominent role played by two Welsh Neck Church members and a former pastor in the Regulator drama, none of the turmoil of the period found its way into the Church Book. When the next political crisis, between Great Britain and her colonies, developed, the Church Book was again largely silent, though it did record a decision in October 1770 to appoint a day of fasting and prayer "in consideration of the gloomy appearance of the state of this Church in particular; that of religion in general; and that of our nation and colonies."[178] The lack of political information was part of a more general silence: Bedgegood recorded very little in the Church Book during his second pastorate. In part, this silence may have been because of lack of activity. We know there were no baptisms between 1767 and 1774; it may also be the case, though we cannot be sure, that the active moral discipline of his early years also decayed.

While Bedgegood failed to add new members and perhaps also did little about disciplining old ones in the 1767-1774 period, he did preside over the acquisition of property and the building of a new meeting house. The decision to build a new meeting house was made under Pugh, on 22 March 1766.[179] On 16 April 1768 the church received a gift of two acres from Daniel Devonald, an official conveyance of the land on which the 1744 meeting house already stood. The new building was erected beside the old one. The grant of the land prompted the appointment of John Sutton and Abel Edwards as trustees to make decisions with regard to church property.[180] The new meeting house, forty-five by thirty feet, was finished in 1769.[181] Bedgegood enjoyed a salary of £400 in South Carolina currency in 1772, with £50 in perquisites; he seems to have been personally prosperous, and he owned 300 acres and sixteen slaves when he died on 1 February 1774.[182]

---

[176] Townsend, *South Carolina Baptists,* 276; Furman, *South Carolina Association,* 61.

[177] Brown, *Regulators,* 57, 107-111.

[178] WNCB, 15.

[179] Pugh, *Diaries,* 54.

[180] WNCB, 15.

[181] Edwards, "Baptists in South-Carolina," 16. Most early Baptist churches were designed as simple rectangles, and Welsh Neck seems to have been no exception. Townsend, *South Carolina Baptists,* 294-295.

[182] Townsend, *South Carolina Baptists,* 68-69; WNCB, 16.

Bedgegood left Welsh Neck in a stable situation. There had been some-what more than sixty-six members when he first took over in 1759; by 1772, numbers were down to forty-five, but these were individuals whose long-term membership demonstrated strong commitment to the church.[183] The roll of members included leading landowners of the local community, whose involve-ment with the Regulators had helped to make Welsh Neck the center of a new court district and political constituency. The Welsh Neck Baptists, though not part of the established Church of England, were certainly not a socially marginal group. Despite the scandal involving his two marriages, Bedgegood's almost twelve years of service between 1759 and 1774 marked a period of continuity, in contrast to the tumultuous decade to come.

B. Elhanan Winchester and the African American Church, 1775-1779

Elhanan Winchester was the pastor of Welsh Neck for only four and a half years, but in that short time he changed the church dramatically by baptizing almost a hundred African Americans. He also played a significant role in the political campaign to disestablish the Church of England in South Carolina, and to put all Protestant denominations in the state on an equal footing. Winchester's experiences at Welsh Neck started him on his journey to Universalism, and thus Welsh Neck was an important, if unwilling, contributor to the Universalist movement. His pastorate tested the community's Regular Baptist identity, which reasserted itself after the Revolution.

Winchester's First Years at Welsh Neck

Elhanan Winchester was born in Brookline, Massachusetts on 30 Septem-ber 1751 to a New Light family of Welsh extraction.[184] He was the eldest of (eventually) fifteen siblings, and his parents could not afford to provide him with much formal education. Yet, being of delicate health, he eschewed the ro-bust sports of his peers, and dedicated his time to study. He taught himself Latin, along with some French, Greek, and Hebrew. He had an extraordinary memory. His mother, Sarah, died when he was nine, and his father remarried.[185]

Winchester, always pious, had an intense conversion experience in 1769, and was baptized by immersion by the Rev. Ebenezer Lyon of Canterbury, Con-

---

[183] WNCB, 2. Sixty-six names are included on the 1759 list, but the transcriber mentions that there were others that could not be deciphered. Edwards provides the num-ber of members for 1772. "Baptists in South-Carolina," 16.

[184] Stone, Edwin Martin, *Biography of Reverend Elhanan Winchester* (Boston: H.B. Brewster, 1836), 13; Anne Lee Bressler, *The Universalist Movement in America, 1770-1880,* (Oxford Scholarship Online, 2001), 15.

[185] Stone, *Winchester,* 13-22.

necticut. In the same year he married his first wife, Alice Rogers. He soon gained a reputation for powerful preaching, thanks to his intense enthusiasm, his powerful eloquence, and his remarkable command of Scripture. He gathered his followers into a church at Rehoboth, Massachusetts, but his embrace of strict Calvinism and closed communion alienated a congregation that was inclined to Arminianism. He refused to forsake his principles in order to keep his position, and moved on to join a Regular Baptist church at Bellingham, Massachusetts. He preached widely throughout the eastern part of the state for the next few years, but did not have a church of his own.[186]

In 1774 he went to Hopewell, New Jersey to be inoculated against small-pox. There, he heard of a need for ministers in South Carolina, and, once his quarantine was over, headed to Charleston.[187] He spent February 1775 in the southern port, and then, hearing of the vacancy at Welsh Neck, visited the church there and was called to become their minister on 12 March 1775. He had left his wife, Alice, in New England, and returned to bring her south. En route, during the fall of 1775, she became ill and he had to leave her at Fairfax, Virginia. It isn't clear exactly when he returned to Welsh Neck; there are no entries in the Church Book between 12 March 1775 and 8 March 1776, when the church renewed its call to Winchester and formally received him as a member of their congregation.[188] Soon after this renewed call, Winchester left Welsh Neck again, to fetch his wife; sadly, when he reached Fairfax, he discovered that she had died. Instead of returning to his new position along the Pee Dee, Winchester made the strange decision to head north to New England, abandoning his flock for the second time in two years. Perhaps he felt the need to share his grief with old friends and to let his wife's family know in person of Alice's death. He stayed for some months, filling in at First Baptist, Boston during the summer. There, he married Sarah Peck from his old home of Rehoboth and returned with her to Welsh Neck that autumn.[189]

Before Winchester had left Welsh Neck in spring 1776 he had taken an important political initiative. The Revolution was gathering momentum in South Carolina. In 1774 the Continental Congress in Philadelphia had called on all Americans to sign the Continental Association, a boycott of trade with Britain; the decision to sign the Association was for many individuals and communities the decisive moment for joining or rejecting the Patriot cause. The interior of South Carolina was already severely divided; wars with the Cherokees and the

---

[186] *Ibid.*, 22-23.
[187] *Ibid.*, 23. There would appear to have been close communication between Hopewell and Charleston. Oliver Hart, pastor of First Baptist, Charleston before the Revolution, later moved north to become pastor at Hopewell.
[188] Hart, "Diary," 9; WNCB, 19.
[189] Stone, *Winchester,* 23-25.

Regulator-Moderator tensions of the 1760s had left behind armed bands and powerful local animosities. Local and personal issues often influenced people as they decided what stance they would take on the major imperial controversies. When, in early 1775, Patriot leaders in Charleston organized the election of a new Provincial Congress, independent of the royal governor's authority, they could not be sure of support from all areas of the increasingly populous interior.[190]

In this situation, anyone of influence, such as a local religious leader, was of sudden importance. Although Baptists after the Revolution stressed the Patriot credentials of their denomination, in fact Baptists could be found on both sides of the Patriot-Loyalist divide, especially in the first years of the upheaval. For example, the most eminent Welsh-American Baptist in the Thirteen Colonies, Morgan Edwards, was an outspoken Loyalist who found himself under house arrest. While Oliver Hart of Charleston sided with the Patriots, and was sent with the Presbyterian William Tennent and the Anglican planter, Henry Drayton, on a mission to solicit support from the interior, their embassy encountered other Baptist preachers who were working just as actively to dissuade their followers from signing the Continental Association and joining the Revolutionary cause; Philip Mulkey, the leading Separate Baptist, was suspected of Tory sympathies and had to leave South Carolina for a time.[191]

In this uncertain situation, Winchester made a decisive move. On 8 March 1776 he proposed, at the Welsh Neck Church meeting, that representatives from all Baptist churches should convene at the High Hills Church in order to organize a petition in support of religious liberty. Since this meeting would take place in April, and Winchester had to return to Virginia to fetch – as he thought – his wife, he would not be able to attend, but the Welsh Neck members asked him to "draw up some thoughts on the continental association, to be laid before the Churches at their meeting at the High Hills."[192] While this April meeting at High Hills was in some senses a replacement for the Charleston Association meeting of 1775, which had not convened because of the political troubles, it turned into more than just a meeting of Baptist delegates. The High Hills meeting extended an invitation to Dissenting churches of other denominations, all of which had an interest in ensuring that the Revolution, at state and national level, ended church establishments. One result of the High Hills gathering was the "Dissenters' Peti-

---

[190] Jerome J. Nadelhaft, *The Disorders of War: The Revolution in South Carolina* (University of Maine, 1981), 12-21.

[191] Flinchum, "Reluctant Revolutionaries," 175-178, 181-186; Townsend, *South Carolina Baptists,* 178-179; James A. Rogers, *Richard Furman, Life and Legacy* (Mercer University, 1985), 24-31; *Encyclopedia of Southern Baptists* (Nashville, TN: Broadman Press, 1958-1962), s.v. "Mulkey, Philip."

[192] WNCB, 20.

tion," which was presented to the South Carolina legislature in 1777. It proved very influential in ensuring that the state's new constitution, drafted in 1778, ended the privileges of the Church of England. William Tennent, the Presbyterian minister mentioned above, emerged as the chief spokesman for the disestablishment effort, but Winchester and Welsh Neck had played a key role in getting the ball rolling.[193]

Winchester may have had an even larger goal in mind when he proposed the meeting at High Hills. The Church Book talked about the High Hills meeting sending "delegates to the Continental Association" on the religious liberty question.[194] It was very possible that he was thinking in terms of sending a group of South Carolina Baptists to Philadelphia to lobby the Continental Congress against any attempt to create a religious establishment at a national level. Although, with hindsight, such a possibility may seem preposterous, at the time many took the threat of a national establishment seriously. The lead taken by New England in the Revolutionary movement made many worry that it would turn into a Presbyterian bid for power. Fear of such a possibility was causing anxiety among many Baptists in New England and New Jersey, some of whom inclined towards or actually became Loyalists because they felt the Patriots were less likely than the old imperial establishment to respect religious liberty.[195] Winchester, who in March 1776 had spent very little time in South Carolina, and who chose to return to New England for the summer of that year, may well have had the concerns of New England Baptists in mind when he proposed the High Hills meeting. Uniting Baptists from the Deep South with those in New England would have given the latter more leverage in their fight for religious equality.[196]

Winchester returned from his visit to New England sometime in the fall of 1776, and stayed in Welsh Neck through the following year. During 1777 he baptized some thirty persons as part of a revival;[197] one of these was his new wife, who joined the church on 4 May. Sadly, she died two months later. Despite

---

[193] Rogers, *Furman,* 34-38; Nadelhaft, *Disorders of War,* 37-38. Furman confirmed that this 1776 meeting was not a regular convening of the Charleston Association. *Charleston Association,* 15. Winchester continued to support the Patriot cause, joining Hart in a congratulatory address to the South Carolina assembly in 1776, and preaching a sermon celebrating South Carolina's independence in 1777. Townsend, *South Carolina Baptists,* 276-278.

[194] WNCB, 20.

[195] Flinchum, "Reluctant Revolutionaries," 181-186.

[196] Although no attempt was made by Congress to create a national church establishment, the establishments in Massachusetts and Connecticut, unlike South Carolina's, did survive the Revolution, and full religious equality was only achieved in those states in the early nineteenth century.

[197] A revival of religion occurred throughout the Charleston Association's churches in 1777 (Furman, *Charleston Association,* 16).

his success at adding new members, Winchester seemed unhappy at Welsh Neck; after only a year of continuous service at the church, he announced, during the autumn of 1777, that he intended to leave Welsh Neck the following spring. The church invited first Richard Furman and then John Gano to take Winchester's place, but both declined.[198] While the church was seeking his replacement, Winchester married again, this time a local woman, Sarah Luke. The marriage may have convinced him to stay at Welsh Neck, and so the church called him for a further year on 26 March 1778. The Church Book states that this renewed call came only "after some debate," possibly due to his obvious restlessness in the position. During the summer of 1778 he again was away, this time in Virginia. He returned to experience a very sickly winter at Welsh Neck, when many of his parish, including his third wife, died. In the wake of these tragedies, he began to preach with even greater power, sparking the revival of 1779.[199]

The Revival of 1779 and Winchester's Universalism

The most memorable phase of Winchester's brief pastorate at Welsh Neck was the revival that took place during the late spring and summer of 1779. As far as Welsh Neck was concerned, the most significant, long-term ramification of this revival was that it created an African American church associated with the white church; this separate church was later incorporated into the white church. Winchester therefore can be credited with turning Welsh Neck into a biracial congregation. The possible factors leading to the conversions of these African Americans are discussed below. First, however, it is necessary to address the question of what stimulated Winchester to lead this revival, which began among the white population and later included the black community. Two years afterwards, Winchester became an avowed Universalist, and the 1779 re-

---

[198] WNCB, 21-22. Richard Furman (1755-1825) was converted by the Separate preacher, Joseph Reese, in 1771 and was ordained as pastor of the High Hills church in 1774. He joined Hart in promoting the Patriot cause in the interior of South Carolina at the start of the Revolution. During the British occupation he fled the state, but returned after the war to resume his pastorate at High Hills before moving to Charleston in 1787. Largely self-educated, he became a champion of education for Baptists, founding or inspiring several Baptist institutions of higher learning throughout the South. He became a close friend of Winchester's successor at Welsh Neck, Edmund Botsford, whose letters to Furman from Welsh Neck are included in this volume (Rogers, *Furman,* passim; Brackney, *Dictionary of the Baptists,* 238). John Gano (1727-1804) was born at Hopewell, New Jersey and converted at an early age to the Baptist faith. He was ordained in 1756 and spent some time in the South. He served in New York during the Revolutionary War. After the war he focused on evangelizing in the Ohio Valley, and was a key figure in the Kentucky revivals at the end of the century. Brackney, *Dictionary of the Baptists,* 241.

[199] WNCB, 24; Stone, *Winchester,* 25-28.

vival at Welsh Neck played a role in his evolution towards Universalism. Tracing the precise steps of this evolution provides useful insights into Winchester's character and beliefs and into the nature of the Welsh Neck community.

Some historians have explained Winchester's revival by claiming he was already an Arminian or even a Universalist before he came to Welsh Neck. Classifying him as a Separate Baptist also explains his revival, since the Separates were kindling many such movements throughout the South at this time.[200] Yet all the evidence points to the fact that Winchester was chosen by Welsh Neck because he was a strict Calvinist, in keeping with the church's Regular traditions and its covenant.[201] One piece of evidence, mentioned above, is that, before he came to Welsh Neck, Winchester had been ejected from his pulpit by a church that was moving towards a more Arminian creed; he insisted on an adherence to the narrowest definition of Calvinism, and was replaced.[202] Further evidence comes from the Church Book. The initial call to Winchester in March 1775 was recorded as follows: "The Church of Christ at the Welch Tract, Pee-Dee in South Carolina, holding the doctrine of Election, particular Redemption; final perseverance; believers baptism, &c. to the Rev[d] Elhanan Winchester sendeth greeting."[203] The following year, when Welsh Neck renewed its call to Winchester and received him as a full member of the church, it recorded in the Church Book the letter of dismission that Winchester had received from his former, Regular Baptist church in Bellingham, Massachusetts:

> The first Baptist Church of Christ in Bellingham, under the pastoral care of Elder Noah Alden; holding the doctrine of original sin, universal depravity, absolute, eternal, unconditional, personal Election; particular redemption by the blood of Christ; justification by his righteousness imparted; regeneration; effectual calling; practical godliness; final perseverance; resurrection of the dead; believer's baptism, &c.:- To any Church of the same faith and order, where our beloved brother Elhanan Winchester may see cause to

---

[200] Bressler, *Universalist Movement,* 15-17; Sylvia Frey and Betty Wood, *Come Shouting to Zion: African American Protestantism in the American South and British Caribbean to 1830* (Chapel Hill: University of North Carolina, 1998), 102-103.

[201] Townsend argues that Welsh Neck had Arminian leanings, but her source for this statement is nothing more concrete than "tradition." *South Carolina Baptists,* 76. In 1767, the Charleston Association, following in the wake of its individual member churches, had formally embraced the 1689 London Confession of Faith, which was grounded on strict Calvinist principles. As Welsh Neck restored its relationship with the Charleston Association under Winchester, it seems unlikely that anything but strict Calvinism characterized the church and its new minister. Furman, *Charleston Association,* 12-13.

[202] Janet Moore Lindman, "Bad Men and Angels from Hell: The Discourse of Universalism in Early National Philadelphia," *Journal of the Early Republic,* Vol. 31, No. 2 (Summer 2011), 267-268.

[203] WNCB, 19.

join as a member; Greeting: we certify you that the above said brother is a member of this Church; and we all esteem him as a real christian, a man of sound principles, orthodox sentiments, an orderly walker, of up-right conversation, [illeg.] clear gospel preacher; and as such we recommend him unto you; and upon his joining and your receiving him, he ceases to be a member with us, and becomes one with you in all respects.___ Dated Bellingham August 14th 1775.[204]

This letter leaves no doubt that Winchester was regarded as a strict Calvinist and an adherent of the Regular Baptist creed when he formally joined the Welsh Neck church in 1776. Furthermore, Winchester himself later avowed that when he took over at Welsh Neck, he had "been deemed one of the most consistent Calvinists upon the continent, much upon the plan of Dr. Gill, whom I esteemed almost as an oracle."[205] There is no good reason to doubt the strong evidence of Winchester's Calvinistic position at this stage of his life; claiming he must have been an Arminian or Universalist because he stimulated the 1779 revival is arguing *post hoc, propter hoc.*

Winchester later explained the Welsh Neck revival as follows. At some point, probably early in 1778, a friend loaned him *The Everlasting Gospel* by Paul Siegvolk and asked Winchester to comment on its doctrine. Winchester glanced through it casually, spending no more than half an hour; since the work was "very plain and clear," he was able to pick up its arguments quickly. The most striking argument was that the original Greek word *aionion,* usually translated as "eternal" can simply mean "for a long period." Therefore, when Scripture refers to "eternal" punishment for sinners, that punishment might well be finite. Winchester shared this idea with his friend. Both agreed it was interesting, but not to be taken seriously. Since the friend had borrowed the book and then sent it back to its owner, Winchester did not have another opportunity to read it. Despite the brevity of his encounter with this work, its arguments kept intruding into his thoughts "in such a forcible manner that I could scarcely withstand their evidence." Soon afterwards, while he was traveling in Virginia, Winchester heard similar arguments that poor translations had created a false idea of punishment without end. Then, back at Welsh Neck, Winchester was again able to borrow a copy of *The Everlasting Gospel,* this time from a physician friend

---

[204] Ibid., 19.

[205] Elhanan Winchester, *The Universal Restoration Exhibited in Four Dialogues between a Minister and his Friend Comprehending the Substance of Several Real Conversations which the Author had with various Persons, both in America and Europe, on that Interesting Subject,* (Philadelphia: T. Dobson, 1792), viii. John Gill (1697-1771) was a widely-known Baptist minister and theologian who held such high Calvinist views that he denied the value of preaching the gospel to sinners. During the eighteenth century, he was distinguishable from the evangelical Calvinist Andrew Fuller (1745-1815). Brackney, " *Dictionary of the Baptists,* 251.

who had just moved into the area. Once more, he was intrigued, but not con-vinced.[206] Apart from demonstrating how the seed of Universalism was sown in Winchester's mind, these incidents provide fascinating glimpses into intellectual life in the remote rural community of Welsh Neck, where books, relatively rare and costly possessions, were energetically shared and discussed.[207]

This account by Winchester was very specific about how and when he first encountered Universalist ideas. He was also very emphatic that his intellect re-jected these ideas, and that he continued to adhere to his original, strict Calvin-ism. The vital push that moved him towards Universalism was more mysterious; despite his rejection of Siegvolk, he found himself

> much stirred up to exhort my fellow creatures to repent, believe, and obey the Gospel, and [I] began to adopt a more open and general method of preaching than I had used for some years before... [M]y heart being opened, and viewing the worth of souls, I felt great compassion towards them, and invited them with all my might to fly for mercy to the arms of Christ, who died for them, and who was willing to save them. I was gradu-ally led into this way of preaching, without considering any thing about its consistency with strict calvinism, but finding myself very happy, and com-fortable in my own mind, and that this method of preaching was highly useful, I continued to go in the same course.[208]

This "highly useful" method stimulated a revival in the Welsh Neck com-munity, first among whites – of whom he converted 139, he later recalled. Judg-ing by the Church Book, the revival began in May, when six were added to the church, after a year or more with few new members. It was in June that the re-vival really took off, with sixty-two white baptisms.[209] During that month, the same unconscious impulse "constrained" him one day to reach out to a group of slaves who were gathered outside the meeting house. That outreach, too, yielded many converts, almost one hundred. As well as the converts of both races, many others came to hear him, and he was regularly preaching to over 1,000 each Sunday. "This was a summer of great success, and I shall remember that happy season with pleasure while I live."[210]

---

[206] Winchester, *Universal Restoration,* iii-viii, x-xi. Paul Siegvolk, the pen-name of Georg-Klein Nicolai, published *The Everlasting Gospel* in 1753. Bressler, *Universalist Movement,* 15; Lindman, "Bad Men and Angels from Hell," 267-268.

[207] The long controversy over Rev. Lewis's failure to return books he had borrowed from the Welsh Neck library, reported in detail in the Church Book and therefore clearly deemed an important issue, testifies to the value of books in this community. WNCB, 29, 37.

[208] Winchester, *Universal Restoration,* viii-ix.

[209] WNCB, 25.

[210] Winchester, *Universal Restoration,* ix-x.

Having experienced the heady joy of converting so many so rapidly, Winchester's intellect then began to catch up with his heart. By the time he left Welsh Neck in September 1779, he was "fully persuaded that the number of the finally saved would equal, if not exceed, the number of the lost." As he traveled through New England during the winter of 1779-1780, he tested Siegvolk's doctrines on the many learned men he encountered, hoping to find that there were convincing counterarguments to refute them. Instead, these debates increasingly persuaded him that Siegvolk was right, and Winchester began to sound to others more and more like a Universalist. Finally, in Philadelphia, he came across another copy of Siegvolk, as well as Sir George Stonehouse's *Restitution of All Things*. He realized he had to make up his mind about what he believed; he shut himself away to study, and finally concluded that Universalism was right.[211] If his journey to Universalism ended in Philadelphia, his narrative makes it clear that it started at Welsh Neck, both because of the ideas he encountered there and because of the mass conversions of whites and blacks.[212]

Winchester's account of his conversion makes a clear distinction between his intellectual powers, which resisted the truths of Universalism, and his unconscious impulses, which Winchester clearly saw as evidence of God's hand. The lesson that stands out from his conversion narrative is that he came to Universalism through the irresistible force of grace rather than through his own human will; thus, even as he evolved into a Universalist, he retained important aspects of his original Calvinist beliefs. Many early Universalists did not see any contradiction between Calvinism and the doctrine that all of humanity would be saved; indeed, many believed they were improving Calvinist doctrine, rather than rejecting it. Terms such as "elect" and "atonement" could be extended to include the entire human race.[213] It is therefore incorrect to conclude that Winchester's conversions during this summer showed he had abandoned the idea of election.[214] One story related by Winchester demonstrates just how seriously he took the idea of God's active involvement in promoting Universalist ideas. During his visit to Virginia in 1778, he heard that a clergyman had been struck dead after preaching universal salvation from his pulpit. Enemies of the doctrine claimed this sudden death showed God's disapproval. Winchester argued that God had preserved the clergyman just long enough to allow him to share the truth with his congregation. As proof of his argument, Winchester pointed out that he himself had now (1792) been preaching the doctrine for eleven years without being struck down by God.[215] While there may have been some inten-

---

[211] *Ibid.,* xi-xx.

[212] Lindman, "Bad Men and Angels from Hell," 267-268.

[213] Bressler, *Universalist Movement,* 17-19.

[214] Townsend makes this argument. *South Carolina Baptists,* 69.

[215] Winchester, *Universal Restoration,* vi-viii.

tional humor in this final comment, there is no doubt that, long after his conversion, Winchester continued to believe that God was actively at work on the side of the Universalist cause; grace empowered the rational faculties, in Winchester's individual case, as well as in others'.[216]

Twenty-first century historians might prefer more earthly explanations for the unconscious impulses behind Winchester's move towards Universalism. It might have been the case that the death of his third wife unleashed an emotional energy in Winchester's preaching, just as the unusually high number of deaths at Welsh Neck over the winter of 1778-1779 might have moved his listeners to respond to his preaching in the way that they did. Another possible factor behind the revival was anxiety over the opening of the Southern theatre of the Revolutionary War; the British capture of Savannah in December 1778 and incursions into South Carolina during 1779 suddenly brought the war very close to Welsh Neck. On a philosophical level, the democratic impulses behind the Revolution were pushing many Calvinists towards a less elitist concept of salvation.[217] Universalist ideas were appearing in many parts of rural New England, Winchester's native region, in this period.[218] Yet another factor behind this revival might have been the success of Separate Baptist preachers in the South Carolina interior. Although they were not Universalists, their methods of preaching and the large-scale conversions they stimulated could well have influenced both Winchester and his listeners.[219]

In the long term, Winchester's conversion of about 140 whites had little impact on Welsh Neck. His successor, Edmund Botsford, and the older members of the church excommunicated many of Winchester's converts, and white membership shrank dramatically during the 1780s and 1790s. However, Winchester's conversion of almost one hundred African Americans did permanently transform Welsh Neck, and these black conversions need to be examined in more detail.

---

[216] Bressler argues that early Universalists were not only Calvinists, but were also inclined to subordinate reason to emotion and to God's active intervention in man's affairs. Early Unitarians, by contrast, were Arminians who stressed the power of human reason to discover truth. The merger of these two faiths in 1961 has meant that the importance of predestination and the miraculous in Universalism's past has been downplayed. Despite her general depiction of early Universalists, she regards Winchester as an Arminian exception, and therefore atypical. The evidence suggests that her broad argument applies to him as much as to his peers. *Universalist Movement,* 3-8, 15-17.

[217] Flinchum, "Reluctant Revolutionaries," 175-177; Lindman, "Bad Men and Angels from Hell," 267-268.

[218] Bressler, *Universalist Movement,* 17-19.

[219] Townsend, *South Carolina Baptists,* 295-305.

Winchester and the African American Community

The most significant development of Elhanan Winchester's pastorate was the baptism of the first African Americans at Welsh Neck. Before Winchester, no black men or women had been baptized; from this time on, they were a permanent and important element of the Baptist community here.[220] This significant change occurred suddenly, in just over two months before Winchester left Welsh Neck. The first baptisms of five African Americans (four men and one woman) took place on 27 June 1779. A further twenty (thirteen men and seven women) were baptized during July, eighteen on one day (25 July). Forty-seven were baptized on the first two Sundays of August: twenty-three (seventeen men and six women) on 1 August, and twenty-four (fifteen men and nine women) on 8 August. On 20 August these new converts "were constituted into a Church by themselves." Finally, on the last day of August, twenty-six were added to the black congregation through baptism. Overall, ninety-eight Africans or African Americans became Baptists under Winchester's leadership, two-thirds of that number (sixty-five) over the course of three Sundays.[221]

What explains this sudden accession of African Americans to the Baptist community at Welsh Neck? The conversion of African Americans at any church was the product of joint decisions by a number of parties. These parties included the pastor; his white congregation, especially the owners of the enslaved converts; and the black converts themselves. Historians have uncovered several general and long-term reasons why enslaved African Americans embraced Christianity and why whites were willing to encourage and to accept them. Undoubtedly, many of these factors were operating at Welsh Neck, and they are explored in the discussion that follows. One particularly intriguing puzzle is why these general factors suddenly worked such a rapid transformation at Welsh Neck at a particular historical moment, over the course of a couple of months in the summer of 1779.

Clearly, one of the most important figures behind this sudden burst of black conversions was Winchester. Fortunately, his account of his evolution

---

[220] Mechal Sobel states that Welsh Neck was a "mixed church" right from its founding, but there is no evidence in the Church Book for black members until Winchester's time (Sobel, *Trabelin' On: The Slave Journey to an Afro-Baptist Faith* [Greenwood Press, 1979] 314). Winchester states clearly that no-one to his knowledge had ever preached to the blacks before his time, nor had there been any black members. Winchester, *Universal Restoration,* ix.

[221] WNCB, 26-28; Note that at the time the conversions of African Americans took place at Welsh Neck, only 2% of slaves in America had become Christians; the Welsh Neck group, though small, was in the vanguard of African American Christianity (Philip D. Morgan, *Slave Counterpoint: Black Culture in the Eighteenth-Century Chesapeake and Lowcountry* [Chapel Hill: University of North Carolina, 1998] 420-423).

from a Regular Baptist to a Universalist includes an explanation of how these African American baptisms came about. One of the unconscious impulses that was driving him to more open preaching that summer led him to reach out to the enslaved one evening in June:

> About this time I began to find uncommon desires for the conversion and salvation of the poor negroes, who were very numerous in that part of the country; but whom none of my predecessors, that I could learn, had ever taken pains to instruct in the principles of Christianity; neither had any single slave, either man, or woman been baptized until that summer, in the whole parish (which was very large) that I ever heard of...[O]ne evening seeing a great many of them at the door of the house where I was preaching, I found myself constrained, as it were, to go to the door, and tell them, That Jesus Christ loved them, and died for them, as well as for us white people, and that they might come and believe in him, and welcome. And I gave them as warm and pressing an invitation as I could, to comply with the glorious gospel. This short discourse addressed immediately to them, took greater ... effect than can well be imagined. There were about thirty from one plantation in the neighborhood present; (besides others) these returned home, and did not even give sleep to their eyes, as they afterwards informed me, until they had settled every quarrel among themselves, and according to their form of marriage, had married every man to the woman with whom he lived; had restored whatever one had unjustly taken from another; and determined from that time to seek the Lord diligently. From that very evening they began constantly to pray to the Lord, and so continued; and he was found of them. I continued to instruct them, and within three months of the first of June, I baptized more than thirty blacks belonging to that plantation, besides as many others, as in the whole made up one hundred...[222]

Winchester's impulse to preach to the slaves gathered outside the meeting was part of the larger change taking place in his preaching and his religious outlook, a desire, implanted by God, "to exhort my fellow creatures to repent, believe, and obey the Gospel," and his adoption of "a more open and general method of preaching than I had used for some years before."[223] His outreach to the black men and women standing outside was a logical extension of his outreach to the white community. Since God's hand was behind the impulse that was leading him to love humanity in general and to preach more openly, it made perfect sense to Winchester that his preaching was rewarded with startling success, among the blacks as well as the whites who heard him.

Winchester's account placed himself and his theological development at the center of the events that turned Welsh Neck into a biracial religious commu-

---

[222] Winchester, *Universal Restoration,* ix-x.
[223] Ibid., viii-ix.

nity. Yet beneath this self-focused narrative, there are hints that Winchester was being impacted by others, even as he made an impact upon them. Winchester's detailed account of his emotional and intellectual progress towards Universalism makes it clear that it was *how* rather than *what* he was preaching that had changed at this stage. The precise chronology of his theological development, discussed above, demonstrates that the mass conversions, black and white, of that summer of 1779 helped to break down the intellectual barriers that kept him from accepting Universalist ideas; the African American response was part of the set of factors that pushed this important early founder of the Universalist movement towards that creed. As Winchester looked back in later life, after he had emerged as a Universalist spokesman, he stressed that the revival he had led in 1779 at Welsh Neck was a vital moment in his discovery of what he later came to see as true doctrine: "This was a summer of great success, and I shall remember that happy season with pleasure while I live."[224] Winchester's conversion to Universalism did not cause African Americans to flock to hear him; rather, their enthusiasm helped, over the long term, to convince him that Universalist teachings were correct.[225]

Although Winchester saw his gradual move towards Universalism as the central factor in these black conversions, others were also responsible for bringing these enslaved men and women into the Baptist faith. An important precondition for the baptism of African Americans was the readiness of the white congregation—and especially the owners of the slaves who converted—to accept and perhaps encourage the spread of Christianity to the black population. The white church members and slave owners at Welsh Neck have not left behind anything like Winchester's detailed explanation of these conversions, but there are indications in the sources, which can be supplemented by educated guesses based on developments elsewhere at this time, about what might have persuaded the Welsh Neck whites to follow Winchester's lead regarding the conversions of these African Americans.

It seems very clear that slave owners in the Welsh Neck area at least permitted, or perhaps encouraged, their slaves to become Christians. Winchester's account of his first conversions of African Americans shows that he had not gone preaching out on the plantations in search of his first converts; instead, he simply turned to a large group gathered outside the church or the private house where he was preaching. Thirty of these were from Alexander McIntosh's plan-

---

[224] Ibid., viii-xi.

[225] Sylvia Frey and Betty Wood, though usually eager to stress African American agency, are strangely blind to the effect of black conversions on Winchester's evolution. Their suggestion that Winchester was a Separate Baptist and their claim that he had already embraced Universalism before he preached to the African Americans at Welsh Neck are inconsistent with Winchester's own account (*Shouting to Zion,* 102-103).

tation. In fact, these and other slaves had been present on other occasions, at or outside church services; Winchester stated that he had long felt sorry for them before he found the courage or inspiration to address them directly. This regular attendance suggests that McIntosh and other owners certainly tolerated and perhaps invited or pressured their slaves to be present at worship. Another indication of the owners' role in their slaves' conversion is that the listing of enslaved converts in the Church Book is organized by master or mistress. The reader encounters these new Christians with their owners figuratively standing behind them as they are entered in the Baptist roll. When listing blacks in the Church Book, ownership trumped gender, normally the main organizing principle for listing newly baptized whites.[226] One should be cautious about reading too much into this, but the way the converts' names were recorded seems a further indication that baptism and ownership were connected in Winchester's mind, and that all newly baptized slaves became Christians with their owners' permission or blessing.

One interesting point about the owners' role is that, while most owners of baptized slaves were members of the Welsh Neck Church, not all were. There are twenty-five named owners of the seventy-two slaves who were baptized between June and August 1779. Of those twenty-five, thirteen were members of the church, seven probably came from families that had one or many church members, and five were not members, nor obviously connected by blood relationships to church members. The vast majority (fifty-seven) of the seventy-two converts whose owners can be identified belonged to the thirteen church members, but it is significant that fifteen baptized slaves belonged to the twelve owners who had not joined the Welsh Neck Church. Certain owners, at least, were willing to give their slaves some latitude in choosing their own religious identity, even though that choice might well mean the slaves would travel to services without their owners and would believe that they enjoyed a spiritual blessing denied to their masters.

Winchester's memoir and the Church Book strongly suggest that owners played a role in their slaves' conversion. What is less obvious from these sources is *why* they played this role. Both for owners who were church members and for those who were not, allowing their slaves to be baptized was an important decision. What long-term and immediate factors might have lain behind these owners' readiness to allow slave baptisms in the summer of 1779?

---

[226] White converts were normally listed with the men first, followed by the women, unless a husband and wife were baptized or admitted at the same time, in which case the wife was mentioned immediately after her husband. Gender continued to be an organizing principle for the slaves; where several slaves belonging to one owner were baptized simultaneously, the males within the commonly-owned group were listed first, the females second.

There was certainly nothing new about the idea that slave owners should do all they could to bring Christianity to their slaves; saving the souls of slaves had been an official goal of imperial authorities and of the Carolina colony since its founding.[227] However, South Carolina's whites in general, and slave owners in particular, had put little energy into evangelization efforts or had actively resisted them during the first two-thirds of the century.[228] Welsh Neck's failure to reach out to its black population during this earlier period was not abnormal, and it is likely that the reasons behind this neglect were similar to those elsewhere in the colony. One fear was that conversion might make slaves less subservient. While the law clearly stated that converting slaves did not make them free, owners feared that the slaves would feel that, as part of the Christian community, they deserved at least an amelioration of their condition and acknowledgement of their spiritual equality. Another concern was that religious activities might interfere with work. Some owners compelled their slaves to work on Sundays, despite laws against such labor, or wanted them to spend that day growing their own food in their vegetable gardens, relieving the master's costs in feeding them.[229] Security was a concern. Some owners were suspicious of slaves leaving the plantation to attend religious services or instruction.[230] More seriously, owners and the white establishment in general had reason to fear that Christianity might encourage revolt. There were examples of slave revolts across the British Empire that were inspired by Christianity or in which Christian slaves had taken part; these revolts were reported in the South Carolina press and known about through commercial exchanges.[231] Indeed, South Carolina itself had experienced a major scare during one of the first serious efforts to evangelize the enslaved population. In 1740 George Whitefield had published a scathing attack on southern planters for failing to care for their slaves' souls.[232] Whitefield's disciple and ally, Hugh Bryan, had attempted to rectify this failing on his own plantation. The two men published a prediction that failure to follow their example would lead to an apocalyptic upheaval, with God using the slaves as a means of

---

[227] Charles II had included Christianization of slaves in his statement of imperial goals at the time of the founding of Carolina. Albert J. Raboteau, *Slave Religion: The "Invisible Institution" in the Antebellum South* (Oxford University, 1978), 96-98.

[228] Morgan, *Slave Counterpoint,* 420-423.

[229] Raboteau, *Slave Religion,* 98-103.

[230] Townsend, *South Carolina Baptists,* 255.

[231] As early as 1731, recent converts to Christianity in Virginia had joined an uprising, claiming that Christianity – backed by a royal proclamation – had made them free; Christianity also played a role in an uprising in Antigua in 1736 and in the Stono Rebellion in South Carolina itself, in 1739. Frey and Wood, *Shouting to Zion,* 68-73.

[232] George Whitefield, *A Letter to the Inhabitants of Maryland, Virginia, North and South Carolina* in *Three Letters from the Reverend Mr. G. Whitefield* (Philadelphia: B. Franklin, 1740).

punishing whites for their addiction to polite luxuries and superficial religion.[233] The authorities took action against Bryan, and Whitefield fell into such disfavor in South Carolina that he never had the impact on this colony that he had elsewhere in America. In general, most of the successful efforts to bring Christianity to South Carolina's blacks during the first two-thirds of the century were carried out by a handful of highly dedicated members of the Church of England, who proceeded cautiously, ensuring that converts were thoroughly educated in the white man's view that Christianity imposed a duty of loyal service on slaves. This caution could mean control of blacks' access to the Bible, and requiring catechists to swear oaths to serve their masters dutifully.[234] The numbers converted by these painstaking methods were unsurprisingly small.

Several factors from the 1760s onwards altered whites' reluctance to evangelize their slaves. Throughout the Anglophone world, a cultural shift in the late eighteenth century was changing the outlook of male heads of household towards their dependents, from one characterized by "patriarchy" to an attitude of "paternalism." Many slave owners began to view their slaves through sentimental, rather than authoritarian, eyes; in keeping with the general mood of the period, heads of households that included slaves prided themselves on the care and attention they gave to those in their power.[235] The obituary for Abel Edwards, a deacon in the Welsh Neck Church from 1777-1793, conveys this new outlook well: he was praised for being an "[a]ffectionate husband, a tender parent, and a humane master."[236] In its most extreme forms, this cultural shift had spurred a humanitarian interest in public measures to ameliorate the conditions of slaves, and had even stimulated calls for abolishing the slave trade and slavery altogether. The Somerset Case effectively ended slavery in England in 1772; many voices in New England were being raised against slavery in that region.[237] Quakers, first as individuals and then as a body, were taking action against the

---

[233] Harvey H. Jackson, "Hugh Bryan and the Evangelical Movement in Colonial South Carolina," *William and Mary Quarterly,* 3rd Ser., Vol. XLIII, No. 4 (October 1986), 594-603; Kenney, "Garden and Whitefield," 13-15.

[234] Anglican clergy were overstretched and had little clout in a society dominated by planters. Clergy supported by the Society for the Propagation of the Gospel and Bray's Associates were more independent and the latter had been specifically organized with the goal of Christianizing slaves. Raboteau, *Slave Religion,* 104-108. Frey and Wood are disparaging of Anglican efforts, even though, during the first half of the eighteenth century, Anglican missionaries converted more slaves than Wesley, Whitefield, and Bryan, whom these historians praise (*Shouting to Zion,* 64-66).

[235] Fliegelman, Jay, *Prodigals and Pilgrims: The American Revolution against Patriarchal Authority, 1750-1800* (Cambridge University, 1982), 155-194; Morgan, *Slave Counterpoint,* 284-288.

[236] Rippon, *Baptist Register, 1794-1797,* 500.

[237] Patricia Bradley, *Slavery, Propaganda, and the American Revolution* (University of Mississippi, 1998), 66-98.

slave trade and slavery. Within evangelical Christianity, the call to convert slaves that had first been voiced during the Great Awakening in the 1740s was gathering momentum; the Methodist movement on both sides of the Atlantic and the Separate Baptists in Virginia and the Carolinas were openly criticizing the institution of slavery, and preaching Christianity to the enslaved in new and effective ways. These wider currents meant that the sudden addition of black members to Welsh Neck was not an isolated phenomenon; the 1770s saw black membership of churches increase throughout the mainland South and in the British Caribbean.[238] The whites of Welsh Neck were no doubt stirred to think more seriously about the material and spiritual condition of their slaves by these broader currents in the Atlantic World.

The most directly influential of these broader currents on Welsh Neck was probably the Separate Baptist movement. Though Welsh Neck was not a Separate congregation, and remained distinct from the Separates both in theology and style of worship right to the end of the century, the Separate movement made its mark. Shubal Stearns established an energetic center for the Separate Baptists at Sandy Creek, North Carolina in 1755; from there, he and his associates converted poor whites and enslaved blacks, establishing new Separate congregations in Virginia and both Carolinas. Their homespun clothes, their simple manner of addressing their congregations, their readiness to engage in physical contact, and their preaching of instantaneous conversion appealed to non-literate audiences of both races. The Separates in Virginia created one of the first all-black Christian churches in America, on William Byrd's estate. This new movement came close to Welsh Neck in 1762, with the founding of a congregation at Fairforest.[239] There was evidently friendly contact and interaction between the Separates and Welsh Neck, despite their differences. During the interlude between Bedgegood's death and the call to Winchester, the Separate preacher, Philip Mulkey, visited Welsh Neck and baptized four new members.[240] Mulkey also assisted in the constitution of a new church at Cheraw Hill in 1782, a church formed for geographical convenience by several Welsh Neck members; the new Welsh Neck pastor, Botsford, as well as Deacon Abel Edwards assisted Mulkey

---

[238] Sobel, *Trabelin' On,* 221-225; Michael Mullin, *Africa in America: Slave Acculturation and Resistance in the American South and the British Caribbean, 1736-1831* (University of Illinois, 1992), 243-249.

[239] Sobel, *Trabelin' On,* 102; Frey and Wood, *Shouting to Zion,* 99-102. Wood Furman characterized the Separates as follows: "The peculiarities of the Separates were a preciseness in dress and language, somewhat similar to that of the Quakers, and the allowing of private members and women to speak in their assemblies under a persuasion of their being under a divine impulse. Many of them were Arminians, and they generally refused communion to those who did not embrace their peculiarities" (*Charleston Association,* 71-72).

[240] See WNCB, 16.

in setting up this new church.[241] The Separates' outreach to the enslaved was no doubt one influence—as a model and perhaps through direct admonition—on the sudden willingness of Welsh Neck's white congregation and slave owners to follow Winchester's lead in 1779.

The Revolution was another likely influence on the decision by the whites of Welsh Neck to accept some of their slaves as members of the Christian community. The Revolution had a complex impact on the broader turn towards humanitarian and antislavery views in the Anglophone world. On the one hand, political preoccupations could distract Patriots from discussing chattel slavery, causing them to put this question on the back burner while they focused on the issue of white American rights.[242] At the same time, the stark contradiction between Patriots' complaints about political slavery at the hands of king and Parliament, and the existence of chattel slavery, caused some Patriots to see the end of the latter as a logical part of the Revolution's new order. This contradiction was loudly pointed out by the Revolution's opponents: many Britons and Loyalists repeatedly accused the Patriots of hypocrisy on the slavery issue. Under the sting of such criticisms, made more pointed by the *Somerset* decision, some Patriots, including John Laurens of South Carolina, discovered a new readiness to reconsider the institution of slavery and the treatment of their slaves.[243] Embarrassment over slavery was reinforced by security concerns once the war got underway. In 1775, Lord Dunmore, the Royal Governor of Virginia, issued a Proclamation that promised freedom to slaves who fled Patriot masters and joined the British side.[244] When British armies established themselves in Savannah from the end of 1778 and advanced into South Carolina during 1779, Welsh Neck slave owners could no longer take their slaves' submission for granted.[245] Courting their loyalty by making them brothers and sisters in Christ was one way to avert the mass defections that occurred in certain parts of the South during the war; the timing of the first Welsh Neck slave conversions may have related to the progress of the war in South Carolina.[246] The slave owners who al-

---

[241] WNCB, 29. Mallary writes that Botsford was unusual among Regular Baptists in his friendly relations with Separates. Charles D. Mallary, *Memoirs of Elder Edmund Botsford* (Charleston: W. Riley, 1832) 41-43.

[242] Bradley, *Slavery, Propaganda, Revolution*, xiii-xvi, 116-153.

[243] Simon Schama, *Rough Crossings: The Slaves, the British, and the American Revolution* (New York: HarperCollins, 2006), 55-56.

[244] *Ibid.*, 69-83. Winchester had spent significant time in Virginia during 1775 and early 1776; he must have known about Dunmore's Proclamation and the willingness of hundreds of slaves to defect to the British side.

[245] By the end of the war, one quarter of Low Country slaves had defected to the British. Morgan, *Slave Counterpoint*, 283-285, 492-495, 666.

[246] Note that a parallel situation had occurred earlier in the century. In 1739 Spain had offered freedom to all South Carolina slaves who escaped to Florida and converted to

lowed or encouraged their slaves to be baptized included a number of military officers who fought on the Patriot side, preeminently Colonel Alexander McIntosh. It is possible that such men looked at their slaves in a new light at this juncture: the need to resolve the contradiction between their own fight for liberty and their willingness to hold others in bondage perhaps seemed more urgent, now that their slaves were potential collaborators with advancing British armies.[247]

Whatever the precise mix of reasons for allowing their slaves to convert, the slave owners and the white community of Welsh Neck must be regarded, along with Winchester himself, as important figures behind the sudden conversion of these ninety-eight slaves. Of equal importance, of course, were the slaves themselves. One often-overlooked aspect of evangelizing the African American population in British America is that slaves were not compelled to convert; Protestantism's emphasis on the personal faith of the believer meant that whites of all denominations required even the enslaved to decide for themselves about becoming Christians. If that principle left plenty of room for whites to claim that it was too difficult to bring Christianity to blacks, it also gave black men and women space, allowing them to convert on their own terms; they were free to reject Christianity when it was offered to them, even by the established church.[248] It is hard to fathom the slaves' motivations for converting; at Welsh

---

Catholicism. A number of the Kongolese slaves in the Lowcountry were Catholic and they took up Spain's offer, thus sparking the Stono Rebellion. John K. Thornton, "African Dimensions of the Stono Rebellion," *American Historical Review,* Vol. 96, No. 4 (Oct. 1991), 1101-1113. The head of the Church of England in South Carolina, Alexander Garden, accused George Whitefield of being a "popish" agent, working on behalf of Spain by openly criticizing the institution of slavery and publishing prophecies of an apocalyptic slave uprising. Barrington, "Suppressing the Great Awakening," 5-10. Garden's solution to this combination of foreign threat and internal fifth column was to establish a school to spread Protestantism to South Carolina slaves, even though his educational plans included teaching literacy. Coping with the combined threat of British invasion and Loyalist collaboration in 1779 by converting slaves into co-religionists fitted this earlier pattern.

[247] Converting blacks to the Baptist faith in order to keep them on the patriot side was not always a successful strategy. George Liele and David George, two African Americans in the Savannah River region who converted just before the Revolution, ended up as Loyalists, leaving with the British for Jamaica and Nova Scotia respectively. Significantly, their religious community had been denied white leadership by the authorities, in contrast to the Welsh Neck Patriots, who reached out to blacks as the Revolutionary War neared their area (Raboteau, *Slave Religion,* 139-142; Sobel, *Trabelin' On,* 104-107).

[248] Sobel, *Trabelin' On,* 59-64; Frey and Wood, *Shouting to Zion*, 52-53. The religious pluralism that was a much-discussed feature of eighteenth-century British liberty meant that blacks, like whites, had a certain amount of choice between specific Protestant denominations.

Neck and elsewhere, historians largely need to rely on sources generated by whites to understand what Christianity meant to enslaved Africans and African Americans.[249] However, such sources, if carefully used, can reveal some important insights into blacks' motivation for conversion.

An important aspect of understanding slave conversions is the question of what they were converting from; and on this point, scholars have differed enormously. On one end of the spectrum are those who argue that the horrors of the Middle Passage and their arrival in an utterly new land, in a new condition of life, destroyed the slaves' faith in their traditional beliefs, creating a state of *anomie*, a spiritual vacuum that Christianity could readily fill, once language barriers and whites' reluctance to share Christian status had been overcome.[250] On the other side of the debate are those who argue that, despite the dehumanizing experience of crossing the Atlantic and living as the property of others, Africans were tenacious of their traditional beliefs, resourceful enough to adapt them to the new conditions in which they found themselves, and successful in transmitting those beliefs to their American-born children.[251] Scholars in this school deny that there was a spiritual vacuum among the slaves, ready to be filled by Christianity; rather, slaves exercised agency in choosing their faith, and only turned to Christianity when they had good reason – material or spiritual - to do so. Their choice of Christianity often meant, not the abandonment of traditional beliefs, but the use of Christianity to reinvigorate those beliefs.[252]

A sensible middle ground in this debate has been marked out by Albert Raboteau and Mechal Sobel.[253] These scholars argue that, while many elements of African religions survived the crossing to America, others simply could not. For example, a minority of Africans back at home had practiced a version of Islam or Catholicism.[254] In Protestant British America, practitioners of these faiths found themselves bereft of the institutional structures that had supported these religions in certain parts of Africa. Most of the enslaved had practiced

---

[249] Sobel, *Trabelin' On,* xvii; Betty Wood, *Slavery in Colonial America, 1619-1776* (Rowman and Littlefield, 2005), 49-50.

[250] E. Franklin Frazier argued strenuously for cultural loss in *The Negro Church in America* per Raboteau, *Slave Religion,* 52-54; more recently, Jon Butler has reiterated arguments for a lack of continuity between African and African American beliefs in *Awash in a Sea of Faith: Christianizing the American People* per Frey and Wood, *Shouting to Zion,* 35.

[251] Melville J. Herskovits was arguably one of the founders of this school. Raboteau, *Slave Religion,* 48-52; Frey and Wood are a good example of recent proponents. *Shouting to Zion,* xi-xiv.

[252] Mullin, *Africa in America,* 1-5, 174-175 sets out the two schools of interpretation very clearly.

[253] Raboteau, *Slave Religion,* 55-59.

[254] *Ibid.,* 3-5; Wood, *Slavery in Colonial America,* 50.

local African religions, which varied in many ways, but generally shared certain important features. Such faiths attributed a significant role to local gods, who were associated with specific objects and sites; they also accorded an important place to the spirits of deceased ancestors and their burial grounds; kinship groups were vital for many aspects of culture, including religion; and religious life depended on specialists in various aspects of the supernatural. Leaving Africa meant leaving much of this behind; and, though Africans could find substitutes for certain aspects of their lost culture and faith—for example, by regarding their fellow slaves on a plantation as a substitute kin-group—other aspects could not be fully replaced, and these survived or were reconstituted in a truncated form. Practitioners of supernatural skills—conjurors or *obeah* men and women—resurfaced in America, but without the elaborate specializations and the social and political controls that kept their power in line with the community's interests.[255] Most challenging was the fact that the social and political elite in America—the white community—did not ascribe to the transplanted African beliefs, and seemed immune from the power of African spells and spirits. A religion that was effective only among the least powerful inevitably inspired less respect than the religions that had been acknowledged in Africa by all, from kings down.[256] Therefore, as memory of the religious, social, and political unity of Africa faded among slaves who had been in America for many years, and among the second and subsequent generations, African traditions became insufficient to constitute a holistic worldview; naturally, the Christianity of the dominant groups became an object of interest.[257] Still tenacious of certain elements of

---

[255] Sobel, *Trabelin' On,* 31-34; Raboteau, *Slave Religion,* 48-49; Frey and Wood, *Shouting to Zion,* 56-59; Mullin, *Africa in America,* 185. Morgan argues that too few priests or other religious practitioners made the crossing for religious institutions to survive (*Slave Counterpoint,* 657-658).

[256] Sobel, *Trabelin' On,* 66-75.

[257] The growing sense of a distance from African reality was the product of many factors. The second and subsequent generations of slaves would obviously feel that Africa was less relevant to them than to their parents; but where the number of newly imported slaves from Africa remained high, and where blacks lived in large communities with other blacks, isolated from whites, African culture could survive more easily, even among the American born. Ethnic mix was another factor behind cultural survival; where knots of Africans from the same or similar backgrounds lived on the same plantation, it was easier for traditions from the homeland to become reestablished. Frey and Wood, *Shouting to Zion,* 45-47; Sobel, *Trabelin' On,* xvii, 34-39. In coastal South Carolina, where the proportion of blacks to whites was high, where blacks were physically isolated from whites, and where new imports of slaves straight from Africa remained high throughout the eighteenth century, African religious beliefs had a strong chance of surviving. Morgan, *Slave Counterpoint,* 1-2, 58-62, 95-101. In the Carolina interior, including the Pee Dee, the proportion of blacks to whites was lower and blacks had more contact with white culture, making religious acculturation more likely. Morgan, *Slave*

their African background, the enslaved who were acculturated to or born in America turned to those variants of Christianity that best meshed with African traditions. They used elements of the Christian faith to heal a culture damaged by transportation to the New World: for example, Biblical history provided African American Christians with a new past and with hope for the future.[258]

This interpretive middle ground has much to recommend it. It acknowledges the partial truth of arguments for the continuity of African traditions as well as the arguments for cultural/religious *anomie*. It finds a role for the agency of the slaves in creating their own belief system, while acknowledging the disempowering and dehumanizing aspects of slavery. This interpretation provides a theoretical framework for understanding why slaves in the southern colonies, including those of the Welsh Neck area, long kept their distance from Christianity, but then fairly suddenly discovered a value in this new faith in the last third of the eighteenth century.

Along with Christianity's ability to fulfill spiritual needs, more practical reasons may have also influenced many enslaved converts: for example, the hope that masters would show more respect for the marriages and families of Christian slaves than for those of non-Christians. Any step that might prevent families being broken by sale, or that might discourage sexual assault from owners, was worth taking. More generally, slaves could reasonably hope that joining their owner's church would create some sense of a bond that would lead to better conditions.[259] Sometimes, simply finding that they were treated more like human beings and felt less "slavish" when they went to church, was enough of an appeal to spark conversion.[260]

It is important to remember that, early in the eighteenth century, one quarter of South Carolina's slaves had been Native Americans; since most of these Indian slaves were women, and most imported Africans were men, a significant number of the American-born slaves were of mixed race and no doubt of mixed culture, as well.[261] When the Welsh Neck Church revised its covenant in 1785, it included provisions regarding the treatment of "negro or other slaves," very possibly a recognition that there were Indian or part-Indian slaves in their community.[262] Native Americans believed in a world filled with spiritual forces, including the spirits of ancestors; these beliefs would have meshed well with African

---

Counterpoint, 300-301. In general, the survival of African traditions has left far fewer traces in mainland North America than in the British Caribbean. Raboteau, *Slave Religion,* 42, 89-92; Sobel, *Trabelin' On,* 22-23.

[258] Sobel, *Trabelin' On,* 99-100, 125-126.

[259] Wood, *Slavery in Colonial America,* 56-58; Frey and Wood, *Shouting to Zion,* 83-87; Raboteau, *Slave Religion,* 126-128.

[260] Mullin, *Africa in America,* 243-249.

[261] Morgan, *Slave Counterpoint,* 481-485.

[262] WNCB, 35.

world views, as would Indian practices of communicating with that spirit world through rhythmic dance, trances, and dreams. For many Native Americans, as for Africans, traditional worldviews had been challenged by displacement from ancestral lands and by rapid cultural change. Like Africans, Indians tended to adopt Christianity or aspects of it when their native faiths could no longer explain or control the new world in which they found themselves.[263] Raboteau and Sobel don't adequately acknowledge the importance of the Native American element in the enslaved population, but their approaches work for a mixed-race, bicultural, African-Indian slave population as effectively as for a purely African one.

The Great Awakening established a new approach to preaching and evangelizing that, compared to other versions of Protestant Christianity, most closely coincided with African (and perhaps mixed Native American-African) traditions. Although each denomination experienced the Great Awakening somewhat differently, there were some common features among the Anglicans, Presbyterians, Congregationalists, and Baptists that came under the influence of this movement. Preachers influenced by the Awakening tended to be highly mobile, and reached enslaved communities that lived far from white population centers.[264] These preachers taught the essential Christian truths orally, rather than through texts; for slaves who were largely non-literate (especially in English), this approach made Christianity more accessible.[265] Preaching was lively and theatrical. White audiences sometimes responded to these preachers with groans, fainting fits, and even death-like loss of consciousness. Slaves who witnessed these gatherings could recognize familiar religious experiences: many African traditions included rituals of spiritual possession, where initiates went into trance-like states; death-and-rebirth enactments featured in many African faiths.[266] The Baptists—whether influenced by the Awakening or not—offered an additional practice that made sense to Africans: baptism by total immersion in a river recalled specific African rituals.[267] Very important among many Protestants who were influenced by the Awakening was a strong sense of community. Faith was not simply an individual struggle for truth, but the creation of a holy company of the saved; individuals who erred doctrinally or morally had to be expelled for the sake of the spiritual health of the whole. It was the responsibility of the community to keep watch over its members, and to correct or excommunicate them if they failed to adhere to agreed-upon standards. This rela-

---

[263] Axtell, "The Invasion Within: The Contest of Cultures in Colonial North America," in *The European and the Indian,* Oxford University, 1981, 73-76, 82-84.

[264] Raboteau, *Slave Religion,* 131-135.

[265] *Ibid.*, 114-120, 128-131; Frey and Wood, *Shouting to Zion,* 82-83.

[266] Sobel, *Trabelin' On,* 87-88, 97-98; Morgan, *Slave Counterpoint,* 644-648.

[267] Raboteau, *Slave Religion,* 43, 55-59; Sobel, *Trabelin' On,* 128-131, 139-140.

tionship between individuals and the community would have made sense to Africans, who had lived in societies that believed themselves endangered by any member who broke a taboo; these societies exerted themselves to discover and put right any such breaches.[268] Finally, post-Awakening churches, especially among the Baptists, tended to be suspicious of hierarchy and to emphasize the spiritual equality of all members, allowing even the uneducated and unsophisticated to share their personal experiences and to take on leadership roles, such as exhorting. This dedication to spiritual equality extended to black members, at least during the late eighteenth century; enslaved blacks who joined the post-Awakening churches could feel that they were treated with respect and love by fellow Christians, who often addressed them as "sister" or "brother."[269] In keeping with this egalitarianism, from the 1760s until the 1790s many of those influenced by the Awakening were outspoken critics of the institution of slavery. They backed away from this stance in subsequent decades, but before that retreat, antislavery preachers had helped to bring the first significant numbers of blacks into Christian churches.[270]

Among the Baptists, it was the Separate congregations rather than Regular churches, such as Welsh Neck, that most closely resembled the Protestantism that emerged from the Great Awakening. Yet under Winchester, Welsh Neck adopted some of these post-Awakening characteristics. Winchester's "more open and general method of preaching" was no doubt a more emotional and demonstrative type, very different from the learned, polite, gentlemanly eloquence that the congregation had been used to under Bedgegood.[271] After Winchester's departure, his preaching style was remembered—with disapproval—by the older members of Welsh Neck as characterized by "thumping, stamping, [and] raving," instead of as one that induced reflection.[272] Importantly, Winchester did not keep his distance from his black audience. His account of the start of his outreach stresses that he went out to them and addressed them directly, making it clear to them that they, too, were the intended beneficiaries of Christ's sacrifice. Winchester also emphasized that it was known to the enslaved that he had "never had anything to do with slavery, but on the contrary condemned it," in the manner of many post-Awakening preachers. His new approach resembled the broader pattern of post-Awakening Protestantism that widely appealed to the religious sensibilities of African American listeners.

---

[268] Sobel, *Trabelin' On,* 14-21, 82-83, 88; Townsend, *South Carolina Baptists,* 257-259.

[269] Frey and Wood, *Shouting to Zion,* 56-58; Raboteau, *Slave Religion,* 131-136.

[270] Sobel, *Trabelin' On,* 86-89; Morgan, *Slave Counterpoint,* 428-435.

[271] WNCB, 16; Winchester, *Universal Restoration,* viii.

[272] Mallary, *Botsford,* 74-75.

It is important to remember that emotional preaching, criticisms of slavery, and other aspects of the post-Awakening formula were not enough by themselves to ensure mass conversions of African Americans; the black community had to be ready for the evangelical outreach. The limitations of a "New Light" approach in cases where a black audience wasn't ready for Christianity had been illustrated by the Great Awakening in South Carolina. George Whitefield converted only 12 blacks during his 1740 preaching tour in the Lowcountry, and the New Light congregation at Stoney Creek, one of the few permanent products of Whitefield's evangelizing in South Carolina, enrolled only 32 slaves during the first 14 years of its existence.[273] Lowcountry slaves were largely African-born in the mid-eighteenth century. Language barriers, isolation from whites, and attachment to the religions of their homeland made them a tough crowd for conversion.[274] As Sobel has argued, blacks had to be at a point where their African heritage was losing relevance in their new American conditions, a point generally reached by American-born or heavily acculturated African-born slaves. Winchester's converts may well have fitted into that category. The names of the first seventy-two slaves he baptized are provided by the Church Book (the final twenty-six are not individually listed, since they were joining a separately constituted black church). These names are almost entirely Anglo names or the names of places in the Anglophone world. Such evidence isn't conclusive, but does suggest that most of these new Christians were American-born or acculturated to white ways.[275] One reason for Winchester's success may well be that he reached out to a group of slaves who were ready to hear his message, because their African traditions were becoming a distant and increasingly irrelevant memory.

The rapidity of the slaves' response to Winchester's first outreach – his "short discourse addressed immediately to them, took greater effect than can well be imagined" - suggests another reason why they were such a receptive audience. Winchester might have been preaching to a group of black men and women who, like his white listeners, had been prepared for his invitation to convert by Separate activity in the region. His black audience, he recalled, "returned home, and did not even give sleep to their eyes, as they afterwards informed me, until they had settled every quarrel among themselves... and restored whatever one had unjustly taken from another." Establishing harmony in this way was a

---

[273] Frey and Wood wax enthusiastic about the success of Wesley, Whitefield, and the Stoney Creek Church, in contrast to the staid Anglican missionaries who had preceded them. *Shouting to Zion,* 91-95. Yet Alexander Garden's Church of England school in Charleston enjoyed a similarly modest level of success during the same period. Raboteau, *Slave Religion,* 114-120.

[274] Frey and Wood, *Shouting to Zion,* 80-83.

[275] Mullin, *Africa in America,* 22-27.

reasonably easy step to take under the impulse of religious emotion, but their other response to Winchester represented a more profound change: "according to their form of marriage, [they] ... married every man to the woman with whom he lived." Winchester's account suggests that his black listeners already understood that an important criterion for being accepted for baptism was the establishment of formal, monogamous marriages that would be recognized as orthodox by their white, Christian neighbors. Many slaves in America continued African norms of short-term relationships or polygyny.[276] Conforming to formal Christian monogamy overnight seems a profound change in a very private aspect of life, and a significant break with the past. Powerful and inviting as Winchester's preaching to them might have been, taking so momentous a step strongly suggests that these enslaved blacks had been exposed to Christianity before, knew what the white man's faith required in terms of marriage, and were already considering a move, as a community, to embrace the new faith. Mulkey or other Separates might have sowed important seeds while visiting the area;[277] an enthusiasm for Christianity may have communicated itself from one region to the next, as slaves visited neighboring farms and plantations and shared their knowledge about a new version of the white man's religion that made sense to them and that offered them a dignified place in a biracial community. Winchester might well have been merely the catalyst in a process that was already underway, thanks to a well-established Separate movement in the region.[278]

---

[276] Wood, *Slavery in Colonial America,* 51-52; Frey and Wood, *Shouting to Zion,* 48-51. Many African societies regarded short-term relationships among young men and women as entirely normal; men and women formed more permanent relationships after the woman's first pregnancy.

[277] Mullin points out that there were differences among New Lights in terms of appealing to black audiences. Samuel Davies in Virginia, despite an emotional style, an emphasis on the direct experience of God's grace and rebirth, and outdoor meetings, failed to reach many slaves, even among a population as acculturated as the African Americans of Virginia. However, Separates such as Shubal Stearns, who preached in the same area a decade after Davies, did motivate large numbers of slaves to embrace Christianity. Mullin, *Africa in America,* 190-194. Mulkey had been converted and ordained by Stearns. *Encyclopedia of Southern Baptists*, s.v. "Mulkey, Philip."

[278] Lindman, "Bad Men and Angels from Hell," 267-268. Frey and Wood mistakenly classify Winchester as a Separate, and also claim that he was preaching a millenarian Universalism at this point in his career. The millennial content of his sermons, they argue, was key to attracting black converts, who found something to hope for in the Christian message. (The appeal of millennialism to Africans and African Americans is one of their central arguments.) Frey and Wood, *Shouting to Zion,* 102-103. In fact, Winchester was never a Separate and he had not become a Universalist by 1779. His interest in the millennium developed much later, largely in response to the French Revolution (Stone, *Winchester,* 126-129).

One intriguing aspect of Winchester's account of the first black conversions is that it portrays a group of slaves, all on the same plantation (Alexander McIntosh's), who came to church together and together made the decision to heal quarrels, regularize marriages, and take the necessary steps towards baptism. The Church Book reveals that thirty slaves from the McIntosh estate were baptized before the constitution of the black church; further slaves from the same estate may have been included in the twenty-six who were admitted after that church's constitution. The joint action by these slaves may well be evidence of a phenomenon seen elsewhere in British America; slaves re-creating their lost kin and community groups by turning the plantation into a surrogate clan.[279] If that is the case, then baptism and acceptance of a Christian identity would have been a group decision, rather than an act by multiple individuals. It is likely that there were recognized leaders in this group, though it is impossible to identify them from Winchester's memoir or from the Church Book. The African sense of community, adapted to the American environment, is certainly visible in the documents, and provided the momentum for large numbers of slave conversions over a short period of time, a momentum that contributed to Winchester's shift towards Universalism.

Two final points may be gleaned from the Church Book's spare, but intriguing, record. First, it looks as though a decision was made early in the process of black baptisms that the enslaved converts would not be admitted to the white church, but would be constituted as a church of their own. Normally, the Church Book recorded two distinct stages for white converts: their baptism (sometimes coupled with a statement that they "gave in their experiences" of saving grace), and their admittance to the church (when the new members often signed the covenant). The admission to the church usually occurred very soon after the baptism—sometimes the next day, and often the following week. Yet there is no record of blacks being admitted as members of the church; even the very first group of five who were baptized on 27 June did not undergo the second stage of admission. It may simply have been the case that the white members of Welsh Neck, while willing to see African Americans baptized, were not willing to share the close fellowship with them that church membership implied. It may also have been the case that Winchester realized, when he baptized the first slaves, that there were many more to come, certainly enough to constitute their own church. This early decision to create a separate black church might be further evidence of an almost ready-made community of black Christians; it might even suggest that the slaves themselves preferred to remain separate and autonomous. Whether it was the desire of the white members of Welsh Neck or of the

---

[279] Sobel, *Trabelin' On,* 31-34.

newly-baptized slaves or of both, a separate black church was constituted on 20 August 1779.[280]

The final point to be learned about this new black congregation from the Church Book was its gender ratio. Before the constitution of the black church, the Church Book gave the names of the converted slaves. Most of these are gender-specific; moreover, while the converts on each date are first of all grouped according to their owners, within each owner's list male names are given first, female second. This practice makes it further possible to identify gender in most cases, and to conclude that of seventy-two named converts between 27 June and 20 August 1779, forty-nine were male and twenty-three female, or 68% male and 32% female.[281] This male:female ratio is close to the gender ratio for new African imports to South Carolina, but if these were largely Creole or American-born Africans, as their names suggest, then the predominance of men among the converts is striking. In either case, the Welsh Neck Church Book challenges the argument that women dominated black church communities from the very beginning of the conversion process in the eighteenth century.[282]

Even though they were not incorporated directly into the white church, Winchester's conversions marked an epoch in Welsh Neck's history. Long-term changes in white views about the slaves in their midst and in African American views about the value of Christianity suddenly bore fruit in the form of black conversions, under the pressure of Revolutionary turmoil, Separate evangelizing, cultural change among African Americans, and Winchester's own, personal evolution towards Universalism. 1779 was arguably the most momentous year in Welsh Neck's early history. The excitement of that summer was brought to an extraordinary conclusion by Winchester's sudden departure from Welsh Neck in September, a departure that may suggest that his innovations were not universally welcome.

---

[280] WNCB, 26-28.

[281] Morgan argues that Winchester converted 100 blacks, of whom two thirds were male, one third female (Morgan, *Slave Counterpoint,* 425-426). In fact, we only know the gender of seventy-two of the converts, but it may be a reasonable assumption that the final twenty-six fell into the same pattern.

[282] Frey and Wood argue that Welsh Neck was 60% female from 1781-1830; a difficult contention, since there are no lists of church members for the 1780s and 1790s. It is true that more white women than men were church members during the 1770s, when we do have data. However, the gender ratio was the opposite for those black members whose names we know: men significantly outnumbered women. Therefore there are no grounds for concluding as they do that Welsh Neck demonstrates the early importance of black women in Christian congregations across the Pee Dee and Savannah regions (*Shouting to Zion,* 163).

Winchester's Departure

Winchester left Welsh Neck abruptly in September 1779. The circumstances of his departure are unclear, but they are worth examining in detail, since they provide some insights about the continuing Regular Baptist outlook of the older members of the church, and about their reaction to Winchester's baptisms of African Americans. Winchester's 1792 account makes the end of his relationship with the church seem uncontentious and almost accidental. He stated that in September 1779 he decided to visit New England for a while. He engaged Edmund Botsford to fill his place while he was away, but on the condition that Botsford would relinquish the pastorate should Winchester return. Winchester stated he was on his way back to South Carolina in October 1780 when he passed through Philadelphia and was asked to fill in at the Baptist church there. He ended up staying. How credible is this account? It is true that Winchester had taken long leaves of absence from Welsh Neck right from the start of his pastorate; the 1779-1780 absence was arguably just an extended version of a practice that his congregation had tolerated on other occasions. Mallary's biography of Botsford confirms Winchester's account to some extent, describing Botsford's initial service at Welsh Neck as "only in the character of a supply."[283] The Church Book states that Botsford was not formally received as a member of the church until his return in 1782.[284] Furthermore, the close approach of the war drove Botsford from Welsh Neck in June 1780; if Winchester had returned at the end of that year, as he said he was intending to do when he arrived in Philadelphia, he would have found no rival in place, though he would have found a church in chaos, experiencing the instability of a partisan war.[285] Though Winchester doesn't say so, it may be that though he really had originally intended to return, the British occupation of South Carolina and the conflict there helped persuade him to take up the offer to stay in Philadelphia.[286]

Winchester's statement that his departure from Welsh Neck was amicable and possibly temporary is open to question, however. His arrangement for Botsford to take over suggests that he intended to stay away longer this time, and that he might not return; this was an open-ended leave of absence, different from his earlier journeys. More significantly, the fact that he left while explosive changes were under way at Welsh Neck raises questions about the calm, consensual nature of his travels north. Winchester had suddenly enrolled 139 new

---

[283] Mallary, *Botsford,* 60.

[284] WNCB, 29.

[285] Mallary, *Botsford,* 56-59.

[286] Note that Oliver Hart, a prestigious Baptist preacher with much more established ties to South Carolina, fled first to Virginia and then to Philadelphia in late 1780. He, like Winchester, never returned south. Hart took up a position at Hopewell, New Jersey. Hart, "Diary," 14.

white members in the church, more than doubling its size; he had also converted almost 100 blacks, constituted in a separate, associated church. He was preaching to crowds of 1000 just before he left. [287] Why would he go on extended leave when he was in the full flood of an exciting and successful expansion?

The Church Book and a later letter by Botsford to Hart, incorporated in Mallory's biography of the former, allow the reconstruction of a plausible explanation for Winchester's departure in September. On 3 July 1779, about a month after the start of the revival, and after the baptism of the first five black members, the "Church unanimously gave a call to Mr. Winchester for another year." Clearly his new preaching style, the flood of new members, and the baptism of African Americans was not – or not yet – causing controversy. There is a suggestion of uneasiness at this point, however: Winchester agreed to continue as minister on condition that "they continue to be all agreed to a single person and not otherwise" and also that "he might be allowed to depart at any time." Did he feel that he was about to take a new direction, either in preaching or theology, that might raise objections? His 1792 account of the steps that had led him to Universalism supports the idea that during this revival, his old soteriological certainties were beginning to crumble in the face of the mass of new converts, white and black, suddenly entering his church. While he firmly denied that he had embraced Universalism until 1781, after he had become established at Philadelphia, he also said that Siegvolk's arguments for Universalism were nagging at the back of his mind throughout the 1779 revival at Welsh Neck. The conditions he attached in July to his acceptance of another year as pastor might have reflected his rising sense of doubt about fundamental theological issues.

If the church was ready to support Winchester unanimously in July, the progress of the revival seems to have eroded that unity. When Botsford later led a revival at Welsh Neck, he was at pains to distinguish his approach from his predecessor's. In a letter to Oliver Hart dated 10 September 1790 he wrote:

> This revival differs from that under Mr. Winchester in the following particulars. 1st Its beginning and progress have not been so rapid. 2dly. It is chiefly among the whites. 3dly. The affections of the Church were centered in him; now, both the old and young members have their love, in a very remarkable manner, drawn out to each other. 4thly. The work under him was carried on, apparently, all by his preaching; now the spirit of prayer , in a very remarkable manner, is poured out on the Church, and most of the old, and a few of the late members, pray in public. 5thly. In the former revival, several of the old members were very uneasy at his conduct, especially his manner of receiving all that came; now, the greatest love and harmony subsist, and none are received but with the consent of the whole.

---

[287] Winchester, *Universal Restoration*, x-xi.

Botsford added, presumably as a favorable comparison between his own preaching and Winchester's, that when he spoke, his voice was "just loud enough to fill the house. No thumping, stamping, raving, or any thing like it; generally, you might almost hear a mouse run across the house in time of worship."[288]

Though Botsford was not present during Winchester's revival, no doubt he heard many critical comments about it from his congregation. Clearly, Winchester was adding too many new members too rapidly, without sufficient evidence that they were truly called by God, in the eyes of the church's old guard. Winchester's conviction that God had saved the majority of mankind, his first step towards his later Universalism, was increasingly at odds with the Regular Calvinism of Welsh Neck's long-term members. Those older members may also have felt that Winchester was filling the church with his own acolytes and sidelining the church's leaders. One of the comments Botsford wrote in the Church Book on Winchester's pastorate reinforces the statements he made in the letter to Hart, above. Soon after leaving the Pee Dee, Winchester "fell into the error of universal restoration" and was the "means of dividing the Baptist Church" in Philadelphia.[289] The mention of the schism in Philadelphia was perhaps a covert or unconscious reference by Botsford to divisions Winchester had created at Welsh Neck, where the "old members were very uneasy at his conduct," in contrast to the "greatest love and harmony" that characterized Welsh Neck a decade later. These comments by Botsford suggest that the unity that had attended the first months of the revival, which must have initially seemed refreshing after the somnolent Bedgegood years, eroded quickly between July and September.

Botsford's comment that his own revival, unlike Winchester's, was "chiefly among the whites" is cryptic, but intriguing. In fact, most of those converted by Winchester were white, while, when Botsford left Welsh Neck, it had a slight majority of black members. Winchester never enrolled any blacks in the church; from the start of the slaves' conversions, it seems, the intent was to form them into a church of their own. Why was Winchester's revival remembered as one dominated by African Americans? It is possible that the answer lies in Botsford's comment about Winchester's preaching being at the center of the revival, and at Winchester's loud, "thumping, stamping, raving" style. Historians have noted that African Americans were attracted to dramatic, expressive preaching. Did their response to Winchester's large outdoor meetings make these meetings seem "African" to the church's old guard, even if many, possibly a majority, of those who were present, were white? There are many known examples of African worship practices having an impact on the style of mixed-race

---

[288] Mallary, *Botsford,* 74-75.
[289] WNCB, 28.

meetings, and it may be that influences of this kind were being felt in the final weeks of Winchester's pastorate.

Another indication that the African American aspect of Winchester's revival had caused concerns can be found in one of the notes that Botsford entered in the Church Book regarding Winchester's new members. "[A] great many of those baptized by Mr. Winchester have been excommunicated, both white and black; but the greater number of blacks; many of the latter upon examination appeared to be very ignorant of the nature of true religion."[290] While the old guard at Welsh Neck was ready to offer Christianity to blacks, Winchester seems to have gone too far. His openness to the black population's demand for baptism, rather than the absolute numbers of blacks baptized, may explain why Winchester's revival was remembered as an African one.

There is no evidence that the Church expelled him—and the Church Book was not shy about recording decisions to get rid of unwanted ministers, as in the cases of the Revs. Williams and Pugh.[291] Yet Winchester may well have felt a sense of uneasiness or hostility among some of his congregation, and therefore made the choice to leave—a decision that was not unwelcome to some of the older members.[292] It is interesting to reflect that most of the newly-admitted members probably approved of Winchester's preaching style, admission criteria, and theological outlook. If he had wished to make a stand, he could certainly have gathered a party in his support—possibly a majority.[293] Botsford's comment, quoted above, that "[t]he affections of the Church were centered in him" suggests that he had a strong personal following. His decision to leave instead of

---

[290] Ibid., 28.

[291] Ibid., 3, 5, 7, 10.

[292] Frey and Wood may be correct in saying that "Regular Baptists ... looked askance at Winchester's noisy revivals," though the Church leadership's rejection of Winchester's new preaching style was not as immediate or absolute as these scholars suggest, given the unanimous call to Winchester back in July to serve for another year. Frey and Wood leap to incorrect conclusions when they state that the old guard was unhappy about "the ecstasy of grace that brought swelling numbers of Africans into the Baptist communion. No sooner had Winchester left the province than the interim pastor, Joshua Lewis, excommunicated the majority of those baptized by Winchester, both black and white" (*Shouting to Zion,* 103). In fact, Botsford, not Lewis, immediately succeeded Winchester, and he did not reexamine Winchester's converts until 1782. If there was anxiety among older Welsh Neck members about the criteria Winchester was employing in baptizing new converts, their reaction was nothing like as extreme as Frey and Wood suggest—nor is there any reason to assume it had something to do with a distinctly African conversion ecstasy. When Botsford examined Winchester's converts and ejected those deemed unsuitable, many whites were ejected, also.

[293] Winchester had converted about thirty whites during the mini-revival of 1777 and 139 during the bigger revival of 1779. At the time of his departure, around 160 of the 220 white members were the products of his ministry. WNCB, 20-22, 24-28.

standing his ground may have resulted from the fact that he had never been very comfortable at Welsh Neck or possibly from his dislike of controversy. When his Philadelphia church later divided over his Universalism, he did all he could to avoid open disputes, at least according to his own account of events.

Whatever the exact truth about the reasons for Winchester's departure from Welsh Neck, there is no doubt that he had an immense impact on the church. Its members would have to decide which aspects of Winchester's legacy to embrace, and which to reverse.

Winchester's later career

When Winchester stopped in Philadelphia on his way back to South Carolina in October 1780, he was close to being fully convinced of the truth of Universalism; within three months, his study of Stonehouse and Siegvolk had completed his conversion. In January 1781 his private conversations about Universalism caused leading members of the Philadelphia church to confront him about his beliefs. When he avowed his Universalism, his opponents engineered a *coup*; they forcibly excluded Winchester's supporters, a majority of the congregation, from the church, and then voted to replace him as their minister. Winchester's version of events states that he did not preach his Universalist ideas from the pulpit, and was willing to keep his new beliefs to himself; he also stated that he did nothing to raise a party in his favor within the church, in keeping with his behavior at Welsh Neck. Threats of excommunication persuaded some of Winchester's adherents to withdraw their support, so that the courts ended up awarding the church and its property to the anti-Universalist faction. Winchester and his followers met at the University of the State of Pennsylvania for four years, until they were able to purchase a meeting house of their own.[294]

While Winchester's account of the schism in the Philadelphia church centers on his personal conversion to Universalist ideas, there was probably more to this controversy than the convictions of one individual. One of Winchester's recent predecessors at First Baptist, Philadelphia was Morgan Edwards, one of the most distinguished Baptist leaders in America. The obituary of Edwards in the *Baptist Register* suggested that he had a private inclination towards Universalism; he expressed an admiration for many Universalists and in his sermons and publications steered clear of debates over the dogmatic tenets of Calvinism.[295] It seems very possible that there was a significant group inclined to or at least open to Universalism before Winchester took charge, and that the support at Philadelphia for his position was not simply a personal attachment to his char-

---

[294] Stone, *Winchester,* 41-57. The University shortened its name to the University of Pennsylvania in 1791.

[295] Rippon, *Baptist Register, 1794-1797,* 308-309.

ismatic personality. Winchester's account of the Philadelphia schism recalls his self-focused account of the African American conversions at Welsh Neck.

Winchester was not the first advocate of Universalism in America. George De Benneville of Germantown, who had arrived in Pennsylvania in 1741, deserves that distinction; John Murray, who emigrated from England to Massachusetts in 1770, also preceded Winchester in an open defense of Universalist beliefs.[296] However, Winchester rapidly became the best-known champion of the Universalist cause, in part because he published prolifically in defense of the doctrine, and in part because the famous Philadelphia physician and Patriot, Benjamin Rush, became an early supporter of Winchester.[297] When representatives from various Universalist congregations from New England and elsewhere met for their first convention at Oxford, Massachusetts in 1785, Winchester, rather than Murray, was elected moderator.[298]

In the summer of 1787 Winchester, in an impulsive gesture that recalls his sudden departure from Welsh Neck, told his Philadelphia congregation that he felt called to preach in England. Since there was a ship about to depart for that country, he announced that he would be leaving in two days. Once in London, he preached at various churches until he acquired a following and a chapel of his own. Rush had given him a letter of introduction to the radical Dissenter Richard Price, and Winchester made contact with prominent figures such as Joseph Priestley and John Wesley. He continued to preach Universalist ideas at his London chapel and on tours throughout the southeastern counties, but from 1790 the focus of his publications was prophesy, using the Book of Revelation and other scriptural texts to predict the Second Coming of Christ and the Millennium that would follow. The spur to this new interest was the French Revolution,

---

[296] George De Benneville (1703-1793) was born in England to Huguenot exiles. He became convinced in his teens that God had saved all of mankind, and as a young man he preached these ideas in France, where he was condemned to death and only reprieved at the last minute. He was well known for an account he published of another, later near-death experience, when he visited heaven and received confirmation of his Universalist ideas; he awoke to find himself lying in a coffin, since he had to all appearances been dead for almost two days. John Murray (1741-1815) had been an associate of Wesley and Whitefield in England. He became convinced of universal salvation there, and brought these ideas to America in 1770. His preaching contributed to the start of a broader Universalist movement in New England (Stone, *Winchester*, 77-80, 102-104); Lindman, "Bad Men and Angels from Hell," 261-262; Bressler, *Universalist Movement*, 14-15.

[297] Bressler, *Universalist Movement,* 15-17. Winchester began his promotion of Universalism with his publication of *The Mystics Plea for Universal Redemption* (Philadelphia, 1781). He kept up a steady stream of arguments in favor of his doctrine, the best known of which was *Dialogues on Universal Restoration* (London, 1788), which was reprinted in numerous editions on both sides of the Atlantic (Stone, *Winchester,* 114-116; Evans, *American Bibliography*; Lindman, "Bad Men and Angels from Hell," 279-281).

[298] Stone, *Winchester,* 93-94.

which Winchester regarded as the time of troubles before the Second Coming, predicted in Revelation. Winchester's writings on the Millennium influenced both Priestley and Rush, with whom Winchester corresponded during his time in England. Rush referred to Winchester as "our Theological Newton" because of his ingenious reading of the prophetic passages of Scripture. Both men drew on Winchester's arguments in their assessments of the French Revolution and its impact on history.[299]

Winchester returned to America in 1794, preaching in Boston, Philadelphia, and New York before settling in Hartford, Connecticut. He responded to Thomas Paine's *Age of Reason* with *A Defence of Revelation*, and Winchester's attacks on Paine and on atheism won him prominent supporters in the Federalist camp: John Jay and Timothy Pickering both encouraged Winchester to publish his arguments against Paine's radical ideas.[300] When Winchester died in 1798, he was an internationally known figure who had come a long way from his remote parish on the Pee Dee. However, those years at Welsh Neck were all-important in introducing him to Universalist ideas, and it was the enthusiasm of his white and black converts there that first convinced him salvation would be given to more than a tiny number of the elect.

C. The Pastorate of Edmund Botsford, 1779-1796

Winchester's successor at Welsh Neck was Edmund Botsford (1745-1819), who took over on a temporary basis in November 1779, after Winchester's departure two months earlier. Botsford fled in June 1780, when the British gained effective control of South Carolina, but he returned at the beginning of 1782. At that point, Welsh Neck gave him a formal call to be their pastor, and he served the church until the end of 1796, when he left for a new position in Georgetown. His main contributions to Welsh Neck were reestablishing regular church life after the chaos of the Revolution, integrating the white and black churches created by Winchester, and tying Welsh Neck even more closely to the Charleston Association.

Botsford's Early Life

Charles Mallary, who preserved and supplemented a memoir written by Botsford in 1807, characterized him as "a plain, good man" though not "a per-

---

[299] *Ibid.,* 126-146, 195-199; Clarke Garrett, "Joseph Priestley, the Millennium, and the French Revolution," *Journal of the History of Ideas,* Vol. 34, No. 1 (Jan.-Mar. 1973), 61-66; Charles D. Russell, "Islam as a Danger to Republican Virtue: Broadening Religious Liberty in Revolutionary Pennsylvania," *Pennsylvania History: A Journal of Mid-Atlantic Studies,* Vol. 76, No. 3 (Summer 2009), 266-270.

[300] Stone, *Winchester,* 216-239.

son of great genius, nor extensive learning."[301] He was born at Woburn, in Bedfordshire, England, on 1 November 1745, the second son of Edmund and Mary Botsford. Edmund senior was an ironmonger and greengrocer. Once prosperous, he had loaned money to an irresponsible brother and become impoverished. Edmund junior was orphaned at age seven, after first his father, then his mother died. The younger children of the family were split up among various relations, and Edmund went to live first with a maternal aunt, Mrs. Osborne, then with an old friend of his mother, Mrs. Barnes. The Barnes family were Baptists, and Edmund grew up attending church. He became fascinated with the idea of becoming a minister and he used to dress in a black cloak and an apron and, standing on a chair, preach sermons to his schoolmates.[302]

One incident that seemed to presage this future career was a dream that Edmund had when he was eight or nine years old, and that he related in his memoir over fifty years later. He dreamed he was standing on Priest's Hill in the Duke of Bedford's park at Woburn, when Christ descended in a bright chariot, calling Edmund by name. He gave Edmund a large sword, and instructed him to look at the chariot whenever he needed the strength to use the weapon. Edmund realized that his schoolmates were also there, and were similarly equipped with swords. The lads soon needed both their weapons and the inspiration of the chariot; they were attacked by an army of giants, and then by two further armies, each of which outnumbered the boys. With Christ's help, they prevailed. In his memoir, Botsford argued that, while dreams are "generally vain and frivolous things," that this one came true both for him and for one of his schoolmate-warriors, William Butfield, since both boys later became ministers and went to battle for Christ.[303]

It is likely that an inspiration for this dream was an incident in one of Botsford's favorite childhood books, John Bunyan's *Pilgrim's Progress*. Bunyan's main character, Great-Heart, meets Valiant, who tells him about his victo-

---

[301] Mallary, *Botsford*, v-vii. Mallary's work lies somewhere between a biography and an autobiography. Extensive passages from Botsford's memoir and correspondence have been reproduced, allowing Botsford to speak for himself, but Mallary has added his own commentary and details, based on interviews with Botsford's friends and family.

[302] *Ibid.*, 13-14.

[303] *Ibid.*, 14-19. This very elaborate narrative of a childhood dream is a useful reminder about the difficulties of distinguishing African elements in American Baptist culture from English or other European ones. Sobel argues that a common – and definably African – aspect of conversion narratives among African American Baptists was an experience where the convert heard God call out his or her name; such experiences often took place in dreams. Sobel, *Trabelin' On*, 107-110. Botsford's memoir suggests he had a very similar experience during his childhood in England. Rather than being a distinct, African element in the Afro-Baptist faith that evolved in the United States, the calling by God may be one of those cases where Africans could recognize in white Baptist culture certain elements that meshed with their own cultural legacies.

ry over three strong foes who attacked him at once. On looking at Valiant's sword, Great-Heart declared that it was a "right Jerusalem blade," the name of the sword given to Botsford by Christ in Botsford's dream. According to his later memoir, Botsford had learned "several parts" of *Pilgrim's Progress* by heart.[304] Not only did this story enter into his dreams, but it inspired him to write "A Spiritual Voyage" in later life, a Bunyan-like allegory of the Christian's journey to salvation, through numerous perils and temptations.[305]

If Botsford seemed destined for a religious life when he was a boy, his adolescence suggested otherwise. (Perhaps the general conventions of biographies, plus the compelling *topos* of God calling a sinner to be his chosen messenger, shaped Botsford's narrative here. His sins were not especially heinous.) He was guilty of "many pranks" that alienated all but the ever-loving Mrs. Barnes. In one escapade, he ran away to sea, a vocation that had always fascinated him. He returned home, however, before he had gotten very far: on his first night he took shelter in a hedgerow, only to find, when the sun rose, that he had been sleeping under a corpse hanging from a nearby tree. He had noticed a horrendous smell as he was settling to sleep. He took the corpse as a sign that he should abandon this particular career. He did run away to join the army later on, during the final years of the Seven Years' War. He saw no fighting, since his regiment was stationed in Scotland.[306] His chief adventure was escaping a flogging for falling asleep on sentry duty, because of the mercy shown by the officer in charge.[307] When the war ended, Botsford returned to Mrs. Barnes and was reconciled to his friends and relations. He worked as a groom and in other capacities for local gentlemen, winning a good reputation for his steady conduct.[308]

Though happy in his work, Botsford was urged by a friend of his, George Harris, to join him in emigrating to Charleston. Botsford's childhood dream of going to sea was stirred to new life. Friends and family found the means for

---

[304] Mallary, *Botsford,* 13-15.

[305] "A Spiritual Voyage" is reproduced at the end of this volume.

[306] Since Scotland had rebelled under Bonnie Prince Charlie during the previous War of Austrian Succession (1744-1748), it was prudent to post soldiers in the northern kingdom during this later conflict. However, Scotland remained quiet, and so Botsford's service during that dramatic war was uneventful. Stephen Conway, "War and National Identity in the Eighteenth-Century British Isles," *The English Historical Review,* Vol. 116, No. 468 (Sept., 2001), 883.

[307] Botsford commented that the officer's merciful restraint showed an intelligent approach to winning the loyalty of subordinates. Botsford suggested that everyone in authority would be wise to adopt this approach. His opinion on this issue was consistent with the growing trend during the eighteenth century to praise "paternalistic" authority that sought to rule through reason and love, rather than force; Botsford similarly advocated a paternalistic approach by slave owners towards their human property. Fliegelman, *Prodigals and Pilgrims,* 9-35; Botsford, "On Slavery."

[308] Mallary, *Botsford,* 19-24.

them to pay their passage, and the two young men left on 18 November 1765, arriving on 28 January the following year. Harris did not last long in Charleston; he joined a company of strolling players and left for Barbados within a few months. Botsford, who had already been experiencing "convictions" of his sinfulness before he left England, now, in his isolation and financial uncertainty, found those convictions intensified. In this state of turmoil, he heard Oliver Hart preach, and thus began a long and close relationship between the two men; Botsford referred to Hart as "my Father" for the rest of his life. Botsford alternated between feeling convinced of his sinfulness and then assured of his salvation; each of these periods of assurance was then revealed to be hypocritical complacency. This struggle ended on his twenty-first birthday, 1 November 1766, when he finally saw the full depths of his sin and the full mercy of God, who had saved him. He communicated these experiences to Hart, who accepted them as authentic and baptized Botsford on 13 March 1767.[309] Hart continued to be impressed by Botsford and urged him to train for the ministry. Botsford began his formal training on 1 February 1769. He was provided with funds from the "Religious Society," an organization founded by Hart in 1755 to support the religious education of talented young men.[310] Mallary represented Botsford's vocation for the ministry as an extraordinary example of divine providence: the "wayward orphan" who was destined for the "gibbet" had become a man of God.[311] This depiction seems somewhat over-dramatic. Instead, Botsford can be seen as a serious and pious child, brought up in a Baptist household, who naturally turned back to his faith as a young adult at a time of loneliness and confusion. Of course, dreams and portents and the salvation of a straying sheep make for a better story.

Botsford was licensed to preach in February 1771. He assisted Hart in Charleston until June, and then briefly assisted Francis Pelot at Euhaw. Botsford was then called to serve a newly formed congregation at Tuckaseeking on the South Carolina-Georgia border. He stayed here a year, traveling widely up and down the Savannah River valley to reach the scattered population; he became known as the "flying preacher." Daniel Marshall, a celebrated Separate preacher, was working in the same area; he and Botsford formed a friendship that was unusual at a time when Regular and Separate Baptists tended to treat each other in a very "unchristian manner." Marshall complimented Botsford on his preaching (though he felt it was not quite up to the standard of the Separate Baptists

---

[309] *Ibid.*, 27-34.

[310] David Benedict, *A General History of the Baptist Denomination in America, and Other Parts of the World* (Boston, MA: Lincoln and Edmands, 1813), 708; Furman, *Charleston Association*, 11-12. Mallary does not mention this aspect of Botsford's training; perhaps Botsford omitted it from his own memoir.

[311] Mallary, *Botsford,* 36-38.

Philip Mulkey and Joseph Reese); Botsford married one of Marshall's converts, Susanna Nun, in 1773. Botsford was ordained by Hart and Pelot at Charleston on 24 March 1773, and then on 28 November the same two ministers helped Botsford turn his converts in the Savannah River region into the formally constituted church of New Savannah.[312]

Edmund and Susanna settled at Brier Creek, Georgia in 1774. A legacy from Edmund's older brother in England allowed them to live comfortably amidst a congregation that was too poor to provide much material support. Botsford steadily made converts – a total of 148 in the area by 1779. This happy life was disrupted by the "horrors" of the Revolutionary War. With the British capture of Savannah on 29 December 1778, and the Battle of Brier Creek on 3 March 1779, Georgia was suddenly under British occupation, and the Botsfords had to flee. They took with them their "three children, the youngest (a daughter) being not then two months old; and a negro man." The only possessions they were able to carry were a cart, loaded with a bed, a blanket, and a sheet.[313] In later years, Botsford regretted the loss of his first church and home, and especially of his library.[314] However, his memoir claimed that neither he nor his wife regretted their sacrifice. "Indeed, instead of murmuring, it was rather a matter of boasting that we had suffered so much in the cause of our country." Botsford explained his patriotism as follows: "In my greatest difficulties, I never regretted engaging on the side of my country. In America I had embraced religion, married a wife, had children, experienced great kindness, and in America I wished to end my days. I considered the war on the side of Britain unjust, and therefore felt myself justifiable in my opposition to that country." He also hoped that an independent United States would provide full religious equality for the Baptists, and an end to the taxes and harassment that even in America had burdened them. He left his wife and children with a friend, and served as chaplain to Brigadier General Andrew Williamson, one of the Patriot leaders who had fought at Brier Creek.[315]

Botsford's Early Years at Welsh Neck

While serving with the army, Botsford was invited to become "the spiritual guide" to the Welsh Neck Church. Botsford's memoir doesn't make it clear who issued the invitation. It may have come from Winchester before his departure, or

---

[312] *Ibid.*, 38-48; Hart, "Diary," 6. Hart has 14 March 1773 as the date of Botsford's ordination.

[313] Mallary, *Botsford,* 51.

[314] John Rippon, ed., *The Baptist Register for 1790, 1791, 1792, and Part of 1793. Including Sketches of the State of Religion among Different Denominations of Good Men at Home and Abroad* (London: Dilly, Button, and Thomas, 1793), 104.

[315] Mallary, *Botsford,* 52-55, 59-60.

from the Welsh Neck community after Winchester left, but in either case, his position at this point was "only in the character of a supply" preacher. Botsford "felt it his duty to accept." He visited the church and preached in October 1779, and the community asked him to move there with his family. He later recalled the warm welcome given by Welsh Neck. "Never... was greater kindness shown to any one in distress. Myself and family were provided with every comfort, and that in abundance."[316]

Unfortunately, the war soon caught up with him. Charleston fell to the British on 12 May 1780, and British armies defeated the last Continental force at Waxhaws on 29 May. Botsford felt himself in danger because of his service to the Patriot forces, and decided to flee.[317] His mentor, Hart, also felt vulnerable because of his earlier advocacy of the Patriot cause, and had therefore left Charleston on 2 February 1780, before the British siege began.[318] Hart had found his way to the Pee Dee region, and the two ministers fled together, deciding to take refuge with one of Hart's brothers, who lived in Virginia. As a testimony to how war could break down denominational barriers and put doctrinal differences into perspective, Botsford and Hart spent their first months in Virginia ministering to a Presbyterian congregation, who accepted, though with some surprise, their ministers' determination to baptize by immersion. With the news of Gates's defeat at Camden, South Carolina seemed permanently lost. Hart headed north to stay with another brother in Philadelphia.[319] Botsford was now joined by his wife, who had left Welsh Neck, sadly losing a son to cholera on the journey north. The Botsfords settled in Brunswick County, Virginia, dur-

---

[316] Ibid., 55, 60.

[317] Brigadier General Williamson, with whom Botsford had served, was captured at Charleston and accepted parole. There was no reason why parole would not have been offered to Botsford on similar terms. However, rumors were rife at this point in the war; the defeat at Waxhaws was widely reported as a "massacre," and Botsford may have believed that indiscriminate punishments would be meted out against all Patriots. His biographer explains his flight as follows: "Mr. Botsford had not raised the musket, but he had fought with his tongue, and, by his warm appeals, urged forward his countrymen to a manly vindication of their rights, against the arrogant claims, and formidable invasion, of the mother country. He had now become too conspicuous for his patriotism and love of liberty, to render it safe to trust himself in the hands of the tories, or British. And besides, he was an Englishman himself, and this made him a *rebel* of the highest grade" (Mallary, *Botsford,* 55). The last comment is a strange one: plenty of recent immigrants from Britain fought on the Patriot side, and, since British authorities regarded all colonists, whether born in America or in Britain, as equally subjects of the Crown, there is no reason to think that Botsford's origins in England would make him liable to particularly severe punishments.

[318] Hart, "Diary," 13.

[319] Ibid., 14; Mallary, *Botsford,* 57.

ing the remainder of the southern campaign.[320] During that time, Botsford preached to as many as 2,000-3,000 at a time, taking advantage of the dislocation of the established church during the upheaval.[321]

In December 1781, after Yorktown and General Nathanael Greene's recovery of the South Carolina interior, the Botsfords returned to Welsh Neck, arriving at the beginning of the new year. He found his congregation in a sorry state, as his memoir explained: "The war had made sad havoc of friends and property; and as for religion, it was almost forgotten."[322] The church members were glad to see him back, and on 5 January 1782 gave him a formal call to be their pastor. He was given a piece of land about two miles from the church, where he built a home he called "Bethel." He now set himself to reorganizing and revitalizing the church after the disruption of war.[323]

One significant development that took place as soon as Botsford had returned was the withdrawal of three members, including a recently-appointed deacon, Thomas Lide, to join a newly-formed church at Cheraw Hill. Ten more Welsh Neck members who lived closer to Cheraw Hill joined them later in 1782. The pastor of the new church was the Rev. Joshua Lewis, who had preached on occasion at Welsh Neck during Botsford's absence. Their application to constitute their own church was submitted to Welsh Neck on 5 January 1782 and the new congregation came into formal existence a week later. This separation seems to have been entirely amicable, based on geographical convenience rather than differences in theology or style of worship.[324] Botsford and Deacon Abel Edwards, among other Welsh Neck members, participated in the formal constitution of the Cheraw Hill Church. [325] The only dispute that did emerge over time involved Lewis's failure to return books he had borrowed from Welsh Neck's library.[326]

---

[320] Mallary, 56-59.

[321] Rippon, *Baptist Register, 1790-1793,* 106-107.

[322] Mallary, *Botsford,* 59-61. Strictly speaking, the church leaders had already taken the first steps towards getting the church back on its feet. They had called on the Rev. Joshua Lewis and the Rev. John Thomas to assist them while Botsford was absent, had elected three new deacons, and had started disciplinary action against errant church members. WNCB, 29.

[323] Mallary, *Botsford,* 59-61.

[324] The Church Book states explicitly that "living more convenient" to Cheraw Hill was the reason for members' dismissal there. WNCB 30.

[325] WNCB, 29. The Rev. Philip Mulkey also assisted, another illustration of Mallary's statement that Botsford, unlike most Regular Baptists, got on well with the Separates. Mallary, *Botsford,* 41-43.

[326] Mallary, *Botsford,* 62-63. Lewis had worked with Botsford back in Georgia; the two were long-term colleagues. Hart, "Diary," 7. The dispute over the failure to return the borrowed books began on 31 March 1787 and was still a focus of church energies in 1794. WNCB, 37, 41.

One important task facing Botsford was restoring the character of the Welsh Neck community as a body of worshipers who shared the same beliefs and adhered to a defined code of conduct. He continued the work begun by the church's leaders in late 1781 of calling members to account for "disorderly walking." Messengers were sent to those who were misbehaving throughout 1782; unfortunately the Church Book provides little information about specific offenses, though it does state that one church member, Gideon Parish, was accused of plundering. After he confessed, he was forced to make restitution.[327] This was perhaps an example of the church trying to heal divisions between local Whigs and Tories, whose violence in the interior of South Carolina had been unrestrained during 1780-1781. It is also possible that Parish had stolen from someone on his own, presumably Whig, side, and that was why he alone was being called to account.

In this first year of Botsford's pastorate, the problem with unworthy church members was more serious than usual. There had always been a few individuals who failed to live up to the church's expected standards of behavior. Now, however, the church was dealing with the aftermath of Winchester's 1779 revival. As Botsford's memoir explains, the older members of the church had been increasingly unhappy, even when Winchester was still pastor, with his willingness to admit new members too freely.[328] By 1782 it was known that Winchester had fallen "into the error of universal restoration," and this development made many of his baptisms even more suspect. The disciplinary procedures during Botsford's first months were aimed not merely at maintaining "upright walking," but at purging the church of members who, many felt, should never have been admitted in the first place. The lack of church member lists after 1779 and the incomplete record of baptisms and excommunications in the Church Book makes it impossible to know exactly how many of Winchester's white converts were expelled, but Botsford's comment on Winchester's pastorate states that it was "a great many."[329] The church's determination to rid itself of unworthy members was demonstrated at the 3 July 1784 meeting, when the members present resolved that anyone who was summoned to explain misconduct, and either failed to appear at the very next meeting, or to send a reasonable excuse for their absence, would be immediately excommunicated. This peremptory procedure differed significantly from the former practice under Bedggood of sending multiple messengers, and then placing members under suspension before proceeding to the extreme measure of excommunication.[330] The functioning of the church as

---

[327] WNCB, 29.
[328] Mallary, *Botsford,* 74-75.
[329] WNCB, 28.
[330] Ibid., 32. In practice, the church showed more patience in certain cases, such as the disciplining of Elizabeth Walsh in 1785 and Mary Walsh in 1786, than this draconian

a loving community depended on its members being able to believe that all of their "brothers" and "sisters" were chosen by God for salvation.

The final step in restoring the Welsh Neck Church to its Calvinistic roots was the revision of the covenant in 1785. On 3 April, three senior members were appointed as a committee for this purpose; their recommendations, reported at the 18 June meeting, were unanimously adopted, and on 2 July, the members formally signed the new covenant. The most significant change in the covenant was the inclusion of new language about the treatment and evangelization of slaves (see below for a discussion of this issue), but also important was the firm reiteration of the church's Calvinist beliefs, stressing that members must believe in "particular and personal redemption" and "particular redemption through the incarnation." While the church under Botsford was willing to accept and to build on Winchester's outreach to African Americans, it firmly rejected his attempt to alter the church's theology regarding salvation. Fifty-two members signed the covenant on 2 July; though it was noted that several members were missing and would sign later, this was still a much reduced number from the two hundred or so white members of the church at the end of Winchester's pastorate.[331] All those who had been attracted to the church by Winchester's doctrine that a majority of mankind was destined for salvation were now excluded, or else agreed, by signing the covenant, to conform to the Calvinist creed of the Regular Baptists.[332]

Botsford and the African American Church

While "a great many" whites were excommunicated, Winchester's black converts were purged in a somewhat different manner. As the 6 April 1782 Church Book entry explained, Botsford decided to disband the black church that had been constituted by Winchester, and then to admit those blacks who were "truly pious" to the white church. The incorporation of the black church into the white church meant that Welsh Neck was conforming to the usual pattern in the

---

rule might suggest, even though both were converted during Winchester's 1779 revival. WNCB, 33-34. However, Townsend's claim that the lack of record of crimes committed by church members after 1782 reflected a "broad and tolerant spirit" under Botsford is clearly incorrect (Townsend, *South Carolina Baptists*, 75-76). Excommunications were numerous, and the lack of detail simply reflected the increasingly sparse nature of the Church Book under Botsford; the Church Book itself states that its policy "[f]rom the commencement of 1786...[was] to record in this Book only such things as are deemed necessary to be kept on record" (WNCB, 38).

[331] Since forty-six of Winchester's black converts had been accepted into the church in April 1782, and ten more African Americans had been admitted since that time, it seems almost certain that all of the fifty-two signatories were white. See below for a fuller discussion.

[332] WNCB, 36.

rural South. Most all-black churches were in the cities. Rural communities preferred to exercise closer supervision over black religious communities.[333] Seven senior members of the white church joined Botsford on a committee that reviewed the requests of African Americans who sought to be admitted. Forty-six were initially deemed worthy, though a note added at a later date explained that "several more have been received since."[334] Botsford's comment on Winchester's converts stated that "many...have been excommunicated, both white and black; but the greater number of blacks." If non-admittance to the white church is seen as the equivalent of excommunication, then somewhere between forty and fifty of Winchester's black converts were "excommunicated" in this manner.[335]

Botsford explained in the Church Book that the blacks who were excommunicated or not admitted to the white church had been found to be "very ignorant of the nature of true religion."[336] Although it is of course possible that poor or confused knowledge characterized some of those who were excluded, it is also likely that some of those purged held different, rather than inferior, ideas about religion from those laid out in the Welsh Neck covenant. Among the expelled blacks, the continuation of African traditions, which had been overlooked by Winchester, may have provoked the disapproval of Botsford and his allies; it was quite common for many Africans who converted to the Baptist faith to retain elements of their traditional worldview in a new, hybrid, "Afro-Baptist faith."[337] The Welsh Neck Church Book and other documents from the period provide little information about the African American members' worldview, but these sources contain a number of clues that, interpreted in the context of what is known about African cultural survivals elsewhere in America, indicate some strong possibilities for what was taking place in Welsh Neck's black population.

---

[333] Raboteau, *Slave Religion,* 137-138.

[334] WNCB, 30. After the first wave of admissions of members of the black church, four further slaves were baptized on 5 June 1784, including Moses, who belonged to General McIntosh's estate, which had supplied the largest and earliest contingent of Winchester's converts (WNCB, 32). Further slave converts entered the church, usually in twos or threes, at regular intervals thereafter.

[335] Ibid., 28.

[336] Ibid., 28.

[337] Sobel, *Trabelin' On,* 17-23. The Baptist focus on adult baptism as the result of an experience of God's saving grace distinguished their focus from the Anglicans, who dominated conversion efforts in South Carolina during the first half of the eighteenth century. The Anglicans emphasized the education of children, believing that adults were too mired in their "heathenish" culture to embrace Christianity. Frey and Wood, *Shouting to Zion,* 68-70. By converting adolescents and adults, the Baptists absorbed many who had been brought up in an African or African American culture, making the perpetuation of African traditions more likely.

One element of traditional African faiths that often made its way into Christianity was a belief that supernatural powers pervaded the natural and material world. Most African religions—especially those influenced by Islam or Catholicism—did believe in a high God, the ultimate power in the cosmos.[338] However, that chief divinity tended to be portrayed as a distant being, and most religious practices focused on lesser divinities or on ancestral spirits.[339] Accepting Christianity meant according the high God a central role in worship—a shift of emphasis rather than an absolute change for many Africans.[340] To what extent lesser divinities and spirits were fully renounced would vary from one individual to another. Catholicism's success among Africans in the Caribbean and Brazil derived in part from the Africans' ability to supplicate and propitiate Catholic saints in the same way they had turned to local divinities in their traditional faiths.[341] The African preference for evangelical Protestantism over more reserved and formal variants, such as the Church of England, derived in part from the sense that supernatural forces were present in evangelical worship, whether in a rebirth experience that resembled African rituals of possession by a god, or in healing through prayer.[342] African American converts could maintain their traditional emphasis on the importance of ancestral spirits by putting their own spin on Christian ideas: while white Christians believed their souls would be reunited with deceased relatives in the afterlife, some black Christians believed that deep prayer and trances could bring contact with the deceased in the here-and-now.[343] There is evidence that many Africans who adopted the Baptist faith continued to believe in certain magical practices, and even used Christian prayer as they would have used traditional propitiations of lesser gods, to seek benefits for themselves or to inflict harm on others.[344] It may be that sorcery, especially with the goal of hurting enemies, became even more widespread among Africans and their descendants in the New World, and that African practices were supplemented with magic from European and Native American traditions.[345]

---

[338] Morgan, *Slave Counterpoint,* 634-638; Frey and Wood, *Shouting to Zion,* 33-34.
[339] Raboteau, *Slave Religion,* 8-13, 16; Sobel, *Trabelin' On,* 6, 10-14, 16-17.
[340] Robin Horton argued that the trajectory of many African faiths in the seventeenth and eighteenth centuries was towards a stronger emphasis on the high God; accepting Christianity was less of a renunciation than a development of traditional beliefs. Frey and Wood, *Shouting to Zion,* 1-3.
[341] Raboteau, *Slave Religion,* 87-89.
[342] Sobel, *Trabelin' On,* 58-59, 80-82, 122-125.
[343] Mullin, *Africa in America,* 208-212.
[344] Raboteau, *Slave Religion,* 13-16, 33-35; Sobel, *Trabelin' On,* 131-135.
[345] Morgan, *Slave Counterpoint,* 612, 619-620, 623-629; Mullin, *Africa in America,* 175-185; Sobel, *Trabelin' On,* 42-48; Frey and Wood, *Shouting to Zion,* 59-62. Note that Botsford admitted in his memoir, without any sense of embarrassment, that he had engaged in conjuring as a boy. He and his friends each poured s small amount of molten lead into cold water to see what shape it would take as it solidified; the shape would indi-

The belief in such magic was still a force among African American members of the Welsh Neck community decades later, after its move to Society Hill: in 1826 Jim, a slave and church member, with the support of two other enslaved members of the congregation, murdered Rachel, a fellow slave and church member, because they were convinced that she had practiced witchcraft against them.[346] Botsford's dismissal of many of Winchester's converts as "ignorant" may have reflected the fact that many black converts were viewing Christianity in their own hybrid fashion. Behind his brief and dismissive entry in the Church Book lay a complex reality of enslaved individuals and communities negotiating their own position between African tradition and the white man's world.

Another aspect of African tradition that sometimes conflicted with Christianity was marriage. Many African societies were polygynous, and many of those brought to America continued to practice polygyny.[347] Baptists, in common with most other Christian denominations, insisted that black members practice monogamy according to European and Christian norms.[348] The only exception allowed, and then only after much debate, was that enslaved spouses who had been forcibly separated by sale could remarry; for example, in 1793 the Bethel Association, to which many churches close to Welsh Neck belonged, decided in favor of such remarriage, since circumstances made it impossible for these slaves, with the best of wills, to maintain a normal Christian marriage.[349] In general, however, lifelong monogamy was the rule for enslaved as well as for free Baptists; since only one quarter of Africans were sold on from the plantation that first purchased them, and masters in South Carolina made increasing efforts to sell spouses together as the eighteenth century wore on, there was enough stability to make marriage according to Christian norms a real possibility.[350] Winchester recorded that the first Africans he preached to immediately went back to their plantation and, "according to their form of marriage, had mar-

---

cate the pourer's future career. From this practice, the young Botsford convinced himself that he was to be a sailor (Mallary, *Botsford*, 19-20). If the adult Botsford related this incident simply as an amusing anecdote from childhood, it does demonstrate that the practice of conjuring, widespread in the African American community, was very familiar to whites.

[346] Frey and Wood, *Shouting to Zion*, 209-210.

[347] Wood, *Slavery in Colonial America*, 51-52; Frey and Wood, *Shouting to Zion*, 48-51.

[348] Unusually, and in contrast to the Baptists, the Moravians allowed black converts to keep multiple wives if they were already married to more than one; after conversion, however, members were not allowed to add additional spouses. Mullin, *Africa in America*, 245.

[349] Raboteau, *Slave Religion*, 120-126; Townsend, *South Carolina Baptists*, 257-259.

[350] Morgan, *Slave Counterpoint*, 507-510, 519-524.

ried every man to the woman with whom he lived;"[351] these black men and women understood the importance of formal, monogamous marriage as a precondition for conversion. Yet, in a deeply personal aspect of life such as marriage, old customs die hard, and when "Bill a negro man being charged with adultery & not giving satisfaction was excommuni[cated]" by Welsh Neck in 1798, it is impossible to know whether Bill had been guilty of philandering, or had been practicing legitimate polygyny in his own mind.[352] The purge of Winchester's converts under Botsford for "ignorance" could well have reflected different, tradition-based attitudes towards marriage as well as towards the supernatural.

If Botsford was dismissive of many of Winchester's black converts, he certainly believed that some African Americans were fully capable of becoming good Christians and valuable members of the Baptist community. He praised black converts for often being more loving to each other than white Christians were. He noted that "[m]any of them can read and are remarkably fond of hymns" and that "[t]hey sing delightfully."[353] He frequently expressed pleasure at black responsiveness to his preaching and liked to portray himself as popular with African Americans. When he fled from South Carolina, he left his wife, children, and a slave he had brought from Georgia behind at Welsh Neck; when his household later caught up with him, his memoir records that "[t]he poor negro was almost frantic upon seeing once more his kind master. He jumped, hallowed, fell down, embraced his master's feet, and in every possible way gave vent to joy."[354] In 1785 Botsford wrote to Hart that during his annual visit to Charleston, "[n]umbers of blacks come to see me, and some whites; and many I must go and see." He spoke "of having much satisfaction in preaching to the negroes" during his 1786 Charleston visit.[355] He celebrated the large black membership in many Baptist churches, from Virginia down to Georgia, and complemented the achievements of an all-black church in Georgia, presumably referring to Andrew Bryan's congregation in Savannah. He said he was "very fond of teaching" African Americans and boasted of having preached to as many as 300 blacks at a time.[356] When he lost his second wife, Caty, in 1796, he was consoled by being able to help two African American slaves with "soul trouble;" he wrote to Furman that "I think it affords me more satisfaction to find the Lord

---

[351] Winchester, *Universal Restoration,* ix-x. Of course, since Winchester's enslaved audience consecrated their relationships "according to their form of marriage," these African Americans may have understood the permanence and exclusivity of these marriages differently than Winchester did.

[352] WNCB, 43.

[353] Rippon, *Baptist Register, 1790-1793,* 105.

[354] Mallary, *Botsford,* 58.

[355] *Ibid.,* 63-64, 65-67.

[356] Rippon, *Baptist Register, 1790-1793,* 105.

is at work upon those 2 poor creatures, than I should be to call the globe my own."[357] By the end of his tenure at Welsh Neck, Botsford was failing to arouse religious convictions among whites, but he was still enjoying success among the African American population.[358]

Though Botsford felt a sense of empathy towards African Americans and praised their piety, he was far more willing to accept the institution of slavery than Winchester. Botsford certainly felt no qualms about owning slaves. The 1790 census showed that he owned four.[359] His 20 April 1790 letter to Furman stated that these slaves consisted of a boy and a "Wench" in the house, and two field hands, whom he had loaned or leased to his neighbor, McIver. He seems to have acquired more slaves over the next few years, since he reported in early 1797 that after his Welsh Neck property was sold and his debts settled, he would be down to four "Servants" again.[360] Botsford's slave ownership was not unusual among Baptists; in the 1790 census, Baptist slaveholding in South Carolina conformed to the general pattern in the state, with about 1/3 owning slaves.[361]

Botsford's unpublished essay "On Slavery" provides further insight into his views on this institution. He wrote "On Slavery" some ten to fifteen years after he had left Welsh Neck, when he was living in Georgetown, an area far more dependent on slavery than the Pee Dee; however, the views he expressed in this short work seem consistent with briefer statements from his Welsh Neck years. Botsford regretted the existence of slavery. He accepted that "[t]he punishment inflicted on the Negro is often severe," and that South Carolina's slavery "in its best state is a very great evil." However, although he said "I do not mean in this Essay to vindicate Slavery," he did offer extensive mitigating arguments for the institution. He argued that "[f]ew things have been more misrepresented than the labour of the Slave on a rice plantation in S° Carolina. Their labour is by no means excessive." The hardest labor – pounding the rice – was now done by machinery. The slaves normally worked only from ten o'clock in the morning until two o'clock in the afternoon. At harvest time, they worked longer, but "[h]arvest is hard labour all the world over...the Negroes do not labour harder than the poor man in England, nor does he [sic] perform so much." Certainly, the slaves were working in the hot sun, "but I never saw a Negro who would not prefer working in the rice field in the hotest [sic] day in Summer, to almost any kind of work in cold weather. The Negro does not love cold, nor does he complain of the heat." They were provided with food that is "plain, but wholesome, & they have as much as they can eate." They usually had gardens

---

[357] Botsford to Furman, 10 March 1796.
[358] Botsford to Furman, 3 May 1796.
[359] Townsend, *South Carolina Baptists*, 70.
[360] Botsford to Furman, 24 March 1797.
[361] Townsend, *South Carolina Baptists,* 280-281.

for growing additional food and keeping pigs and chickens. They were given sufficient clothing. The slave "has considerable time to work for himself," and could therefore supplement the food and clothing allowances with his own earnings. "I have seen many families in England among the labouring poor much more wretched than hundreds of the Negro Slaves with whom I have been acquainted." As for the slaves in the interior of the state, "generally speaking they fare better, in each of the particulars mentioned [than slaves in the rice region]. A great many live nearly as well as their masters" and looked down on poor whites.[362]

Of course, material conditions were not everything: "That which appears the most horrid to a stranger is the loss of freedom." Yet "the Negro does not view freedom in the same light as most considerate men do. Many Negroes were born slaves in Africa & America. And many in Africa who were not born slaves, their lives were miserable, & to my knowledge many prefer their present to their former state." While "[t]he punishment inflicted on Negroes is often severe," those who were industrious were not ill-treated; it was only the idle who were "at the mercy of the Overseer." Fortunately, "[m]ost owners of slaves, now, employ, or wish to employ humane men."[363] Botsford knew from experience in his own household just how severe punishment could be for slaves who stepped out of line. In 1795 one of his two field hands was accused of robbery. Fortunately, he was "cleared even of ... suspicion" of the crime, a great relief, since the man who was found guilty, a slave belonging to one of Botsford's neighbors, was punished with 100 lashes and the loss of an ear. If the robbery had involved burglary, the penalty would have been death. Botsford knew well that the veneer of humanity towards slaves could often give way to brutal violence.[364]

Given the precariousness of the slave's situation, Botsford believed that Christianity had an important role to play. Many slaves had become "truly pious" and these acted as a "restraint on some of a bad character." One wealthy planter told Botsford that the "truly religious" refrained from stealing and prevented others from doing so.[365] This depiction of Christianity as a promoter of obedience among slaves echoed the opinion Botsford had published in *The Baptist Register* some two decades earlier: slave owners "begin to discover that their slaves are of increasing value to them when they become religious."[366] Yet, if conversion could mitigate the conflicts in the master-slave relationship, it was also ultimately subordinate to that relationship, with masters intervening in the process of salvation, a process that, for whites, was between the individual, his

---

[362] Botsford, "On Slavery," 2-4, 6-7, 9-11.
[363] Ibid., 9, 14, 5-6
[364] Botsford to Furman, 7 October 1795.
[365] Botsford, "On Slavery," 12.
[366] Rippon, *Baptist Register, 1790-1793,* 105.

church, and God. Thus, even slaves who had provided convincing testimony of an experience of God's grace were not baptized until their master had given permission. If permission could not be obtained, the usual effects of God's grace were frustrated: Botsford noted that "two or three" slaves who had related their experiences and had been accepted as true recipients of salvation were not going to be baptized, since "they are sold & shortly to go off."[367]

The attitudes manifested by Botsford in "On Slavery" and elsewhere may make him appear to modern eyes as an outright apologist for slavery. However, it is important to judge him in the context of the time and place in which he lived. For all of his concern in "On Slavery" to prevent slavery from being "represented [as] much worse than it really is," his overall judgment was that "[u]pon the whole, slavery is attended with many evils & I wish not to defend it." An important aspect of Botsford's view of slavery was that the conditions and treatment endured by the slaves were far better in the early nineteenth century than they had been "forty or fifty years ago." He hoped "that their condition will continue to meliorate, till some way & means shall be fallen on for their emancipation." If that must be "a work of time," at least things were moving in the right direction, and Christianity was a force for progress towards better conditions and therefore an ultimate end to the institution.[368]

Botsford was more critical of slavery than many of his southern contemporaries. While many Baptists in the south had condemned slavery during the 1770s and 1780s, most were moving in the early nineteenth century towards the notion of gradual emancipation.[369] George Liele, a prominent African American missionary in Jamaica who had been converted to the Baptist faith during his youth along the Savannah River, was ready to assure slave owners that Christianity would reinforce the master-slave relationship; his church only baptized slaves whose masters vouched for their obedience.[370] "On Slavery" was written at a time when many whites in South Carolina were becoming advocates of

---

[367] Botsford to Furman, 12 October 1796.

[368] Botsford, "On Slavery," 1, 13-14.

[369] During the 1770s and 1780s, certain Baptist preachers had been among the most outspoken critics of slavery, urging their members to free their slaves and have nothing to do with the institution. John Leland of Virginia achieved the most dramatic success in this area; under the influence of his preaching, Robert Carter III of Nomini Hall freed 300 slaves, and the Baptist General Committee of that state formally condemned slavery in 1789. However, as the Baptists became less marginalized and more respectable in the new republic, from the 1790s on, they backed away from their antislavery stance, allowing members to make up their own minds on the question, and treating abolition as an ultimate ideal, rather than an urgent imperative (Sobel, *Trabelin' On,* 86-89). The readiness to treat black members of churches as equals also changed; seating and burial arrangements became segregated, and whites ceased to address blacks as "brother" and "sister" (Morgan, *Slave Counterpoint,* 434-435).

[370] Rippon, *Baptist Register, 1790-1793,* 335, 339.

slavery as a positive good. If some traces of this idea found their way into Botsford's claim that slaves in South Carolina were better off than they had been in Africa, his continued adherence to the idea that slavery was fundamentally evil made him relatively radical, compared to others in the Georgetown area.

The incorporation of black converts into the white church, and the steady admission of further black members who were deemed "truly pious," influenced the revision of the church covenant in 1785. The most significant change involved guidelines for slave owners' behavior towards their slaves:

> We promise that if we should be possessed of negro or other slaves, that we will act a truly christian part by them; by giving them good advice, laying our commands on them to attend the worship of God in public on Lord's days & in private in our families when convenient & we also promise, that we will not treat them with cruelty, nor prevent their obtaining religious knowledge, & will endeavour to prevent their rambling: and will encourage those who can read, at proper times to instruct others; & in all things endeavour to act in our families, as to obtain the blessing of God.[371]

These guidelines are notable for several reasons. First, they recognized that members of the church had duties not only to fellow church members and their children, but also to their slaves. These duties included not only humanitarian behavior—refraining from cruelty—but also providing wholesome advice and discipline—preventing them from "rambling". The most important Christian duty towards slaves was requiring them to attend services and allowing them to seek instruction, even to the extent of encouraging slaves who could read to instruct others. The new provisions mingled a humane tone, in keeping with the late eighteenth-century sentimental notion that slaves were part of church members' "families," with a strong note of control. An important ramification of this revised covenant was the principle that Welsh Neck's mission was to bring slaves to Christ, and that the accession of new black members would be a normal part of the church's future. These new provisions in the covenant chiefly concerned the relations of owners with slaves who were not church members, though the prohibition of cruelty and the requirement to prevent rambling and give good advice would also apply to baptized slaves. The addition of these provisions suggests that the baptism of slaves under Winchester and the incorporation of some of his converts into the white church under Botsford had stimulated a new attitude among the whites towards all slaves, who were now seen as potential Christian brothers and sisters, with the master-slave relationship being a means of realizing that Christian potential. These new provisions reflect very

---

[371] WNCB, 35. Note the reference to "negro or other slaves," probably an indication that church members were aware that many slaves were wholly or partially Native American.

clearly the shift in eighteenth-century culture, noted by many scholars, from "patriarchy" to "paternalism."[372]

The element of paternalism is important, because it is clear that Christian spiritual brother- and sisterhood only went so far. It is significant that only fifty-two members signed the revised covenant on 2 July 1785. Although the Church Book stated "several" were absent and would sign later, this modest number of signatories probably excludes the fifty-six or so black members of the church.[373] It would be interesting to know whether the one free black church member, Hanibel, who had been baptized on 22 August 1784, was invited to sign.[374] Was race or status the criterion for signing the covenant? Since it is clear from the covenant itself that blacks were encouraged to learn to read as a preparation for baptism, there must have been significant numbers of African American church members who were capable of signing; it seems unlikely that literacy was the determining factor regarding who signed. Although blacks and whites were now part of the same church, it is hard to conceive of slaves being invited, even re-quired, to admonish whites for sin: "We promise to watch over the conversation of each other, & not willfully to suffer sin upon one another without a gentle reproof," though this provision might well govern the expected behavior of en-slaved church members towards each other.[375] It seems likely that, despite the incorporation of African American members into the Welsh Neck Church, the church remained two distinct communities. This reality was further demonstrat-ed in the proposed design for a new meeting house that was drawn up in 1790: one feature was "a Shed the length of the House...for use of the negroes."[376] Even in the old meeting house, the black members may have sat in a separate part of the church; segregated sitting was normal for biracial Baptist churches.[377]

Segregation, while demeaning in many respects, might also have reflected and allowed for a great deal of *de facto* autonomy; generally during this period, where black congregations were part of white churches, they often held separate services, elected their own officers, and made their own decisions about mem-bership.[378] We do not know how far the black members of Welsh Neck held

---

[372] Fliegelman, *Prodigals and Pilgrims, passim.*

[373] WNCB, 36.

[374] Ibid., 33.

[375] Note that slaves were certainly expected to adhere to the church's standards of behavior, and could be excommunicated if they failed to do so, as in the case of Scipio on 4 November 1786. Ibid., 37.

[376] Ibid., 39. Although the meeting house proposed in 1791 was not built, when the church moved to a new site at Society Hill at the start of the nineteenth century, the new meeting house similarly included segregated seating for black members. Townsend, *South Carolina Baptists,* 75.

[377] Raboteau, *Slave Religion,* 137-138.

[378] Sobel, *Trabelin' On,* 181-187, 205-210.

their own religious meetings or chose their own leaders, unrecognized by the white church. We do know that in March 1791 a special committee of seven senior white church members, including Botsford, was appointed to hear the conversion experiences of prospective black members and to "settle any matters among them." [379] The committee is evidence of white efforts to supervise aspects of black religious life, and further evidence of distinct black and white communities within the church. Yet, while new black members had to receive the approval of a white committee, the recruitment and preparation of such members was very probably a process dominated by the black members of the church. As the 1785 covenant quoted above stated, white members should "encourage those [slaves] who can read, at proper times to instruct others." The white committee of approval was simply the final stage of a long preparation by blacks of new black members.

The existence of two distinct, parallel communities at Welsh Neck is further suggested by various remarks about the revival of 1790-1791. Botsford's 10 September 1790 letter to Hart stated that his revival was "chiefly among the whites." Moreover, the deliberately quiet, rather than demonstrative, prayer that Botsford fostered at his Monday evening meetings was not typical of the style of worship that normally drew African Americans into white churches.[380] Even so, the revival among whites at Welsh Neck seems to have been accompanied by a jump in African American membership. The Church Book unfortunately stopped recording baptisms of both races at this point, but the formation in March 1791 of the committee mentioned above suggests a significant volume of new interest among blacks in joining Welsh Neck. What explains this accession of new black members? The atmosphere of excitement stimulated by the white revival seems to have attracted more blacks to church on Sunday, and Botsford's depiction of black interest captures quite vividly the existence of two distinct communities: "Aug. 9 [1790]. Yesterday was a day to be remembered, our large meeting-house was crowded, and a number of blacks without the doors." Botsford did preach directly to black audiences, to as many as 300 at a time, when, significantly, "not one *white* [was] present but myself." He was not the only person preaching to African Americans in the Welsh Neck area. He noted that "We have several [blacks] in our church who go to the plantations, and preach to their own colour on Lord's-day evenings, and at other times when we have no service in the meeting house."[381] It seems very likely that a black-led revival among the enslaved population was taking place at about the same time as Botsford's revival among the whites. Not only would such an explanation point to black agency in the Welsh Neck Church, but it might indicate the con-

---

[379] WNCB, 39.

[380] Mallary, *Botsford,* 74-75.

[381] Rippon, *Baptist Register, 1790-1793,* 105, 108.

Historical Introduction

tinuous existence of an Afro-Baptist community of worship that had been tapped by Winchester, had absorbed those of Winchester's converts not admitted to Welsh Neck under Botsford, and was now again proving a ripe field for black members of the Welsh Neck community to procure further recruits.[382] The different momentums behind the white and black revivals at the start of the 1790s can be seen in the racial balance of church membership at the end of Botsford's pastorate. One note in the Church Book states that there were sixty-four black and sixty-three white members at the beginning of 1797; another reference puts white membership at only thirty-one.[383] In either case, Welsh Neck, despite Botsford's revival being "chiefly among the whites," had become a majority black church, whether that majority was slight or substantial. The revival among the black population seems to have had more staying power than its white equivalent.[384]

Botsford's Later Pastorate

Redefining the church's membership, black and white, was naturally Botsford's main focus, but he undertook other tasks as well. One consistent preoccupation was safeguarding and adding to the church's material possessions. He took care to obtain title deeds for the land on which the church was built and for further acreage left to the church by Colonel Kolb. He also worked to ensure that monetary legacies left to the church were actually received. For over two years, from 1 October 1785 until 1 December 1787, the church negotiated with Josiah Evans and Thomas Evans to get hold of bequests to the church by Thomas and Josiah James. They finally concluded an agreement: Thomas James had left £100 in South Carolina currency, while Josiah James had left £10,000 in currency. These amounts were translated into sterling, the hard money of the day, as 6 shillings and 9 pence and £28 respectively. Further legacies of unspecified amounts came to the church from James Wilson and Josiah Evans, along with a substantial legacy of £100 sterling from the late Deacon Abel Edwards in

---

[382] It is known that there were numerous unofficial (to whites) black churches in rural areas that retained many African ways, and were only loosely connected to recognized congregations (Sobel, *Trabelin' On,* 181-187).

[383] WNCB, 42.

[384] Frey and Wood incorrectly state that "the Botsford-led revival of the 1790s created several hundred black converts." They may be correct in their assumption that the black members of Welsh Neck recruited and converted other blacks in the region, accounting for the black majorities in many local churches in the 1820s, but, if so, this momentum occurred despite, rather than because of, Botsford's revival, which was chiefly focused on whites (Frey and Wood, *Shouting to Zion,* 159). A more plausible explanation of the foundations of black Baptist communities in the Pee Dee region can be found in the Separate Baptist evangelizing of the 1760s and 1770s and Winchester's revival of 1779.

1794.[385] Another source of income was pew rental, which was recorded in the Church Book for the first time in 1792. Books were valuable church property, also; Botsford took part in cataloguing the books in the church's library and recovering those that were missing.[386]

An important aspect of protecting and extending the church's possessions was the legal incorporation of the church. The church petitioned for incorporation on the same day the revised church covenant was adopted, 18 June 1785, and the incorporation was finalized later that year. Incorporation defined the most basic beliefs of the church, though in far less detail than the covenant, and it created a permanent mechanism—a body of Trustees—for watching over the church's property. Given the recent disturbances and the likelihood of gaps in the office of pastor, putting the church's possessions in the care of a legally recognized body made sense. On 31 March 1786, ten senior members of the church, including Botsford, were appointed trustees: any three could transact business.[387]

In addition to his work for Welsh Neck, Botsford took on another, formidable task; helping to revive the broken church in Charleston. From 1783 to 1786 he visited the city each year, on occasion spending several weeks there, as he did from February to April 1785.[388] During the British occupation, Baptist church life had collapsed. Many of the congregation were scattered, and the church building itself had been used as a British army hospital. Hart had fled before the beginning of the siege, and was delaying his return, ultimately deciding not to come back. Botsford had fond memories of the Charleston church; it was there that he had felt the experience of God's grace and had been baptized. The church had also provided him with funds for his ministerial education. He therefore located some of the church's former members and persuaded them to restore the church building and reconstitute a community of worship. Botsford presided when he was present, and he steadily added new converts, white and black. He also saved and reorganized the Charleston church records. Indeed, he said he would have gladly moved to Charleston if he had not felt committed to Welsh Neck. All in all, he did much to prepare the ground for Richard Furman, who took over the church in 1787.[389]

Botsford's work at Charleston went hand-in-hand with his close involvement in the Baptist church throughout the state. In his first year back on

---

[385] WNCB, 30, 37, 38, 41.

[386] Ibid., 37, 40, 41. It was discovered that twelve were missing from the last list that had been prepared, under Bedgegood. It was assumed that these were the books borrowed by the Rev. Joshua Lewis when he left for Cheraw.

[387] Ibid., 36-37; Townsend, *South Carolina Baptists,* 74-77.

[388] WNCB, 34.

[389] Mallary, *Botsford,* 63-67. Rogers, *Furman,* 54.

the Pee Dee, Welsh Neck hosted the annual meeting of the Charleston Association, a sign of vigor and broader leadership on Botsford's part.[390] Botsford was also included on the revived Standing Committee, appointed by the Association to transact business between its annual sessions.[391] Welsh Neck hosted the Association again in 1791, and sent representatives to the Association each year, with Botsford usually among their number. Welsh Neck contributed to the Association's education fund, and helped support the cost of printing the sermon delivered by Henry Holcombe at the 1791 meeting.[392] When the Charleston Association decided to send an official and substantial Circular Letter to its members each year, Botsford was asked to write the second of these: "On the Duty of Christians in Matters of Controversy" (1794).[393] On a more local level, Botsford also had regular quarterly meetings with eight or nine churches in the Pee Dee district; these are mentioned in 1790, 1795, and 1796, though the last was poorly attended.[394]

Botsford's interest in the broader Baptist Church beyond Welsh Neck was further evidenced in his contributions to the *Baptist Annual Register*. John Rippon (1750-1836), pastor of the Carter Lane Church in London, established the *Register* in London in 1790 to create an organ where Baptist churches could exchange news on a regular basis, learn about their denomination's history, and be inspired by accounts of its members' exemplary lives and success at spreading the faith.[395] The *Register* came out twice a year, and was republished in collected editions for 1790-1793, 1794-1797, and 1798-1801. Rippon's chief interest was in creating stronger ties between America and England, but the full scope of the project encompassed "America, England, Ireland, Scotland, Wales, the United Netherlands, France, Switzerland, Poland, Russia, Prussia, and Elsewhere..."[396] "America" included the British Caribbean, where the Baptist faith was spreading rapidly, among blacks as well as whites. "Elsewhere" included India and Sierra Leone, where British trade and British rule were providing an

---

[390] WNCB, 31.
[391] Richard Furman and Evan Pugh were the other members of this committee. Botsford, Furman, and Pugh were reappointed to this committee in 1786, with Joseph Cook, Joshua Lewis, and Henry Holcombe as additional members. Furman, *Charleston Association*, 18.
[392] WNCB, 39-40.
[393] Furman, *Charleston Association*, 98-104.
[394] Rippon, *Baptist Register, 1790-1793*, 105; Botsford to Furman, 20 July 1795 and 18 July 1796.
[395] Rippon, *Baptist Register, 1790-1793*, i-vi; Brackney, *Dictionary of the Baptists*, 484-485.
[396] Rippon, *Baptist Register, 1790-1793*, Dedication Page.

entrée for Baptist missionaries.[397] For isolated churches in rural South Carolina, such as Welsh Neck, struggling to recover after the Revolution, the *Register* provided an exhilarating "imagined community" of fellow Baptists on four continents, and a sense that they were part of a much larger and generally successful story of growth; news from Welsh Neck, Charleston, and other places familiar to South Carolinians appeared amongst articles on Baptist churches across the world, so that the *Register* wasn't simply a publication about exotic locales, but portrayed Welsh Neck in the context of an intercontinental fellowship.[398]

The *Register's* news about Baptists in North America, the Caribbean, Africa, and India represented the denomination as multi-racial; the achievements of black church leaders, particularly in Georgia and Jamaica, received significant coverage, so that readers encountered an image of a Baptist church where blacks and whites were co-workers in evangelization efforts.[399] The *Register* also published letters and notices about sermons that were critical of both the slave trade and slavery itself, reflecting the decisive stance on these issues among London evangelicals and some Baptists in the northern states at this time.[400] It is significant that Welsh Neck church members were willing to subscribe to, and presumably to read, a publication that often approached race and slavery in a way that was very different from the reality along the Pee Dee.[401] If Welsh Neck readers had turned to their own pastor's letter in the 1790 edition of the *Register*, as it seems natural they would do, they would have seen two contrasting views of slavery in juxtaposition: Botsford celebrated the numbers of blacks who were entering Baptist churches throughout the southern states, and interpreted this development as proof that "their owners begin to discover that their slaves are of

---

[397] Eg. Rippon, *Baptist Register, 1790-1793,* 353-373; *Baptist Register 1794-1797,* 215-218.

[398] Benedict Anderson's concept of how print could foster an "imagined community" was developed to explain the origins of popular nationalism, but it also seems applicable to the *Register's* role in fostering in its readers a sense of an international community sharing a single religious identity. Anderson, *Imagined Communities* (London:Verso, 1983), 5-7. Welsh Neck appeared in this international company as the venue for the Charleston Association meeting of 1791, with Botsford as the scheduled preacher. Rippon, *Baptist Register, 1790-1793,* 114.

[399] Eg. Rippon, *Baptist Register, 1790-1793,* 332-343; 540-541.

[400] Eg. *Ibid.,* 118, 321; Rippon, *Baptist Register, 1794-1797,* 198.

[401] In his 12 December 1791 letter to Furman, Botsford pledged "three dozen" subscriptions to the *Register,* suggesting a very wide readership in the small Welsh Neck community. Although Rippon charged one shilling per issue in London, the costs of transportation meant that purchasers at Welsh Neck were paying five shillings per issue. Botsford to Furman, December 1792; Rippon, *Baptist Register, 1790-1793,* vi. Even during hard economic times, Botsford's neighbors were willing to purchase the latest editions of the *Register* when they would not buy other sermons and books that Furman had sent to Botsford as recommended reading (Botsford to Furman 10 March 1796).

increasing value to them when they become religious." In the same 1790 letter, Botsford commented enthusiastically on the conversion to the Baptist faith of the prominent Virginia planter, Robert Carter. Botsford's point was that Carter's conversion demonstrated the progress of the Baptists and the crumbling of the old Episcopal establishment; but Rippon added a note that stressed Carter's condemnation of slavery and the slave trade after his conversion. The note quoted Carter as saying that *"[t]he toleration of slavery* indicates VERY GREAT DE-PRAVITY of mind."[402] Welsh Neck readers would have seen themselves as part of a denomination that held divergent opinions about the compatibility of slavery and Christianity.

Theologically, Rippon advertised himself as a Calvinist, but one open to recognizing goodness in men of other sects. The *Register* declined to publish "angry disputations," but its ecumenism was limited. Its very first issue denounced Arminianism, a doctrine that spread "the seeds of popery," and it included a harsh characterization by Botsford of Virginia's Church of England priests: "it would be difficult to find such another set of drunkards, whoremongers, etc. practicing vice openly and boldly."[403] An indication of the *Register's* theological outlook can be found in a letter it published from a Presbyterian minister in America. The letter celebrated ecumenical ties among different Protestant denominations, but claimed that all Protestants were abandoning Arminian principles in favor of a stricter Calvinism.[404] The *Register's* stance reflected Welsh Neck's (and Botsford's) relationship with Separate Baptists, who were seen as brothers and allies, but only on the assumption that the Separates were moving in the direction of strict Calvinism.

Botsford's contributions to the *Register* were his first known foray into print. He was extremely diffident about his intellectual abilities; in his letters to Furman, he acknowledged his inferiority to the Charleston pastor.[405] His shortcomings as a scholar drove him to embark on a course of serious study soon after he took over at Welsh Neck; as he explained to Hart, he needed to tie together the scraps of knowledge he had acquired into a more coherent whole.[406] This determination to improve his mind explains his request to borrow the church's books from Mrs. Wilds, who had them in her keeping, since he had left his own books behind when he had fled Brier Creek.[407] The *Register* provided

---

[402] Rippon, *Baptist Register, 1790-1793,* 105-107.

[403] *Ibid.,* vi-viii, 53-59, 107.

[404] *Ibid.,* 103-104. Botsford's ecumenism was demonstrated in his warm approval of Furman and a local Presbyterian minister, Dr. Keith, preaching at each other's churches. "[T]his looks like brethren, I hope a liberal spirit will continue to be cultivated..." Botsford to Furman 10 April 1796.

[405] Botsford to Furman, 11 January 1789, December 1792, and 20 July 1795.

[406] Mallary, *Botsford,* 61-62.

[407] WNCB, 30.

an outlet in which he could see himself in print, even if only in the shape of newsletters and obituaries, rather than theological discourses.

Rippon and the *Register* provided him with the solution to another problem: revitalizing spiritual life at Welsh Neck. After the activity of the first few years, when unworthy members were purged, the African American Baptists brought into the white church, and a new church covenant drafted and signed, Welsh Neck seemed to be stagnating. During the year and a half after the signing of the revised covenant in 1785, the church had lost one black and twelve white members through excommunication, dismissal, or death, while gaining only two. Attendance at monthly church business meetings had been between twenty and thirty in 1783 and 1784; by the end of 1786 it could be as low as ten. In these circumstances, it was only natural, on 2 February 1787 to appoint a day of fasting and prayer for the revival of religion. That day failed of its purpose. Deaths, excommunications, and dismissals continued, with only two baptisms, both of new black members, throughout all of 1787, 1788, and 1789. The most common entry in the Church Book for these years is "Nothing to record."[408] It was in this context that Botsford took up an idea put forward by Rippon: holding Monday evening prayer meetings once a month in common with Baptist churches in England and elsewhere.[409] Such meetings provided a chance for church members to share their spiritual needs and experiences in a format that was different from Sunday services; the meetings also allowed Welsh Neck to feel part of a broader, transatlantic community of Baptist worship. As Botsford put it: "to unite with our English Friends we held their monthly time of Prayer."[410]

Botsford's leadership in these prayer meetings may have acquired an emotional intensity from a personal tragedy he experienced at this time: his wife, Susanna, died on 9 March 1790.[411] He left an extensive record of his feelings after this loss in his memoir, in letters to Hart and Furman, and in a newsletter he wrote for the *Register*. On 6 April 1790, he described his loss to his spiritual "father," Hart, as follows:

> Of all the trials I have experienced, the one I am now groaning under is the most severe. It is no less than the loss of my dear Mrs. Botsford. She departed this life on the 9th ult. She was seized with a violent cough, which terminated in a nervous consumption, and inflamation of the bowels. She was confined to her bed about two weeks; proper medical assistance was not wanting; prayers from our many friends were, I believe, sincerely addressed to heaven for her; but God saw fit to issue the mandate to surrender

---

[408] Ibid., 37-39.

[409] Rippon, *Baptist Register, 1790-1793,* 108.

[410] Botsford to Furman, 4 August 1790.

[411] Interestingly, Winchester's revival of 1779 similarly began after the death of his wife.

life. She was favoured with the exercise of her reason, I believe to the last moment; though through extreme weakness and obstructing phlegm was not able to articulate so as to be understood for the last twenty hours. Some of the last expressions which we understood were, 'I am quite calm and resigned – all my dependence is on Christ alone for salvation. Dont grieve for me." The last words I perfectly understood were, 'death is hard work, but it will soon be over.' On being asked at that time if she had comfort in her, she plainly replied, 'yes, O yes.'[412]

His struggle with despair over his wife's death was relieved by what he believed to be a special gift of grace from God. He wrote to both Hart and Furman about the strength he found suddenly one night that enabled him to surrender entirely to God's will, instead of complaining at his fate. One month after the powerful emotional and spiritual experiences following Susanna's death, the Monday evening prayer meetings and a notable revival at Welsh Neck got underway. Botsford described these meetings as follows:

Our public monthly prayer meetings are held on the first Monday in each calendar month. We introduce by prayer, singing, prayer, and a short discourse suitable to the occasion. Then prayer, and an exhortation to the brethren to pray. They then pray, generally allowing a few minutes between. When all have prayed that choose, (for I do not press it upon them in public, though at other times I do) I then ask if any of such, or such a class, request our prayers for them; observing that I desire none to present themselves but such as intend to lead a religious life. When they come, I ask for a short account of the state they conceive themselves in. I pray; then drop a word of exhortation suitable to their cases; then desire them to take their seats. I then ask if any others desire to be prayed for; when no more come, conclude with singing and dismission.[413]

In his correspondence with Furman and in the account he wrote for the *Baptist Register,* he particularly stressed the impact of the revival on "youth of both Sexes."[414] Botsford was so impressed by the success of these meetings at Welsh Neck that he suggested at the quarterly meeting of district churches on 2 July 1790 that others adopt the practice. Apparently "several" others did so, though all agreed that daytime meetings were more practical than evening gath-

---

[412] Mallary, *Botsford,* 71. Many details of this account, including Susanna's final words, were repeated in Botsford's published letter in Rippon's *Baptist Register, 1790-1793,* 104-105. For another account of her death, see his letter of 20 April 1790 to Richard Furman in this volume.

[413] Mallary, *Botsford,* 75. These prayer meetings were contrasted with Winchester's noisy revival in Botsford's letter to Hart, discussed above.

[414] Botsford to Furman, 4 August 1790 and Rippon, ed., *Baptist Register, 1790-1793,* 105.

erings, because of the long distances that many had to travel to their local churches.[415]

The new air of hope generated by the revival at Welsh Neck prompted the formation of a committee to examine the rebuilding of the meeting house. When the committee reported on 4 September 1790 the cost of renovations was estimated at £120 sterling, over four times the total amount left by the legacies of Thomas and Josiah James. On 5 March 1791 the church also agreed to support the Charleston Association's fund for educating young men for the ministry, a renewed version of the fund established by Oliver Hart before the Revolution that had supported Botsford's training.[416] If these ambitious plans reflect an optimistic outlook at that particular juncture, disappointment soon followed; while the monthly Monday evening prayer meetings continued at least through the end of 1791, the revival didn't last. One severe blow was the excommunication in September 1791 of Charles Lide, a young man whom Botsford had converted the year before and regarded as a "prodigy."[417] After the revival of 1790-1791, a return to religious apathy followed; entries in the Church Book for 1792 almost uniformly report: "Church met. No record." The sputtering revival at Welsh Neck was all the more marked because the Baptists across the southern backcountry were enjoying a period of "explosive growth" in this period.[418] Neither an attempt to revive the Monday evening prayer meetings at the start of 1793, nor a visit by the famous revivalist, John Gano, in May managed to restore life to the church. Botsford's severe illness in the fall of that year cannot have helped matters, either; he told Furman in November that he had been confined to his house for over five weeks, and "really thought I was going to enter the joy of my Lord."[419]

A Church Book entry in March 1793 contrasted the 220 white members at the end of Winchester's pastorate with the remaining forty-eight whites.[420] The decline continued to the end of Botsford's pastorate. There are hints that the falling off of membership may have been partially due to theological differences, rather than mere apathy. On 4 October 1794, Abel Goodwin was excommunicated for "immorality and apostacy [sic]"; at a time when the Church Book

---

[415] Rippon, *Baptist Register, 1790-1793,* 107-108.

[416] Though Botsford approved of the purpose of the fund, he initially opposed creating a legal corporation to administer it, fearing individual Baptist churches would lose their independence to the Charleston Association. Botsford to Furman, 31 August 1789.

[417] WNCB, 39-40; Botsford to Furman, 4 August 1790 and 17 August 1791.

[418] Flinchum, "Reluctant Revolutionaries," 173-175.

[419] Botsford to Furman, 18 November 1793. Botsford suffered from *tic douloureux.* Townsend, *South Carolina Baptists,* 70. He had been charged by the Charleston Association with preparation of the annual Circular Letter, but was too sick to complete the task. Rippon, *Baptist Register, 1794-1797,* 73.

[420] WNCB, 40.

rarely recorded the reasons for disciplinary measures, including excommunication, this entry stands out for its explicit bluntness.[421] In 1796 Botsford complained to Furman that "Infidelity increases, & hence a neglect of attendance on the Word." He also noted that Captain McIntosh, once a stalwart pillar of the church, had embraced principles "the reverse of those derived from the Scriptures." Since Botsford continued his lament by saying, "What a mercy my dear & Honored Sir it is that you and I were not left to embrace such, which at this time are so fashionable," it sounds as though Botsford was concerned about incorrect religious beliefs rather than a simple lack of religion. Unfortunately, he did not specify the nature of these "fashionable" principles.[422]

Meanwhile, Botsford was facing financial problems. He had left almost all of his personal property behind when he had fled Brier Creek in 1779; for the next three years he had been a refugee, dependent on the charity of others for support. When he returned to Welsh Neck in 1782 he had been given a small plot of land on which he had built a house, but he lacked a regular income. In 1789 he had complained to Furman about the shabbiness of his "pine barren spot of a few acres" which he had only two hands to help him cultivate. He lamented his own lack of "industriousness," but at the same time prided himself on not allowing his mind to become preoccupied with the acquisition of wealth.[423] He seems to have abandoned any serious effort at farming the following year, when he loaned or leased his two field hands to his neighbor, McIver.[424] His lack of activity meant that he failed to profit from high grain prices in 1791 along with his neighbors, for "as I plant... little, little must be my share, may I be content with my little." Yet he was not content; he was in debt, and hoped for the settlement of an "Affair" in Ireland that would allow him to pay off all he owed.[425] Botsford's poverty was especially irksome given the fact that most Baptist pastors in this period tended to own more property than most in their congregations.[426] In March 1795 the church agreed to lend him £100 sterling (presumably, Abel Edwards' legacy, which the church had received the previous October), though a later note says the loan was never executed. In both 1795 and 1796 he was given the interest on the church funds, a small step towards the endowed salaries that some Lowcountry churches were establishing for their

---

[421] WNCB, 41.

[422] Botsford to Furman, 3 May 1796 and 12 October 1796.

[423] Botsford to Furman, 11 January 1789.

[424] Bostford to Furman, 20 April 1790.

[425] Botsford to Furman, 17 August 1791; his first wife, Susanna, had been Irish, so it is possible that the money he hoped for from Ireland was connected with her. He was still hoping for news about the Irish "Affair" five years later. Botsford to Furman, 18 July 1796.

[426] Townsend, *South Carolina Baptists*, 280-281.

pastors.[427] However, in these years the entire community was suffering hardship. "[T]imes with us are bad, very bad," he wrote to Furman. "[V]ery few in... our neighbourhood have made any thing for market."[428] Botsford himself was "over head & ears in debt" – to the tune of £300 - and did not even have a horse that would carry him to Charleston to fill in for Furman for a few weeks. He complained that members of his church "conceive themselves not able to help me" and "act as if they thought I could live on air." Many who had provided financial support in the past were now failing to do so. [429] Contrary weather and flooding suggested that 1796 would be as bad as earlier years.[430]

Personal tragedy compounded financial woes. Botsford had married his second wife, Catherine Evans, or Caty, in 1791. They had a daughter, also named Caty, in 1793, but the new Mrs. Botsford had a history of difficult births: baby Caty "was the first live born child she has had of 7." (Presumably, Mrs. Botsford had been married before.) Three years later, on 7 February 1796, Mrs. Botsford died "in child-bed;"[431] in keeping with the time and society in which they lived, the couple had not taken steps to avoid pregancies that were likely to be problematic. Botsford was hit hard by the loss of his second wife; he received some glimmerings of religious consolation, but they were not as powerful as those that had visited him when he had lost Susanna. Two months after Caty's death, he told Furman that "I am still much in the dark & very uncomfortable; in many respects my Way seems hedged up; most appearances are very gloomy."[432] Even before Caty's death, the religious and financial problems at Welsh Neck had made him talk with his wife about moving; her death seems to have ended any ties he felt to the area.[433] The church at Georgetown seemed ready for him to take over. Botsford had often visited Georgetown. He liked the people and felt at home among them, but doubted his abilities to fill so important a position; he asked Furman for encouragement. Such encouragement must have been forthcoming. In June, he announced at the church meeting that he would be leaving Welsh Neck at the end of the year. He visited Georgetown in September or October and was given a formal call, which he accepted.[434] He handed the Welsh Neck books over to Deacon Evander McIver at the November meeting, and was

[427] *Ibid.,* 294-295; WNCB, 42.
[428] Botsford to Furman, 10 March 1796.
[429] Botsford to Furman, 10 April 1796 and 3 May 1796.
[430] Botsford to Furman, 18 July 1796.
[431] Botsford to Furman, 27 April 1793 and 10 April 1796.
[432] Botsford to Furman, 10 March 1796 and 10 April 1796.
[433] Botsford to Furman, 3 May 1796; Mallary, *Botsford,* 78. Botsford felt few ties to the living members of his congregation; but one factor that discouraged him from leaving Welsh Neck were deceased "Children who lie near me." Botsford to Furman, 18 July 1796.
[434] Botsford to Furman, 12 October 1796.

formally dismissed in December.[435] Disposing of his property and settling financial issues forced him to miss the Association meeting in 1796, but by early 1797 he was reporting progress in winding up his affairs at his old residence.[436] After his many frustrations as pastor at Welsh Neck, he was not disappointed in his expectations regarding Georgetown; he and his flock proved compatible, and he held the position for the remaining twenty-two years of his life.

After Botsford

During the first half of 1797, a small number of church leaders met each week to take care of church business; procuring a new pastor was the most pressing issue. The Rev. David Lilly and the Rev. Evan Pugh provided occasional religious services during this time. In June, the Rev. David Cooper agreed to attend Welsh Neck one weekend in every month, and some sort of regular church life recommenced. In late 1797 and early 1798 there were nine new baptisms and one excommunication, all of African Americans. In April 1798 the Rev. David Lilly agreed to serve as full-time pastor of the church for one year. At that same meeting the church members decided to build a new meeting house in a different location, at Society Hill. The last record of the church while it was still located at Welsh Neck was in November 1798; the records after that date have been lost, according to a note inserted by the transcriber of the Church Book. When records resumed in 1803, the church had moved to its new home on Society Hill.[437]

---

[435] WNCB, 42.

[436] Botsford to Furman 12 October 1796 and 24 March 1797.

[437] WNCB, 43-44.

Part II

The Welsh Neck Church Book

1

1737
[O]rigin of the Church[1]
In the year 1737 a party of emigrants from the Welch Tract in the State of Delaware removed to Pee-Dee River South Carolina which place they designated the Welch-Neck in rembrance of their former residence. The following are the names of the individuals who composed this party which was embodied into a church. viz. [James James originally written here and erased]

[James James—again written and erased][2]
Philip James and his wife
Abel James and his wife
Daniel James and his wife
Daniel Devonald and his wife
Thomas Evans and his wife
Thomas Evans Jr and his wife
John Jones and his wife
Thomas Harry & wife
David Harry and his wife
John Harry & wife[3]

---

[1] Most dates in the Welsh Neck Church Book are written in the margin, along with brief headings. In the current re-transcription, these marginal dates and headings are italicized and placed at the top of the paragraphs next to which they appear.

[2] James James was twice written into the Church Book and erased, probably because of uncertainty on the part of the transcriber as to whether he should be counted as a founding member of the Welsh Neck Church. He was the leader of the group of migrants who came to South Carolina from Delaware, but he died soon after their arrival, before a church could be formally constituted. Edwards, "Baptists in South-Carolina," 4, 17; Townsend, *South Carolina Baptists*, 62-63n.

[3] Morgan Edwards states that of the three Harry brothers, only John was married. Edwards, "Baptists in South-Carolina," 17. However, three women with the surname Harry—Elizabeth, Sarah, and Catherine—were dismissed from the Welsh Tract Church in Delaware in 1735 and 1737. *Welsh Tract Baptist Meeting*, I, 83-86. Either Edwards was wrong, or perhaps two of the Harry women were sisters, rather than wives, of the three brothers.

Samuel Wilds and his wife
Samuel Evans and his wife
Griffith Jones and his wife
David Jones and his wife[4]
Thomas Jones and his wife

[C]onstitution
[J]anry 1738
In January 1738, the above named persons were constituted a Church under the style and title of the "Baptist Church of Christ at the Welch-Neck."_ The following pages will disclose so much of the proceedings of said Church as have escaped the ravages of time. It is a subject of regret that so much valuable information has been lost, but as the deficiency can be supplied by no human effort, the remainder should be treasured with the more care.
Philip James son of James James Esq was the first Pastor of this Church
He was ordained 1743, and died 1753.
[N]ames of the
[Fir]st Pastors
Revd John Brown succeeded Mr James, but continued for a short time when Rev[d] Joshua Edwards was called to the pastoral office. He had the care of the Church six Years.[5] Mr. Edwards was succeeded by the Rev[d] Robert Williams.__ With this we have some account of the transactions of the Church. The records previously have been lost.

2

1759
March 12th a list of Members

---

[4] Edwards records these last two names as "David James" and "Thomas James." "Baptists in South-Carolina," 17. There is no later record of a David Jones in the Church Book; there is a Thomas Jones, but he entered the church through baptism in 1760. WNCB, 7. While there is no David James in the later church book, a Thomas James was listed as a member of the church in 1759. WNCB, 2. A Thomas Jones and a David Jones were dismissed from the Welsh Tract Church in Delaware in 1737. Townsend, *South Carolina Baptists,* 61-63. It seems that Morgan Edwards, who probably viewed the original Church Book, is more accurate than the transcriber here.
[5] Joshua Edwards became the first pastor of the newly constituted church at Cashaway in 1756. Townsend, *SC Baptists,* 85. He was ordained on 15 July 1751. Edwards, "South Carolina Baptists," 21-22. His pastorate at Welsh Neck can therefore be dated 1751-1756.

In 1759 March 12th a list of the members was taken which is as follows.[6]

1 Philip Douglass, (Died October 17th 1766)[7] 43 Anne Jones (now Douglass)
                                             D'd Ap'l 12th 176[?][8]

2 Elizabeth James Mrs Philip J.[9]   44 Sarah James

3 Hannah Evans[10]   45 Mary Hollingsworth

4 Martha Rogers[11]   46 Howel James

5 Wm Terrel & }   47 John Sutton

6 Anne his wife } april 2nd 1743   48 Mary Plathro
                                             (Died Febry 21st 1766[12]

7 Barbary Monochon (died June 19th 1761)[13] 49 Jacob D'Surrency

---

[6] There are four lists of church members in the transcribed Welsh Neck Church Book, including the brief list of church founders on page one. There are some indications that these lists were originally kept separately from the Church Book. They were incorporated into the Church Book when surviving records were transcribed to produce the current document. One indication that these lists were once separate documents is that some death dates were noted on this 1759 list, but not recorded in the Church Book. Two death dates—those for Philip Evans (# 18) and Abel Wilds (# 28)—relate to periods when the Church Book was not being maintained. A further indication that membership lists were originally separate is that on 30 June 1798, a resolution at a Church Meeting called for the "List of Church Members" to be examined, even though no such list had been included in the Church Book for twenty years (see below, WNCB, 44).

Assuming that membership lists were originally separate documents, then the inclusion on this 1759 list of members who had already died (Sarah McDaniel, # 26; Eleanor Harry, # 27; Mary Jones, # 30; and William Hollingsworth, # 37) would make sense; this list would be a cumulative document, with names added as they joined, rather than a "snapshot" of members on 12 March 1759. The fact that this list, unlike the later 1775 and 1778 lists, is not neatly divided into a list of men followed by a list of women also suggests that it was added to over time. Since only three of the original male founders of the church are on this list (the female founders are not named, and therefore cannot be traced to this document) it seems likely that this 1759 list must have been started at some point after the founding in 1737 but before the first recorded death in 1744. If that theory is correct, there was considerable turnover of membership during the first few years of the Church, unless most of the founding members' names were among those that were too "entirely defaced" to be "decyphered".

The numbers next to the names on this list are faint, and may have been added some time after the list was incorporated into the transcribed Church Book.

[7] Agrees with entry below, WNCB, 13.

[8] Anne Douglass died on 12 April 1766 per WNCB, 12.

[9] "Mrs Philip J." is very faint—these words have either been erased or were added later.

[10] Died 9 January 1761 per WNCB, 7.

[11] Died 26 January 1761 per WNCB, 7.

[12] Below, WNCB, 12, a "Mrs. Mary Prethro" died on 21 February 1766.

[13] Spelled "Barbara Monaghon" when death recorded (WNCB, 9).

8 Samuel Wilds
9 John Evans
10 Thomas Evans (died Janry 28th 1785)[14]
11 Daniel Monochon (" April 30th " [15]
12 Sarah James
13 Sarah Bowdy
14 Elizabeth Wilds[16]

15 William James
16 Griffith John (died Augt 1765)[17]
17 Abel Evans (" June 4th [18]
18 Philip Evans, died 5th Decr 1771[19]
19 Margaret John
20 James James Novr 21st 1769. died.[21]
21 William Jones died July 2nd
22 John Perkins dismissed 1778[22]
23 David Evans
24 Volentine Hollingsworth died Augt 6th[23]
25 Elizabeth Powers died Octr 1st
26 Sarah McDaniel died May 12th 1744
27 Eleanor Harry (now Jones)
died April 20th 1745[25]
28 Abel Wilds died 15th May 1781.[26]
29 Samuel Evans

50 Mary Cleary
51 Sarah James
52 Thomas James
53 Walter Downes
54 Rachel Downes
55 Sarah Booth (now Wilds)
56 Jane Poland
(Died Novr 30th 1766
57 Naomi Harry (now Underwood)
58 Mary Edwards
59 Mary Wilds
60 Elizabeth Evans
61 James Rogers[20]
62 Joshua Edwards
63 Charity Edwards
64 Thomas Edwards
65 Sarah Edwards
66 Anne Robbyn[24]
=

N.B. There were several
other names to this list, but so
entirely de-faced, that they
could not be deciphered—

---

[14] Death not recorded on this date in WNCB.

[15] Death not recorded on this date in WNCB. A Daniel Monahon is recorded as dying on 30 January 1761 per WNCB, 7.

[16] This Elizabeth Wilds was probably a founding member and wife of Samuel Wilds, #8. If so, she died 11 February 1761 per WNCB, 7. Another Elizabeth Wilds was married to a George Wilds and was dismissed to Cashaway 6 September 1761 (WNCB, 9).

[17] Died 3 August 1765 per WNCB, 12.

[18] Death not recorded on this date in 1765 in WNCB.

[19] Not recorded in WNCB; there are no entries in WNCB for 1770-1774.

[20] Dismissed 17 October 1767 per WNCB, 14.

[21] Death not recorded on this date in WNCB.

[22] Agrees with entry below, WNCB, 22. Date of dismissal was 3 January 1778.

[23] Volentine Hollingsworth died on 26 March 1760 per WNCB, 4.

[24] An Anne Rollyn is recorded as dying on 1 May 1768.

[25] The "now Jones" statement suggests that this entry was originally made on a list compiled before her death in 1745.

[26] Death not recorded in WNCB, which was not maintained between 1779 and August 1781.

30 Mary Jones, died Decr 1757
31 Sarah James
32 --------- Jones (now McIntosh), died Decr 30th 1764[27]
33 Martha Roach (now Evans)
34 James Harry, dismissd to Cashaway
35 Hannah Howel (Died Decr 24th 1761)[28]
36 Alice Lucas
37 William Killingsworth (Died Octr 1757)[29]
38 Samuel Reredon
39 Edward Jones
40 Jenkyn David
41 Eleanor Evans (Died Febry 16th 1765[30]
42 Margaret Evans

3

1759
Call of Rev[d] Mr Bedgegood
As Mr Williams could not give proper attendance to his office, the Church unanimously presented a call to the Rev[d] Mr Nicholas Bedgegood of Charleston to minister to them in the word and ordinances of the Gospel, for the term of one year. which call he accepted. __

April 5th
Samuel Reredon formerly suspended for obscene conversation, applied to be restored to his former privileges; but not giving satisfaction, his suspension was continued.
  The Rev[d] Mr John Brown & Sarah his wife were dismissed to Cashaway Church by letter requested.[31]

July 1st
William James was baptized, and received into full communion.

---

[27] Below, WNCB, 11, "Jane McIntosh" died on 30 December 1764.
[28] Agrees with entry below, WNCB, 10.
[29] "Killingsworth" is written over "Hollingsworth". A William Killingsworth's death is recorded on 1 November 1760 per WNCB, 7.
[30] Agrees with entry below, WNCB, 12.
[31] Cashaway Church was located about 12 miles SE of Welsh Neck (as the crow flies), on the Great Pee Dee River. It was originally a branch of Welsh Neck and was constituted as an independent church on 28 September 1756. Townsend, *South Carolina Baptists,* 84; "Cashaway Church Book," 1.

Jacob D'Surrency was suspended for breach of Church Covenant in absenting himself from public worship.

Walter Downes was suspended, having behaved in a very disorderly manner__ He was found guilty of not filling his place in the Church, spending his time in idleness- drinking to excess, and acting in contempt of Church authority. The Church also sent him a letter of admonition.

August 9th
David Harry Senr died.
The Rev[d] Mr. Williams applied for liberty to absent himself from the Lord's Table and Church Meetings, which the Church thought would be irregular to grant, and being credibly informed that he charges them with such crimes as to prevent his communion, two messengers were sent to desire him to appear at the next monthly meeting, that the Church may either be convinced of their faults, or vindicate their innocence, and the order of God's House. They also sent to recal their Letter of Dismission granted him formerly, upon his declaring his intension to remove.

Sept[r] 2nd
Mr Williams not appearing as desired, nor having returned, and refusing to return the dismissory Letter, messengers were again sent for the purpose above. It was agreed that the Church Covenant shall be read once a quarter at the Monthly Meeting: in order that by the divine blessing, the members may be animated in the discharge of the several duties incumbent upon them.

A Letter was ordered to be sent to John Perkins to advise him to apply for a Letter of Dismission, living at a distance from us and convenient to another church.

[Se]ptr 19th
Departed this Life, John Jones.

4

1759
Oct[r] 6th
Robert Lloyd and John Booth were baptized and admitted to full communion. The Church being informed by two credible witnesses, that the Rev[d] Mr Williams disowns himself a member, and says that it is not a Church of Christ, and his disorderly actions speaking the same; it was agreed to send him a Letter of admonition in the spirit of meekness.
Three messengers were appointed to go to the Association to meet in Charleston November 12th

It was determined by the Church, that if any member <u>travels up or down the river</u> on a <u>Sabbath</u>-<u>day</u> without an absolute necessity (of which the Church shall be judge) such member shall be censured.[32]

Decr 14th
Sarah Killingsworth died.
   "   *15th*
Nicholas Rogers died.

<u>*1760*</u>
Janry 4th
James Finley died.
   "   *5th*
The messengers which were sent to Mr Williams (vide Octr 6th) having informed the Church that he refused to read their Letter, and that he cast the greatest contempt upon their mesage, they still being unwilling to use severity, and desirous to win him by Kindness, concluded to send him another Letter of admonition.___ A Letter of admonition was sent to Jacob D'Surrency under suspension. (vide July 1st

Febry 2nd
Mr Williams refusing to receive the Letter sent him by the Church a second time, and professedly disowning the Church's authority, he was suspended. John Booth was publicly suspended for publicly quarrelling with his neighbour, and using profane language.

March 8th
Rachel David, wife of Jenkyn David, was baptized.
The Church gave Mr Bedgegood a call to the pastoral care of them, which he accepted for the term of time during which divine Providence may render it his duty to remain among them.
Also admitted a member by Letter from Charleston Church.
   "   *26th*
Volentine Hollingsworth departed this life.

---

[32] Less than a month earlier, the daughter church at Cashaway had imposed a similar rule on its members: "Concluded that no member shall at any time work up or down the river on the Sabbath Day without a lawful reason, nor shall any member charge hire for his boat on the Sabbath Day when not working, and no member hired to work in boats shall charge for his work on the Sabbath Day [except] on special necessity and the reasons shall be produced to the church and the church shall judge whether lawful or not." "Cashaway Church Book," 12 September 1759.

April 5th
James James was suspended for beating his neighbour.
Anne Williams absenting herself from her place in the Church two messengers were sent to ask her reason for it.

5

1760
June 1st
The messengers that were sent to Anne Williams giving the Church information, that she slights the message and reproaches the Church, averring that she never more will commune or own herself a member, two persons were appointed to admonish her of her fault and extort her to repentance. __And as Mr. Williams remains obstinate, the same were sent to him for the like purpose.
Philip Douglass ordered to be publicly suspended for drinking to excess and to the public reproach of Religion.
William James Junr ordered to be publicly suspended for the same crime.

July 5th
The messengers sent as above could not see Mr Williams in proper time, and are to take another opportunity. Mr Williams still behaving in contempt of the Church was suspended.
An enquiry was decided to be made why Eleanor the wife of Abel Evans doth not live with her husband.__and proper exhortation to be given her.____An addition ordered to be made to the old Church Covenant, and to be signed by all the members.
The first friday in every month ordered to be kept as a day of public prayer, during the present public calamities and war.[33]
Ordered that at every quarterly meeting after sacrament the Deacons shall receive such donations (for the use of the Church) as God shall be pleased to influence the hearts of the members to give.
__a letter to be sent to Mr Wm Rowel and his wife living at the Congarees directing them to apply for a Letter of dismission.

---

[33] "Present public calamities" probably refers to the Cherokee War, which broke out on 19 January 1760 and continued until the end of 1761. Cherokee raids on backcountry settlements created a flood of refugees into fortified settlements and towards the coast. Both sides engaged in scalping and other acts of a savage nature. Although the Pee Dee was at the opposite side of South Carolina from the worst of the fighting, the dislocation of people and commerce and the sense of panic affected the Welsh Neck area, too. Brown, *Regulators*, 3-12.

Augt 2nd

Church Covenant Adopted

In pursuance of an agreement made the last meeting the following Covenant contains our solemn explicit obligations as a Church of Christ to God and each other.

Knowing that is it our Happiness and Duty to pay a solemn regard to the Laws of Love, and the Ordinances of the Gospel which are commanded and instituted in God's Holy Word; We do for the better regulation of our Conduct towards God and each other renew our Covenant; and do solemnly promise the services and conscientious regard to the following articles. And to this we desire to be the more induced by a remberance of our past Neglects and for which we would be humbled before the Lord and one another.

We promise to walk in all holiness & humility with brotherly love that our fellowship may be acceptable to God: agreeable to the Churches of Christ and comfortable to ourselves.

We promise to watch over the conversation of each other and not willfully to suffer sin upon one another without a gentle reproof, and that we will endeavour to stir one another up to Love & to good works by mutual exhortation and a holy example.

6

1760

Augt 2nd

We promise to pray for one another bearing each other's burdens and to fulfil the Law of Christ; and also to pray for God's presence & power in our assemblies, & that our Church may flourish & many be added to it who shall be saved.

We promise to endeavour to keep the unity of the spirit in the Bonds of peace; to bear with one another's infirmities, putting on bowels of Compassion as the elect of God, to forbear rash judging, evil surmises and reproachful or censorious Language; and also that we will not expose the weakness and faults of any to others either within or without the Church without some special necessity & in point of duty; and always in conformity to the Rule given us by our Saviour in Matthew 18th ch:

We promise each for ourselves that if God gives us children to bring up whether our own or others, that we will use our utmost endeavours to bring them up in the nurture and admonition of the Lord, that we will keep a strict watch over their conduct, and at all convenient seasons, give them such advice, admonition and correction, as their case shall appear to require; and that we will take due care to have them taught to read and to learn the Chatechism; and also that we will use our authority to keep them as much as possible from wicked company & vain pleasures__knowing that a companion of fools shall be destroyed, and that Lovers of pleasure are not Lovers of God. And we likewise promise that if we should be remiss in the practice of these duties, that we will submit to, & thankfully receive the friendly reproof of a private brother or the Church.

We promise to meet together every Lord's day and at all other opportunities as divine Providence shall permit; Keeping our places in the House of God as becometh Saints, "not forsaking the assembling ourselves together as the manner of some is." We promise to strive together for the Truth of the Gospel, and the purity of Gospel institutions; desiring by the Grace of God to live & die in the faith of God's elect, constantly and steadily adhering to the glorious doctrines of Free Grace, and the plain scriptural administration of the words and ordinances.

We promise, that according to the ability which God shall be pleased to give us we will freely contribute to the support of the ministers, whom the Lord shall be pleased to make our Shepherd, and that we will endeavour daily to pray for a blessing upon his labours.

These & all other evangelical duties we resolve and promise by the grace & strength of our Lord Jesus, honestly to perform, & for our being at last admitted into the Church triumphant in Heaven, we desire to trust entirely upon his precious blood & spotless righteousness.

This covenant was signed by the Pastor & Church. We deem it was unnecessary to copy the names, as they can be seen by referring to the original [34]

7

1760
Augt 2nd
1 Baptized
Thomas Jones was baptized and received into full communion.
[illeg.] in re[illeg.]ing excluded member
John Booth made application to be restored to his place, and giving a clear verbal account of his repentance & as nothing could be laid to his charge since his suspension, the Church could not fairly reject him; but as some circumstances gave them occasion to be jealous over him, lest he was deceiving himself, they informed him of it, and left it to his own conscience to judge for himself whether it would be best to take his place, or to remain as he is till he has farther examined his heart . Upon which he concluded to delay for that purpose

---

[34] This marginal note was inserted to the bottom left of the Covenant.

Septr 6th

Philip Douglass appeared before the Church and in an humble and penitent manner acknowledged the greatness of his sin, & begged pardon of God and men. This he consented should be declared before the whole congregation; which was done by the minister, and he was then received to enjoy his privileges as a member, but continued suspended from his office as a deacon.

It was concluded by the church, that if a member is restored after a public suspension, it shall be done in a public manner.

Novr 1st

It was concluded that two members should be sent with a Letter to the Association.__William Killingsworth died.

Decr 7th

A messenger was sent to Mr Williams and his wife to advise them to consider their case, and repent of their sins, and that otherwise it was concluded by the Church to cut them off from all communion and fellowship.

1761

Janry 4th

Mr. Williams and his wife being regardless of the Church's admonition sent as above, the Church ordered them to be ejected, and this was done on Sabbath January 5th following.

" *9th*

Hannah Evans died.

" *26th*

William James Esqr. And Martha Rogers died.

" *28th*

Sarah James wife of Wm James Esq died.

" *30th*

Daniel Monahon died.

" *31st*

James James who was suspended Apr^l 5th 1760 was this day restored to his place.

A messenger was sent to Jane Poland on account of her absenting herself from public worship; and for selling liquor at a horse race; to desire her appearance before the Church.

Febry 11th

Elizabeth Wilds died

8

1761
April 4ᵗʰ

Jane Poland appeared and acknowledged before the Church the crimes laid to her charge, but no sufficient marks of repentance appearing, she was suspended from communion, and which suspension is to be publicly declared in the congregation.

John Booth giving the Church farther satisfaction as to his repentance, he is to take his place tomorrow, upon a public acknowledgement of his humiliation for his crimes.

Martha Martin was received upon examination and a good character given her by the minister of the Church to which she belonged.

1Baptized

Elisha James was baptized and received to full communion.

A messenger was sent to Jacob D'Surrency under suspension, to admonish him, that unless he satisfied the Church as to his repentance for crimes laid to his charge, he is to be excommunicated on the sabbath next after monthly meeting in June next.

admission of pedo-baptists to the communion of the Church

It was concluded upon by the unanimous voice of the Church that all those who were educated in the belief of Infant Baptism by sprinkling, and as they labour under the prejudice of such an education can't see it their duty to submit to Immersion, having been already sprinkled, who shall nevertheless satisfy the Church as to their real conversion, shall be admitted to sit down with us at the Lord's Table upon their signing such a covenant as shall be thought proper by the Church. But it is concluded nevertheless, that all such who may at any time apostatize from the Truth in which they have been educated by getting themselves sprinkled, and refuse to submit to the mode of Immersion shall be debarred from communion, notwithstanding they might be able to give a clear verbal account of a work of Grace on their hearts, for this would render it suspicious.[35]

May 2ⁿᵈ

Alexander McIntosh, and Roderick McIver, members of the Church of Scotland were upon their confession of faith and experience in Godliness, and upon signing a covenant, admitted to the Lord's Table.

---

[35] It seems likely that the debate and resolution about admitting those who had only been sprinkled was spurred by the membership applications of Alexander McIntosh and Roderick McIver.

As many difficulties attend persons, who apply for communion with us, their relating their experience before the whole Congregation, it is concluded that such persons shall first apply and communicate the dealings of God with their souls, to the minister and such others of the members as the Church shall think proper; that they may relate it to the Church. Nevertheless such persons must appear before the Church to make a confession of their faith.

9

1761
May 2ⁿᵈ

Philip Howel having been guilty of speaking reproachfully of one of the members in a public place, and using very rash and unbecoming speeches in other respects, and being suspected of having drank to excess at a public Tavern, he was publicly suspended on Sabbath May 3ʳᵈ.

June 6ᵗʰ

Some circumstances appearing in favour of Jacob D'Surrency, though he did not appear before the Church, another messenger was sent to him, his excommunication being deferred.

James Harry having been accused of being disguised with liquor was suspended.

" *19ᵗʰ*

Barbara Monaghon died.[36]

July 4ᵗʰ
Open communion rescinded

Whereas the Church found it impossible to maintain communion at the Lord's Table with Christians of other denominations without causing great divisions in other churches; it was therefore concluded that it would be best in order to prevent such dreadful consequences to desist from it.

Jacob D'Surrency made confession of some of his faults and promised reformation, desiring the Church to suspend her excommunication and entreating their prayers. His request granted _ but remained under suspension.

---

[36] Presumably, this is the "Barbary Monochon" on the 12 March 1759 list, which also states that her date of death was 19 June 1761.

August 1st
Elizabeth Simonson (formerly James) was suspended upon suspicion of her having been guilty of very abusive language.

Septr 6th
Elizabeth Simonson's case having been examined into, and it being found not so bad as was represented, and she acknowledging with sorrow what had been amiss her suspension was taken off.

James Harry made humble acknowledgements of his sin for which he was suspended on June 6th, and was again received to communion.

Joshua Edwards, having been guilty of drinking to excess and in an illegal manner taking some negroes into his possession; is publicly suspended.

Robert Edwards residing at Cape Fear made application for a letter of dismission, which was granted him.

James Harry, Mary Harry, and Elizabeth Wilds (the wife of George) having their residence near the Church at Cashaway, requested a Letter of dismission; which was granted.

Abel Edwards was received into full communion with us by Letter from Cashaway.[37]

10

1761
Octr 3rd
William Thomas and his wife & John Bowen, were received to full Communion by Letters from the Church at Cashaway.[38]

Sent a Letter and Messenger to the Association.
Decr 24th
Hannah Howel died.
1762
Janry 2nd

---

[37] Abel Edwards was the son of the Rev. Joshua Edwards, pastor of the Welsh Neck Church from 1751-1756 and then of neighboring Cashaway. Abel's father was suspended from his position as minister at Cashaway in 1760 for drunkenness, though he later became minister at Catfish. The Joshua Edwards who was suspended in the entry above was a different individual, possibly Abel's brother; the Rev. Joshua Edwards had twelve children, one of whom was named Joshua. "Cashaway Church Book," 23 February 1760; Rippon, *Baptist Register, 1794-1797,* 500; Edwards, "Baptists in South-Carolina," 21.

[38] The Cashaway Church Book records on 27 September 1761 the dismission to Welsh Neck of a John Thomas and his wife, along with John Bowen. Later entries in the Welsh Neck Church Book record the suspension, repentance, restoration, and dismission of a William Thomas, but there is no record of a John. WNCB, 12, 13.

Mr Williams (under excommunication) having made application to the Association in Charleston, the Church received a Letter of advice relative to his affair; and advised that they should receive a letter of acknowledgement, made and signed before the Association, as a sufficient satisfaction, and that thereupon he should be restored.[39]

The letter from Mr. Williams together with the unhappy circumstances of his affair, were considered, and a Letter sent him in answer signifying that upon his declaring himself free to commune with the Church, which is looked upon as a necessary sign of his repentance, he should be restored again to his place.

David Evans and Martha Evans having been guilty of criminal conversation before marriage were suspended in the public congregation till a proper repentance be manifested; on Sabbath January 3rd.

A messenger was sent to Jacob D'Surrency to desire his appearance before the Church, that an enquiry might be made into his late conduct at a Horse-Race, it having been reported that he had drank to excess.

Febry 6th

As Mr. Williams refuses to comply with the Terms proposed, he continues excommunicated.

Another messenger was sent to Jacob D'Surrency, who has since the above, been accused of drinking to excess.

A messenger was sent to Philip Howel, and one to Walter Downes under suspicion, as messengers of care.

Sarah Hicks was received to union and communion by Letter from Cashaway Church.

March 6th

Philip Howel, having lately conducted himself unworthily at a public sale, and not having received the last message, was sent to, that he might be admonished for his faults.

April 3rd

---

[39] The Charleston Association was founded on 21 October 1751 by the Rev. Oliver Hart, on the model of the Philadelphia Association. Welsh Neck was one of the three original members. The Association had no power over individual churches; its role was to be a forum for communication and a source of advice and support for the independent congregations that joined. In the present controversy over the Rev. Williams, the Association could advise Welsh Neck to accept him back, but it had no authority to order any particular action, and Welsh Neck was free to impose its own conditions on restoring Williams to communion. S.v. "Charleston Association," *Brief Baptist Biographies,* Vol. II, 346-347.

A messenger of care was sent to William James under suspension.
Another messenger was sent to Jacob D'Surrency.
Do.. to David Evans to admonish him for his late disorderly conduct having
drank to excess & attempted to dance in public company. Do..Martha Evans as a
messenger of [care].

11

1762
May 1st
George Hicks and Mary White were baptized.
  Martha Evans having appeared and acknowledged her fault before the Church
and given her satisfaction as to her repentance, it was concluded that she should
be admitted to Communion.
Jacob D'Surrency was again sent to.

June 5th
1 Baptized
William James professing repentance was restored to the communion.
Under many considerations it was concluded that Church Business should be
transacted on the Saturday before monthly meeting,__ Saturday
George Hicks and Mary White baptized May 1st received the right-hand of
fellowship.

Augt 1st
Mary Hicks was baptized 31st July.
2 Baptized
Sept 4th
Tabitha James was baptized.
A complaint having been made against William Jones for Excess in drinking he
was privately suspended till further enquiry be made about it
  A messenger was sent to Jane Poland, under suspension for some misconduct.
A messenger to Griffith John for non-attendance on God's worship.

Oct 2nd
1 Baptized
Lydia Eustice was baptized. Elizabeth Counsel examined (was formerly
baptized in Nola) and received.

Martha Faox received by Letter of dismission from Catfish.[40]

1763
Febry
David Evans making acknowledgement of his crime before the congregation
was restored to Communion.
William Jones publicly suspended for drinking to excess.

March 5th
1Baptized
Susannah Young was baptized.

June 4th
Elizabeth Simonson privately suspended, upon an apprehension that she lives in
wilful separation from her husband.
  The suspended members were sent to by a messenger of care.

1Baptized
July 2nd
Robert Hicks was baptized[41]
1764
Septr 1st
Mr William James being guilty of Drunkenness and some other misbehaviour all
of which he confessed before the Church; for which the Church concluded to
suspend him publicly which was done 2nd Septr 1764.
  Mr William Jones was restored to his place publicly 2nd Septr 1764
Elizabeth Simonson was restored to her place.
Novr 15th
Mrs Mary White died
[De]cr 30th
Mrs Jane McIntosh died.[42]

---

[40] Catfish was originally a branch of Welsh Neck. It became an independent church
in 1752. Townsend, *South Carolina Baptists,* 78. It was situated approximately 25 miles
SE of Welsh Neck.

[41] There is a significant gap of over a year in the Church Book at this point. The
original transcriber provided no explanation. The gap might be due to the scandal over
the discovery that the Rev. Bedgegood had married his second wife while his first was
still living. See the introduction for further discussion.

[42] Mrs. McIntosh's funeral took place on 1 January 1765; the Rev. Pugh preached
on Job 19.21. Pugh, *Diaries,* 42.

12

<u>1765</u>
Febry 16th
Concluded by the Church that public suspension is not to be practiced in this Church. (12th) died Robt Hicks. (16th) Mrs Eleanor Evans died.[43]

March 2nd
Mr William Thomas is suspended for the sin of drunkenness.
    Mrs Poland who had been suspended, was this day restored to her place.
Mr Bedggood dismis^d to the Charles^{tn} Church.[44]
The Rev^d Mr. Bedgegood having sent for a Letter of Dismission is this day dismissed from this Church, to the Church in Charleston of the same faith and order.

May 4th
1 Baptized
Miss Hannah Sutton was baptized by the Rev^d Mr Oliver Hart.
Mr Pugh was appointed to write a letter to Mr Philip Howel to come to the Church.__ Also to go to Mr Joshua Edwards and to Mr William Thomas to admonish them. (March 9th) died Mr John Booth.[45]

June 1st
Mr. Joshua Edwards appeared, declared his sorrow for his being in drink, and that he had grieved the members of the Church; was received into his place.

July 6th
Mr William Thomas came to the Church, and manifested repentance for his sin; and was restored to his place in the Church.

Augt 3rd
Call of Mr Hart

---

[43] The different style of this entry, with the month's deaths recorded under the date of the monthly meeting, may indicate that this entry was the beginning of the Rev. Pugh's record in the Church Book. In his diary for 19 March 1765 Pugh stated that he "Wrote some in ye Church Book." *Diaries,* 44.

[44] In the original Church Book transcription, the Rev. Bedggood's name is at different times spelled with and without a middle "e".

[45] Although it seems odd to record a March death under a May date, Pugh's diary suggests that John Booth did die in the earlier month: Pugh was visiting his widow, Sarah, on 19 March 1765. *Diaries,* 44.

A call was signed for the Rev^d Mr Hart in Charleston to come and be the minister of this place.[46]__ Died Griffith John.

Octr 5th
Messengers appointed by the Church to several persons.__ Abel Wilds to Jacob D'Surrency, also to William James under suspension.
Samuel Wilds to Mrs Cox, who we hear has acted amiss to Philip Howel.
Mr. Pugh, Thomas Evans, & Samuel Evans to Mrs Martin, and David Evans to admonish them, to be reconciled to each other. (which was done)
Concluded by the Church, that David Evans must come and declare his innocency before the Church, in relation to a bad report about him, that has become public.
    Mr. Pugh is appointed a messenger to the Association.

Decr 7th
Mr Hart declines
A full answer was received from the Rev^d Mr Hart declining to accept the Call of the Church.[47]
Mrs Cox appeared was examined, and acquitted by the Church.

1766
Janry 4th
Call of Mr Pugh

---

[46] Oliver Hart (1723-1795) was born, baptized, and ordained in Pennsylvania. He became pastor at Charleston in 1750, where he founded the Charleston Association, of which Welsh Neck was a member. In 1769 he baptized Edmund Botsford, pastor at Welsh Neck 1779-1780 and 1782-1796. Hart also created a fund for educating young men for the ministry; Pugh and Botsford both benefited from this financial support. Hart's prominent work for the Patriot cause led him to flee South Carolina in the face of the British invasion of 1780. He became pastor at Hopewell, NJ, where he served until his death. Hart, "Diary," 1, 13; Rippon, *Baptist Register, 1794-1797,* 507-514; Mallary, *Botsford,* 27-34; Brackney, *Dictionary of Baptists,* 273. Hart had visited Welsh Neck in March and May 1765 (he and the Rev. Pugh went "a-gunning" during his March visit) and so was known personally to the Welsh Neck congregation. Pugh recorded this invitation to Hart in his diary, also. Pugh, *Diaries,* 43, 44; WNCB, 12.
    [47] On 31 August 1765, Pugh had read a letter from Hart in response to the call on 3 August. Whatever this letter said, it must have been indecisive, since only now, on 7 December, was a "full answer" received from Hart, declining the call. Note that twenty years later, when the Charleston church asked Hart to return from his Revolutionary exile, he behaved in a similar fashion, giving several provisional responses before finally stating that he was not going to come back to Charleston. Pugh, *Diaries,* 48; Rogers, *Furman,* 54.

The Rev^d Mr Pugh having received a Call to take charge of this Church as a Minister accepts it, and becomes its Pastor.

Febry 21st
Mrs Mary Prethro died.[48]
April 12th
  " Anne Douglass[49]

13

1766
July 5th
David Baldy and Sarah his wife were received members of the Church, by letter from Catfish Church.
William Thomas and Mary his wife were dismissed to any Church of the same faith and order by Letter.

Octr 4th
Excommunication
Resolved that Philip Howel & William James be excommunicated.
  The Church concluded to send to the Association. The Rev^d Mr. Pugh appointed Messenger.
Mr Bedggood dismissed to any Church

The Rev^d Mr. Bedgegood dismissed to any Church of the same faith and order.
__ __ __A copy of his Dismission.
Copy of letter of Dismission
"The Church of Christ, in the Welch Neck on Pee Dee baptized upon a profession of Faith; holding the doctrines of Grace &c.

  To any whom it may concern. These are to certify that the Rev^d Mr Nicholas Bedggood has been a member with us for the space of six years and eight months, that he was our minister four years and better; and that he is now a member in full communion, with us. During all which time he was unusually beloved:- And as he has requested a Letter of dismission, he is hereby dismissed from us, when joined to any Church of the same faith and order.
          Given at our Church Meeting October 4th 1766.'
  " 12th

---

[48] Pugh preached on Romans 7.9 at Mary Prothro's funeral, on 22 February. Pugh, *Diaries*, 53.
[49] Pugh preached on Psalm 34.19 at Ann Douglass's funeral, on 14 April. Pugh, *Diaries*, 54.

Philip Howel & William James' excommunication publicly read in the
Congregation. The Form of their Excommunication.
Form of an act of Excommunication

Whereas Philip Howel & William James have for a long time passed, been
suspended from the Communion of this Church_ they still persisting in a course
of life, contrary to the rules of the gospel, and of this Church, notwithstanding
all necessary and gospel methods have been made use of to reclaim them;
therefore the Church have thought it proper and necessary to cut them off from
this Body. Pursuant to this conclusion, we now make it known to all, that they
are no longer members of this Body. May the Lord grant, that this ordinance
may be the means to bring them to a sense of their evil ways and to a timely
repentance and to stir up each of us to watch and be sober lest we enter into
temptation.
" *17ᵗʰ*
Philip Douglass died.

Decr 6ᵗʰ
Another Letter of Dismission for Mr. Bedggood is this day signed by the
members.

N.B.
I find the following in Mr. Bedggood's handwriting; the presumption is, that is
was written the first of the year 1767. No date is attached to it, and we are
therefore left to conjecture. From July 5ᵗʰ to Decr 6ᵗʰ inclusive I presume is Mr
Pugh's writing.[50]
Mr B it will be seen, was next after the dismission of Mr Pugh.

14

1767
An investigation
The Church having been long in a declining state Brother Abel Wilds desired
the opinion of the Church as to what they thought the cause of such declension
was. Upon consideration, it was the unanimous opinion, that it was owing to the
general dislike of Mr. Pugh.
Consideration

---

[50] The transcriber is referring to July-December 1766. Yet Pugh stated that he was
writing in the Welsh Neck Church Book as early as March 1765. Pugh, *Diaries,* 44.

This being the opinion of the Church, it was then moved that it might be considered, whether it would be most for the glory of God for Mr. Pugh to continue our minister or to remove to some other place.

But as this was a matter of consequence it was thought advisable to consider it with deliberation. Therefore the Church agreed to give each- their opinion, and to desire Mr. Pugh to do the same on next Saturday.

Resignation of Mr Pugh

The Church met according to the above appointment, and unanimously thought it most conducive to the Honor of God in the welfare of the Church for Mr. Pugh to remove. He acquiesced in their opinion and received a recommendatory Letter.[51]

March 7th
Call to Mr. Bedd

The Church presented a Call to the Revd Mr Bedggood, then minister to a people on James Island_ which call Mr Bedggood accepted.

April 12th
Return

Mr Bedggood returned to us, and preached his first sermon from Colossians 3.11. "Christ is all and in all."

May 2nd

Messengers of care were sent to several members.

June 6th

Very agreeable answers were returned from the above persons.

Augt 1st
L'S in 2 months

It was determined by a majority of voices that the Lord's Supper should be administered once in two months.

---

[51] The transcriber was incorrect in the assumption that Welsh Neck's discussion about Pugh and the minister's "resignation" a week later took place in early 1767. Pugh's diary states that he received news of his dismissal on 13 December 1766. The preliminary discussion must therefore have taken place on 6 December 1766. Pugh was obviously absent from that meeting. If the transcriber is correct in stating that Pugh wrote the Church Book entry for that day, recording the signing of a third letter of dismission for Bedgegood, then someone gave Pugh a radically edited version of what had taken place. Though the 13 December entry in Pugh's diary that records his dismissal is brief, it does suggest he was taken by surprise. Pugh, *Dairies,* 61.

Octr 3rd
Agnes MLemore presented a Letter of dismission to us from the Church at
Catfish.
" *4th*
Mrs MLemore admitted; further business postponed to this day fortnight.
" *17th*
A Letter was signed and sent to the Association_ James Rogers dismissed.
Complaint was made against Martha Martin for defaming one of members; and
a messenger (Walter Downes) was sent to desire her to desist from so evil a
practice; and to answer to the complaint at our meeting on January next (2nd)
(Decr 5th) Rec^d & read the minutes & Letter from the Association, (Decr 6th)
John Abran Esq rec^d as a member by Letter, from Catfish Church.
1768
Janry 2nd
Mrs Martin's case postponed.

April 16th Satur^y
A special meeting._ A complaint was made against Walter Downes for having
told untrue and mischievous stories. He was suspended till farther enquiry._
David Evans suspended for drinking to excess.

15

1768
April 16th Sat-^{dy}
A difference subsisting between James James and Thomas Jones they referred
the affair to the Church, who appointed three members to arbitrate it viz.
Thomas James, Howel James & Thomas Evans.
Deed of Gift to the Church
This day Mr Daniel Devonald signed a Deed of Gift of Two acres of Land
whereon the Church is now situated.
appointment of Trustees
John Sutton and Abel Edwards were appointed Trustees _ with power to appoint
others; any three of whom may appoint others upon the departure of the rest.

May 1st
------ Brown was this day received a member, by letter from a Church in North
Carolina.__ Anne Rollyn died.

June 4th

Walter Downes continues under suspension.

Messengers were sent to Mrs Clay and Mrs Charity Edwards on account of their absence from public worship.

A day of Fasting and Prayer was appointed to be observed on Saturday the 18th inst, and to consult what means we should use in order to obtain a revival of Religion.

Sept[r]

Martha Martin after repeated exhortations and brotherly reproofs continuing in the practice for which she was complained of was this day suspended from the Communion of the Church.

Oct[r]

Messengers were sent to Thomas Edwards to persuade him to the due observance of his Covenant; having neglected an attendance upon the ordinances of the Gospel for a long time.

Messengers were sent to David Baldy, the Church having heard a report of his having had guilty conversation with a woman.

<u>1769</u>

May 6th

Thomas Edwards' reply to the messengers sent in October last induced the Church still to continue hopeful of his return to his duty and to continue their regard to him.

The Church was fully convinced, upon examination of D. Baldy's innocence.

Messengers were sent to Abel Edwards and Thomas Edwards relative to a report propagated by the former against the latter

<u>1770</u>

Oct[r] 13th

Thomas Edwards and Sarah his wife dismissed to Cashaway Church.[52]

Messengers were sent to Sarah Baldy and Walter Downes.

The Church, in consideration of the gloomy appearance of ~~religion~~ the state of this Church in particular; that of religion in general; and that of our nation and colonies; appointed next Saturday as a day of fasting and prayer

16

<u>1770</u>

---

[52] Cashaway received Thomas and Sarah Edwards as members on 18 May 1771. "Cashaway Church Book."

Novr 3ʳᵈ
Mrs. Baldy appeared, and gave satisfaction as to her conduct.

It was unanimously agreed that it is expedient to have the Supper administered in a meeting of the Church only __ with the admission of such serious persons only, who particularly desire to see it.

It was thought expedient that the deacons should be set apart by solemn prayer and imposition of hands: and Saturday the 1ˢᵗ of December was appointed for that purpose.

(This is the last of Mr Bedggood's record. What follows, is in the hand writing of Mr Winchester.[53] In reference to the last article Mr. W says -- N. B. This was never done. i.e. the setting apart of deacons in Decr ----

1774
Febry 1ˢᵗ
The Revᵈ Mr. Nicholas Bedggood died near fifteen years after his first call to this place; and almost seven years after his return, from which time he ministered here till his death. He was regarded a good scholar, and a sound divine, an eloquent preacher and a polite gentleman; and well beloved by his acquaintance: Yet notwithstanding all his abilities and endowments, he was never very successful, especially in the latter part of his life: none being baptized after his return.

Septʳ 3ʳᵈ
3 Baptized
At a Church meeting Thomas Shirley with his wife Martha Shirley, and Anne Hewstess, gave in their experiences, were received by the Church, and baptized by Mr Pugh minister at Cashaway.[54]

Octʳ 1ˢᵗ
3 Baptized
William Edwards Junr with Catharine Edwards his wife and Elizabeth Evans, were received by the Church, and baptized by Mr Pugh.[55]

---

[53] Elhanan Winchester (1751-1798) was pastor of the Welsh Neck church from March 1775 until September 1779. See the introduction for more details about his life and career.

[54] As well as performing these baptisms on 3 September, Pugh had preached at Welsh Neck on 2 July and 6 August. During his August visit, he lodged with Abel Wilds, the man who had led the move to replace him in 1766. *Diaries,* 136, 137, 138.

[55] Pugh preached at both the Saturday meeting (1 October) and the Sunday service (2 October). *Diaries,* 138.

4 Baptized
At a church meeting – John David, John Pledger, Thomas Harry and Sarah Edwards were received by the Church, and baptized by Rev^d Mr Philip Mulkey[56]

2 Baptized
At a Church meeting, David Roach and John Evans Junr were received after baptism, which was administered by the Rev^d Mr. Pugh.[57]

7 Baptized
At a Church meeting Mackey McKnatt, Josiah Evans, John Wilds, William Terrel Junr, Dinah McKnatt, Anne Jones, and Mary Evans were received into fellowship. Baptized by Mr Pugh.

This above contains an account of the members added to the Church, from the death of the Revd Nicholas Bedggood, to the settlement of his successor, the Revd Elhanan Winchester.
What follows doubtless contains the list of those who were previously members and those afterwards added.[58]

---

[56] Philip Mulkey was born in Halifax, North Carolina on 14 May 1732. Reared in the Church of England, he became a Separate Baptist in 1756 under the influence of Shubal Stearns and was ordained in 1757. Mulkey founded the earliest Separate Baptist church in South Carolina in 1759 at Little River, later moving to Fairforest. Fairforest became the center of a network of Separate churches. His involvement at Welsh Neck in 1774 demonstrates the presence of Separate Baptists in the Pee Dee region on the eve of the Revolution. Separate Baptist influence may have contributed to the conversions of African Americans during Winchester's pastorate. See introduction for further discussion. Mulkey died c. 1805. Edwards, "Baptists in South Carolina," 43-48; *Encyclopedia of Southern Baptists,* Vol. IV, s.v. "Mulkey, Philip."

[57] Pugh preached at Welsh Neck on 31 December 1774; it is likely that this is the date for this entry in the Church Book. *Diaries,* 141.

[58] This list is not a complete roster of all the members of the Welsh Neck Church at any particular date. It contains several names of long-standing members, some of whom go back to the list of 1759, but it does not include all of the older members who were still living and active in the Church at this point. This list mostly consists of new additions to the church from 8 June 1777 to the end of the Rev. Winchester's pastorate in September 1779. It does not include any who were baptized in 1774 or in late 1776 and early 1777. It is not possible to find details about baptism or admission to membership for a few of the individuals included on this list. Since "1775" is one of the dates at the top of this list, it is possible that these individuals were baptized by visiting pastors during 1775, when the Rev. Winchester was away. No baptisms for that year are recorded in the Church Book. Since this list omits those who died or were dismissed during the 1777-9 years, it seems to have been put in its present form, with men and women neatly separated, at the end of or soon after 1779. Most of the names on this list joined the church after the next

17

A list of the members of the Church 1775_   1778. 1779

1 Elhanan Winchester Pastor	44 William Hewstess
2 John Edwards	45 James Hewstess
3 Abel Edwards	46 Thomas Ayer
4 Aaron Pearson	47 Henry Sparks
5 Magnus Cargill	48 Burrel Huggins
6 Moses Pearson	49 Charles Mason
7 Joseph Luke	50 Owen Darby
8 William Lang	51 Arnold Colvin
9 John Williams	52 Michael Fitzgerald
10 William Jones	53 Shadrack Fuller
11 John Hughes	54 George Trawelk[59]
12 Obadiah Hudson	55 Paul Baldy
13 Amos Pilgrim	56 Evander McIver
14 William Mason	57 Robert Hodges
15 Daniel Sparks	58 John Hodges
16 Gresset Johnson	59 Thomas Evans Junr
17 Abel Evans	60 Joel McNatt
18 Benjamin James	61 Tristam Thomas
19 Walter Downes	62 William Luke
20 Charles Lowther	63 Josiah James
21 Josiah Pearce	64 Abel Goodwin
22 Sampson Thomas	65 John Edmunson
23 Daniel McDaniel	66 Enoch Evans Senr
24 Robert White	67 Ruth Askew
25 John Stinson	68 Elizabeth Pilgrim
26 Welcome Hodges	69 Martha Evans
27 Gideon Parish	70 Alice Lucas
28 John Downs[60]	71 Rachel Pearson
29 William Hewson	72 Mary Wilds
30 John Stevens	73 Mary Hollingsworth
31 Joseph Mason	74 Mary Andrews
32 William James	75 Sarah Hicks
33 Matthew Griffith	76 Sarah James
34 Enoch Evans Junr	77 Margaret James
35 William Cherry	78 Anne Terrel
36 Alexander Walden	79 Sarah Wilds
37 Joseph Pledger	80 Rachel David
38 John Chambliss	81 Ruth Wright
39 Hall Hudson	82 Mary Jones
40 Abel Kolb	83 Mary Terrel

list, WNCB, 23, was compiled; it would have made more sense, perhaps, to incorporate the list above into the Church Book at the end of the Rev. Winchester's pastorate in 1779.

[59] This name is spelled differently almost every time it appears. It can be: Trewelk, Treweek, Treeweek, etc.

[60] Spelled "Downes" WNCB, 25.

41 Jeremiah Brown
42 Matthew Hewstess
43 John Hewstess

84 Sarah Lang
85 Sarah Pouncey
86 Mary Chambliss

[18]

87 Rebecca James
88 Mary Evans
89 Sarah Hewstess
90 Elizabeth Flenegald
91 Sarah Winchester
92 Winiford Pearson[62]
93 Anne Hargrove
94 Mahetabel Irby
95 Anne Cleary
96 Eddy Johnson
97 Sarah Foster
98 Mary Hudson
99 Peggy Darby
100 Tabitha Williamson
102 Elizabeth Luke[66]
103 Martha McNatt
104 Charity Hurd
105 Elizabeth Hodges
106 Sarah Pledger
107 Sarah Downs[67]
108 Ann Peggy Ayer
109 Feribe Lang
110 Elizabeth Lide
111 Deborah Geer
112 Elizabeth Hicks
113 Martha Pearce (now Sparks)
114 Elizabeth Sutton
115 Elizabeth Thomas
116 Anne Lowther
117 Martha Lampley
118 Hannah Kimbrough
119 Sarah Steward
120 Sarah Evans
121 Catharine Ross
122 Sarah Stubbs

132 Mary Evans
133 Zilphah Walsh
134 Lydia Howell
135 Martha Wilson
136 Mary Wilds
137 Sarah Fearson
138 Sarah Lock[63]
139 Rhoda Booth
140 Mary Cox
141 Mary Pearce now Thomas
142 Nancy Williamson
143 Susannah Bingham
144 Elizabeth Hewson
145 Phebe Pledger
146 Rebecca Scott
147 Sedona Upthegrove
148 Celia James
149 Celete Morgan
150 Mary Evans
151 Mary Griffiths
152 Elizabeth Mason
153 Mary Vaun
154 Mary Anne Fitzgerald
155 Eddy Stinson
156 Rachel Groves
157 Elizabeth Luke
158 Lydia Evans
159 Sarah Kolb
160 Celete Luke
161 Isabel David
162 Eleanor Hewstess
163 Anne Lampley
164 Honor Darby
165 Comfort Pearson
166 Eleanor Hudson

176 Mary Huggins
177 Caty McIver (after Botsford)[61]
178 Grace Brown
179 Anne Baldy
180 Nancy Brown
181 Elizabeth Ayer
182 Sarah Horry[64]
183 Sarah Raburn
184 Rebekah Hodges
185 Elizabeth Evans
186 Martha McNatt [65]
187 Anne Poland
188 Betsey Hicks
189 Anne Evans
190 Elizabeth James
191 Sarah Mumford
192 Mary Harper
193 Feribe Lang
194 Mary Ivy
195 Anne Brown
196 Sarah McIver
197 Jamimah Bruce

---

[61] Caty McIver married Edmund Botsford at some point after his first wife, Susanna, died on 9 March 1790. Caty herself died on 7 February 1796. WNCB, 38, 42.

[62] Winifred per 1778 list, WNCB, 23.

[63] Elsewhere, Sarah Lack; se WNCB, 24, 25.

[64] Spelled "Harry," WNCB, 27.

[65] The number 185 was repeated and the number 186 omitted.

[66] The transcriber of the church book omitted number 101.

[67] Spelled "Downes," WNCB, 25.

123 Sarah Walden	167 Lydia Trawelk
124 Sarah James	168 Elizabeth Medford
125 Elizabeth Counsel	169 Anne Roach
126 Agnes Creele	170 Susannah Lampley
127 Elizabeth Pledger	171 Mary Lide
128 Mary Cooper	172 Agnes Hewstess
129 Mary Walsh	173 Elizabeth Raburn
130 Elizabeth Walsh	174 Sarah Cherry
131 Anne Stevens	175 Bibbe Bruce

[19]

1775
March 12th

The Records of the Church at the Welch Neck on Pee-Dee.
This day the Church and Society being met together, unanimously agreed to give Mr. Elhanan Winchester a call to be their minister for a season, and were pleased accordingly to present him with one after this manner. ___

The Church of Christ at the Welch Tract, Pee-Dee in South Carolina, holding the doctrine of Election, particular Redemption; final perseverance; believers baptism, &c. to the Revd Elhanan Winchester sendeth greeting.

Whereas we are destitute of a minister to administer the word and ordinances amongst us, we have thought fit to present you with this our call to be our minister for one year fixed; and then if you and we should agree, we would put ourselves under your pastoral care. Given from under our hands this 12th day of March 1775. Signed in behalf of the whole. George Hicks. }

Abel Wilds.   } Deacons.

1776
March 8th[68]
Call to Mr Winchester renewed.

This day the Church being met together, were pleased to renew the Call to Mr Winchester, to be their minister, which he accepted for the space of one year, beginning from this day. And the Church that on Sunday the 17th day of this month, the renewal of the call, and his acceptation of the same should be made

---

[68] The gap in the records between Winchester's first call to be pastor in March 1775 and the recommencement of the records in March 1776 was due to his long absence from Welsh Neck. He spent much of 1775 and early 1776 traveling back to New England to fetch his wife, Alice. She became ill during the journey south, slowing his progress. Ultimately, he had to leave her with friends in Fairfax, Virginia, so that he could return to his Welsh Neck congregation. Stone, *Winchester,* 33-34.

public, from which time he will be considered as their pastor, for the space of one year, or while he and the people may agree.[69]

This day brother Elhanan Winchester was received as a member of this Church, being about to take the charge over it in the Lord, as a minister and pastor; he having before obtained a letter of recommendation and dismission from the Church of which he was before a member, which run after this manner.

"The first Baptist Church of Christ in Bellingham, under the pastoral care of Elder Noah Alden; holding the doctrine of original sin, universal depravity, absolute, eternal, unconditional, personal Election; particular redemption by the blood of Christ; justification by his righteousness imparted; regeneration; effectual calling; practical godliness; final perseverance; resurrection of the dead; believer's baptism, &c.:- To any Church of the same faith and order, where our beloved brother Elhanan Winchester may see cause to join as a member; Greeting: we certify you that the above said brother is a member of this Church; and we all esteem him as a real christian, a man of sound principles, orthodox sentiments, an orderly walker, of up-right conversation, [illeg.] clear gospel preacher; and as such we recommend him unto you; and upon his joining and your receiving him, he ceases to be a member with us, and becomes one with you in all respects.____ Dated Bellingham August 14th 1775. Signed in behalf of the Church. Noah Alden Pastor.[70]

[20]

1776
March 8th
A proposition for a meeting of the churches of this Province at the high hills.
Messengers
Brother Elhanan Winchester being received as a member, took the lead of the meeting, and proposed by request, that as the Association did not meet in Charleston this year on account of the troubles there; there might be a meeting of the Churches in this Province, at the High Hills of Santee[71] on the wednesday

---

[69] Presumably, there is a word omitted in this sentence, which should read: "And the Church *resolved* that…"

[70] This letter of dismission from Bellingham is explicit about that church's adherence to the strict Calvinism of the Particular Baptists, and about Winchester's theological stance at this time. When taken in conjunction with the Welsh Neck Church's initial call to Winchester on 12 March 1775, it is clear that Welsh Neck was a strict Calvinist community seeking a pastor of similar beliefs. Winchester's move in the direction of Universalist ideas came after this point. See the introduction for a fuller discussion of this issue.

[71] The church at the High Hills of Santee was constituted in 1772 from the large number of those converted by Joseph Reese in that area over the previous two years or

before the last Sunday in April next, in order to choose delegates to attend the Continental Association, which he judged very expedient and necessary at this season, in order to obtain our liberties, and freedom from religious tyranny or ecclesiastical oppressions; which the Church unanimously agreed to: and chose two messengers viz brethren Abel Wilds and Thomas Evans to the provincial association, at the time and place mentioned.[72]

Voted that brother Elhanan Winchester draw up a letter from this Church to the Association; and as he cannot be present at the same, he is desired to draw up some thoughts on the continental association to be laid before the Churches at their meeting at the High Hills.[73]

March 17th
Call to Mr Winchester
This day the Church and Society publicly renewed their call to Mr Winchester for one year, which he publicly accepted for the time, and is from this day their pastor.

Novr 2nd
1 Baptized
John Geer was received upon a relation of his exercises of mind and baptized

Decr 1st
1 Baptized
Baptized the widow Rebecca James having been examined and received the day before

---

more. Reese was a Separate Baptist. Richard Furman, the recipient of the letters from Edmund Botsford included in this volume, became the pastor of High Hills in 1774. He took a lead in preaching in favor of the Patriot cause during the early years of the Revolution, and so High Hills was a logical place for this gathering of Baptists who wished to ensure that Congress in Philadelphia endorsed the principle of full religious liberty. Rogers, *Furman*, 17, 21, 29-30.

[72] The minutes of this 1776 meeting in the High Hills have been lost. Clayton, "South Carolina Baptist Records," 320; Rogers, *Furman*, 34. The "ecclesiastical oppressions" referred to here by Winchester may have included fears that Presbyterian Patriots would attempt to impose their religious views in Congress or at local level in New England. Flinchum, "Reluctant Revolutionaries," 181-186. See the introduction for a fuller discussion.

[73] Winchester could not be present because he had to return to Fairfax to fetch his wife. He journeyed there in April to find that she had died. Instead of returning immediately to Welsh Neck, he went on to Boston, where he served as substitute pastor at First Baptist, Boston for a brief period. There, he married Sarah Peck and returned with her to Welsh Neck later in the year—hence the gap in the Church Book between March and November 1776. Stone, *Winchester*, 24-25.

1777
April 6ᵗʰ
Tabitha James wife of William James died.

May 3ʳᵈ
This day the Church met and after sermon proceeded to business.
1.James Crocker, giving an account of the work of grace upon his soul and desiring to unite with the Church, was received.
2.Mrs Anne Lide giving an account of her experience was received.
3.Joshua Terrel giving an account of God's goodness to his soul was admitted as a member.
4.Elizabeth Terrel having given the Church satisfaction of a work of grace upon her heart was also received.
5.The Church continue their call to their pastor for another year which he accepts.
6.Mr Winchester is allowed to go to the Hill (Cheraws) once in three Sundays if they desire him, and will do their part towards his support by a majority of the church.[74]

[21]

1777
May 3ʳᵈ
William James being proved guilty of drunkenness was turned out of the Church, or voted out of his covenant, till he repents and gives satisfaction.
Adjourned to Saturday 18ᵗʰ inst.
" 4ᵗʰ
5 persons baptized
This day being Sunday; Sarah Winchester gave herself up to the Lord, and by his will, to the Church, was received, and baptized, together with James Crocker, Joshua Terrel, Elizabeth Terrel, and Anne Lide, who were examined and received the day before, but not baptized till this day.[75]

---

[74] This is the first mention of a distinct congregation at Cheraw Hill, approximately twelve miles north of Welsh Neck. On 12 January 1782 it was constituted as a separate church, and several members of the Welsh Neck congregation were dismissed there in the ensuing months. See below, WNCB, 29.

[75] The stages that individuals progressed through before admittance to Regular Baptist churches are represented in this entry. Sarah Winchester and the others mentioned

Sat^{dy} " 18th
1 Baptized
Met according to adjournment, and proceeded to business.
1 John Pledger gave himself up to the Church, and was received; he having been baptized before.
2 John Bowen excluded from our fellowship, for drinking, swearing, cursing, &c.
3 Walter Downs excluded for drinking.
appointment of Deacons. Names.
4 Agreed to choose two more deacons to assist in the business of the Church, with those already in that office.
5.Mr Abel Edwards and Mr William Terrel Jnr. were chosen, & accepted.[76]
  " 31st
Church met according to order, and proceeded to business.
1 Elizabeth Massy gave herself up to the Lord, and by his will to the church, was received, and will be a member in full communion when baptized.
2 Sarah Sparks and Martha Edwards gave themselves up and were likewise received. No difficulties appearing we are to commune tomorrow.
June 1st
3 Baptized
Sunday. Elizabeth Massy, Sarah Sparks, and Martha Edwards were baptized.__
We had the sacrament of the Lord's Supper openly which is to be our practice for the future.
June 8th
2 Do
John Hughes and Obadiah Hudson were baptized
Sunday " 15th
5 persons baptized

---

here would first have experienced a profound conviction of their sinfulness, followed by a powerful sense of God's saving grace. They would relate these experiences to the church, or, if shy, to a committee of the church, who would share the information with the church as a whole. (See WNCB, 8 for the church's decision to allow applicants for baptism to relate their experiences before a small group of people instead of the whole congregation.) If their experiences seemed authentic, they would be received by the church, and then baptized. This careful procedure was still in force at this date; towards the end of Winchester's pastorate, during the 1779 revival, it seems that short cuts were taken.
[76] William Terrel, Jnr. was not included in the 1775 list; this is the first mention of him. Abel Edwards served with distinction as deacon until his death in 1793, when he was honored before an international readership with an obituary in the *Baptist Register*. WNCB, 40; Rippon, *Baptist Register, 1794-1797,* 500-502.

Daniel Sparks, Moses Pearson, Amos Pilgrim, Mary Terrel, and Elizabeth
Pilgrim were baptized.

" " *22*nd

6 persons baptized

Magnus Cargill, Joseph Luke, William Mason, James Brown, Mary Jones, and
Ruth Wright were baptized.[77]

" " *29*th

3 baptized

Aaron Pearson and Winiford his wife, and Rachel the wife of Moses Pearson
were baptized.

*July 3*rd

Died much lamented, Mrs Sarah Winchester.

" *5*th

At our monthly meeting, John Hughes, Obadiah Hudson, Daniel Sparks, Moses
Pearson, Amos Pilgrim, Magnus Cargill, Joseph Luke, James Brown, Mary
Jones, Ruth Wright, Aaron Pearson, Winiford Pearson, his wife, and Rachel
Pearson the wife of Moses Pearson, were received to communion and fellowship
with this church, they being all baptized before.

" *6*th

3 baptized

Sunday. John Edwards, Ruth Askew, and Sarah Lang were examined and
baptized.

[22]

1777

*Octr 10*th

James Brown going home to New England, received a Letter of
recommendation; and is dismissed, whenever he joins with another Church of
the same faith and order.

" *18*th

1 baptized

William Lang was examined and received by the Church, and on Sunday 19th
was baptized by the Rev^d Mr Furman.

*Novr 1*st

At a church meeting, John Edwards, John Williams, Elizabeth Pilgrim, and Ruth
Askew were received into full communion having been baptized before.

Call to Revd Mr. Furman

---

[77] James Brown was not included in the 1775 list; the other five were.

As our minister is about to leave us in the Spring, on account of his health; agreed to send a letter to Mr Furman and to the Church at the High-Hills of Santee, desiring that he might come and be our pastor.[78]

Agreed that Mr Jenkyn David, and Mr Abel Wilds draw the same; and that Mr Wilds and Mr Winchester be messengers to carry it, and to <u>entreat</u> in our favour in this important matter.

Decr 6th
Call to Revd M[r]. Furman withdrawn
At our Church meeting, hearing that the Rev[d] Mr Dargan formerly of the High-Hills of Santee, was about removing thence, concluded not to send for the Rev[d] Mr Furman, as there is no probability of obtaining him.

William Mason was this day received into full communion he having been baptized before.

<u>*1778*</u>
Janry 3rd
At a monthly meeting of the Church Gresset Johnson and Sarah Pouncey were examined.
Any person of moral character may be evidence for or against etc.
the imposition of hands not required in ordination of deacons.

Agreed by a majority of votes (according to a former vote of the Church not recorded) that any person of a good moral character (of which the Church is to judge) may be an evidence either for, or against a member, where brethren of the Church cannot be obtained.
Agreed by a majority of votes, agreeably to a former vote of the Church not recorded, that ordination consists in the people's choice of a member to office, and his acceptance of the same; and needeth not the imposition of hands to make it valid.

Concluded to send for Mr. Gano to be our minister, and that Mr Abel Wilds and Thomas Evans be a committee to draw up a call for that purpose.[79] Letters

---

[78] Richard Furman (1755-1825) was converted by the Separate Baptist preacher, Joseph Reese, in 1771 and was ordained as pastor of the High Hills church in 1774. He joined Hart in promoting the Patriot cause in the interior of South Carolina at the start of the Revolution. During the British occupation he fled the state, but returned after the war to resume his pastorate at High Hills before moving to Charleston in 1787. Largely self-educated, he became a champion of education for Baptists, founding or inspiring several Baptist institutions of higher learning throughout the South. He became a close friend of Winchester's successor at Welsh Neck, Edmund Botsford, whose letters to Furman from Welsh Neck are included in this volume. Rogers, *Furman*, passim; Brackney, *Dictionary of the Baptists*, 238.

of dismission were this day signed, for our brethren John Sutton, and John Perkins.

A Letter was this day signed, to be sent to the Association. Col Hicks appointed messenger.

Sunday " 5ᵗʰ
3 Baptized
This day Gresset Johnson, Sarah Pouncey and Mary Chambliss were baptized and received into the Church: together with Mary Terrel and Sarah Lang who had been baptized before.

[23]

1778
Febry 5ᵗʰ
Died Mrs Mary Edwards
" *28ᵗʰ*

Amos Pilgrim and Elizabeth his wife being about to remove from this place, were dismissed to any Church of the same faith and order, where they may see cause to join.

1 Baptized
Sunday March 15ᵗʰ
Sarah Winchester gave in her experience and was baptized.[80]
" *28ᵗʰ*
Call to Mᵣ Winchester
At a Church meeting, Col Hicks chosen moderator, the Church concluded, after some debate, to give Mʳ Winchester a call for another year.

Sarah Winchester was this day received a member of this Church.

A List of Members April 5ᵗʰ, 1778.[81]

---

[79] John Gano (1727-1804) was born at Hopewell, New Jersey and converted at an early age to the Baptist faith. He was ordained in 1756 and served in the Revolutionary War. After the war he focused on evangelizing in the Ohio Valley, and was a key figure in the Kentucky revivals at the end of the century. Brackney, *Dictionary of the Baptists*, 241. It was Gano who recommended Pugh as the first recipient of financial support from Hart's fund for educating ministers. Furman, *Charleston Association*, 10-11.

[80] The first Sarah Winchester died 3 July 1777 (see WNCB, 21). Elhanan then married a local girl, Sarah Luke; this explains the apparent resurrection of Sarah Winchester here. Sadly, the second Sarah Winchester, Elhanan's third wife, died on 23 January 1779 (see WNCB, 24).

1 Elhanan Winchester Pastor
2 Col. George Hicks. Deacon
3 Abel Wilds. Deacon
4 Abel Edwards Deacon
5 William Terrel Junr Deacon
6 Jenkyn David
7 William Terrel Senr.
8 Thomas James
9 Thomas Evans
10 John Evans
11 Josiah Evans
12 Thomas Shirley
13 Edward Jones
14 William Edwards
15 Mackey McNatt
16 Joshua Terrel
17 Daniel Sparks
18 Aaron Pearson
19 Moses Pearson
20 John Edwards
21 Magnus Cargill
22 John Hughes
23 John Pledger
24 Joseph Luke
25 John Geer
26 John Wilds
27 David Roach
28 James Crocker

29 John Williams
30 John Evans Junr.
31 John David
32 William Lang
33 Abel Evans
34 William Jones
35 Gresset Johnson
36 Charles Lowther
37 James Rogers
38 Edward Gillman
39 John Abran Esq.
40 William Mason
41 Thomas Harry
42 Obadiah Hudson
43 Sarah Winchest[er]
44 Sarah Hicks
45 Mary Wilds
46 Sarah Edwards
47 Elizabeth Terrel
48 Rachel David
49 Anne Terrel
50 Sarah James
51 Margaret Evans
52 Elizabeth Evans
53 Mary Evans
54 Martha Shirley
55 Mary Jones
56 Catharine Edwards

57 Dinah McNatt
58 Mary Terrel
59 Sarah Sparks
60 Winifred Pearson
61 Rachel Pearson
62 Martha Edwards
63 Sarah Cargill
64 Anne Hughes
65 Mary Andrews
66 Sarah Hewstess
67 Anne Hewstess
68 Anne Cleary
69 Anne Lide
70 Elizabeth Massey
71 Sarah Lang
72 Mary Hollingsworth
73 Elizabeth Simonson.
74 Elizabeth Counsel
75 Elizabeth Flenegald
76 Martha Evans
77 Sarah Wilds
78 Alice Lucas
79 Agnes Creele
80 Rebecca James
81 Ruth Askew
82 Ruth Wright
83 Mary Evans
84 Mary Chambliss

---

[81] This list, unlike the one included on WNCB, 17-18, does seem to be a "snapshot" of members at the date stated. All of the still active members from the 1750s and 1760s are recorded, as are other groups omitted from the WNCB, 17-18 list, such as those admitted in 1774, 1776, and the first half of 1777. The list above provides a helpful portrait of the church shortly before the great revival of 1779; it includes a respectable number of members, but far short of the 200+ that belonged to the church at the end of 1779; all members on this 1778 list were white, and the gender balance was equal.

April 20th

Died Mrs Elizabeth Simonson; She was formerly the wife of the Rev^d Mr James, first Minister of this Church.

[24]

1778
May 3rd
Anne Hargrove was baptized and received to communion.

June 7th
2 Baptized
Mahitabel Irby was received by letter from Cashaway Church.

This day Sarah Pledger the wife of John Pledger, and Eddy Johnson the wife of Gresset Johnson were examined and baptized.[82]

Septr 26th
Died Mrs Sarah Wilds.

Octr 31st
At our monthly Meeting brother Thomas Shirley and Martha his wife, were dismissed to any Church of the same faith and order.
" "

Eddy Johnson was this day received as a member in full communion, having been baptized before.
Petition for an act of incorporation
Agreed that Mr Winchester draw up a petition to the General Assembly in behalf of the Church, to obtain an act of Incorporation, according to the Constitution of this State.[83]

---

[82] The lack of entries for July and August is due to Winchester's absence in Virginia during the summer. Winchester, *Universal Restoration,* iv-v.

[83] South Carolina's new constitution, which disestablished the Church of England and gave all Protestant denominations equal status, was approved on 19 March 1778. Nadelhaft, *Disorders of War,* 38. Among the new opportunities for Dissenting churches was the possibility of legal incorporation. Perhaps the most important benefit of incorporation was that the church's property would enjoy more effective legal protection. Hiatuses between pastors and schisms within congregations could create considerable confusion about the ownership of church property. Welsh Neck did not achieve incorporation at this stage, no doubt because of the imminent escalation of the Revolutionary War, but it was incorporated in 1785 under Edmund Botsford's pastorate. See WNCB, 36.

Decr 5th
At our monthly Meeting Benjamin James and Jane his wife brought a letter from Cashaway Church, and were received members of this.

1779
Jan'ry 23rd
Died Mrs Sarah Winchester.

March 21st
Mr John Geer died.

April 1st
Mr Joseph Luke died.
  " *14th*
Mr William Jones died.
  " *25th*
Mrs Sarah Sparks died.

May 2nd
This day being Sunday Mary Cooper was examined, and baptized.
  " *9th*
Sunday _ Elizabeth Pledger was examined, and baptized
  " *30th*
4 persons baptized
  " . Anne Stevens, Mary Evans, wife of John Evans Junr, and Mary and Elizabeth Walsh were examined and baptized.

June 4th
At our monthly meeting, Mary Cooper, Elizabeth Pledger, Anne Stevens, Mary Evans, and Mary & Elizabeth Walsh were received to full communion and signed the Covenant: having all been baptized before.
  Walter Downes was received to his place again, making a confession, and promising amendment for the future. Likewise Charles Lowther who had long neglected his duty made great satisfaction to the Church, came and took his place in an humble manner; and signed the covenant, which he had never done before. Also, Walter Downes again signed the same.__ Gideon Parish, Sarah Lack, Lydia Howel, Sarah Fearson, Zilpah Walsh, Mary Wilds, Rhoda Booth, Martha Wilson, and Mary Cox were admitted to the ordinance of baptism: all giving great satisfaction: Glory to God!
9 person baptized

[25]

1779
June 9ᵗʰ

Sarah Lack, Lydia Howel, Sarah Fearson, Zilpah Walsh, Mary Wilds, Rhoda Booth, Martha Wilson and Mary Cox were received to full communion and signed to covenant.

16 persons baptized

Also the same day Sampson Thomas Robert White, Josiah Pearce, and Mary Pearce his wife, Nancy Williamson, Susannah Bingham, Elizabeth Hewson, Rebecca Scott, Mary Griffiths, Sarah Foster, Tabitha Williamson, Phebe Pledger, Sedona Upthegrove, Mary Hudson, Celia James, and Elizabeth Hodges were examined and baptized.

Saturday " 12ᵗʰ

Sampson Thomas, Josiah Pearce, Mary Pearce, Nancy Williamson, Susannah Bingham, Rebecca Scott, Elizabeth Hewson Phebe Pledger, Celia James, and Sedona Upthegrove, were received to full communion (all having been baptized before) and signed, the Covenant.__

9 persons baptized

Also the same day Welcome Hodges, Daniel McDaniel, Elizabeth Luke, Elizabeth Thomas, Charity Hurd, Martha McNatt, Mary Evans, Peggy Darby, and Celete Morgan were baptized.

Sunday " 13ᵗʰ

Daniel McDaniel, Robert White, Welcome Hodges, Sarah Foster, Mary Hudson, Peggy Darby, Tabitha Williamson, Elizabeth Luke, Martha McKnatt, Charity Hurd, Elizabeth Hodges, Mary Evans, and Celete Morgan were admitted as members of the Church, and signed the covenant, having all been baptized.

As also John Stinson who formerly belonged to a church in North Carolina.

4 persons baptized

Col Thomas Lide, Ann Peggy Ayers, Sarah Downes and Feribe Lang were baptized.

Saturday " 19ᵗʰ

Gideon Parish, Sarah Pledger (wife of John Pledger) and Mary Griffiths were received into full communion, and signed the covenant; having been baptized before.

Sunday " 20ᵗʰ

Col Thomas Lide, Sarah Downes, Anne Peggy Ayer, and Feribe Lang were received to full communion, and signed the covenant; having been baptized before.

5 persons baptized

This day John Downes, Matthew Griffiths, Deborah Geer, Elizabeth Lide and Elizabeth Hicks were baptized.

Saturday " 26th
4 Baptized
Elizabeth Sutton, the wife of John Sutton, Anne Lowther, the wife of Charles
Lowther, Martha Pearce, and Martha Lampley were baptized.
Sunday " 27th
15 persons baptized
John Downes, Elizabeth Lide, Deborah Geer, Elizabeth Sutton, Anne Lowther,
Elizabeth Thomas, Martha Pearce, Elizabeth Hicks, and Martha Lampley were
admitted as members, and signed the covenant, having been baptized before.
   William Hewson, William James, & Sarah James his wife, Joseph Mason, and
Elizabeth Mason his wife, John Stevens, Sarah Steward, Sarah Evans, Hannah
Kimbough, Sarah Walden, Catharine Ross, Sarah Stubbs, Mary Vaun, Mary
Anne Fitzgerald and Eddy Stinson were examined and baptized.
        continued __

[26]

1779
June 27th
5 baptized Negroes
Likewise at the same time, were baptized Mingo (servant of Mr. Aaron David)
Plato, Stephen, Darion and Leannah servants of Col McIntosh.[84]

July 3rd
At our monthly meeting, William Hewson, William and Sarah James, Joseph
and Elizabeth Mason, Matthew Griffiths, John Stevens, Sarah Steward, Sarah
Evans, Hannah Kimbrough, Sarah Walden, Catharine Ross, Sarah Stubbs Mary
Vaun, Mary Anne Fitzgerald, and Eddy Stinson were received to the
Communion, and signed the covenant, having been baptized before.
Call to Mr. Winchester renewed.
The Church unanimously gave a call to Mr Winchester for another year, which
he accepts, with these qualifications _ that they continue to be all agreed to a
single person and not otherwise: and also if he should not like, he might be
allowed to depart any time.
11 persons baptized

---

[84] This is the first instance of the baptism of enslaved men and women. It was a
landmark moment in the history of the eighteenth-century Welsh Neck Church, with
black members forming an increasing proportion of the total. By the end of Botsford's
pastorate in 1796, black members outnumbered whites (see WNCB, 42).

Enoch Evans Junr, Sarah Kolb, Isabel David, Eleanor Hewstess, Rachel Groves, Elizabeth Luke, Lydia Evans, Celete Luke, and Honor Darby were baptized _ as also <u>two servants</u> of M^{ts} Martha Evans viz Isaac and Tilla.
" *13th*

Enoch Evans Junr, Sarah Kolb, Isabel David, Eleanor Hewstess, Rachel Groves, Elizabeth Luke, Lydia Evans, and Celete Luke were received to full communion, and signed the Covenant; having been baptized before.
2 baptized
Anne Lampley and Anne Roach were examined and baptized.
" *24th*

10 persons baptized
Joseph Pledger, Jeremiah Brown, John Chambliss, William Cherry, Alexander Walden, Hall Hudson, Eleanor Hudson, Lydia Treeweeks, Mary Lide, and Susannah Lampley were examined and baptized
Anne Lampley, and Honor Darby were this day received to communion, and signed the covenant, having been baptized before.
" "

Comfort Pearson was received as a member of this Church; She was baptized in North Carolina, by the Rev^d Mr. Moore Junr.
" *25th*

Jeremiah Brown, Joseph Pledger, John Chambliss, Alexander Walden, William Cherry, Hall Hudson, Anne Roach, Eleanor Hudson, Lydia Trewicks, Elizabeth Medford, Susannah Lampley, and Mary Lide were received to Union and communion with the church, and signed the covenant; having been baptized before.
" "

27 persons baptized
Thomas Ayer, Elizabeth Raburn and Bibby Bruce were baptized. As also Scipio, Sancho, Pompey, Dundee, Fanny, Cretia and Nancy (servants of Col McIntosh) and Boston and Mingo, (servants of Thomas Evans), Robert and Priss (servants of Abel Wilds), Frank (svt of William Ellerbe), Will (svt of Col Kershaw), and Will servant of John Wilds, and Ludlow (servt of Est of Hart), Jethro (svt of Job Edwards), Hampton (svt of the widow Lide), and Sue (svt of Charles Mason).
" *27th*
Died Josiah Pearce.
" *31st*

9 baptized
Monthly meeting, Capt Abel Kolb, Matthew Hewstess, John Hewstess, Agnes Hewstess (his wife), William Hewstess, James Hewstess, Henry Sparks, Burrel Huggins, & Sarah Cherry were baptized.

[27]

1779
Sunday Augt 1st
34 persons baptized

Capt Abel Kolb, Matthew Hewstess, John Hewstess, William Hewstess, James Hewstess, Thomas Ayer, Henry Sparks, Burrel Huggins, Agnes Hewstess, Sarah Cherry, Elizabeth Raburn, and Bibbe Bruce were received to union and communion with the Church, and signed the Covenant, having been baptized before.

This day Michael Fitzgerald, Charles Mason, Shadrack Fuller, Arnold Colvin, Owen Darby, Elizabeth Akins, Mary Huggins, Grace Brown, Catharine McIver, Sarah Raburn, and Elizabeth Ayer were examined and baptized.__ as also Sharper, Dick, Bosen, London, Sam, George, Joe and Toby, Rachel, Peggy, and Patty (servants of Col Alexander McIntosh. Morris, Essex and Joe (svts of Capt Jeremiah Brown), Caesar and Jim (svts of Joshua Edwards), Volentine (svt of Col Kershaw), Sam (svt of Capt Abel Kolb), Harry (svt of Charles Mason), Ned (svt of Benj: Williamson, Chloe (svt of John Wilds, Hannah (svt of Capt Thos Ellerbe), and Beck servant of Josiah James.

" 7th

Charles Mason, Owen Darby, Arnold Colvin, Shadrack Fuller, Michael Fitzgerald, Mary Huggins, Catharine McIver, and Grace Brown, were received to union and Communion with the Church, and signed the covenant, having been baptized before.

5 persons baptized

Also Paul Baldy with Ann Baldy his wife, George Trawicks, Nancy Brown and Sarah Harry were examined and baptized.

" 8th

George Trawicks, Paul Baldy and Anne (his wife) Nancy Brown, Elizabeth Ayer, Sarah Harry and Sarah Raburn were received to union & communion with the Church, and signed the covenant; having been baptized before.

38 persons baptized

Also Capt Tristram Thomas, John & Rebecca Hodges, Thomas & Elizabeth Evans, Joel & Martha McNatt, Anne Evans, Mary Wilson, Elizabeth Jarrel, Betsy Hicks, Anne Poland & Sarah Mumford were examined and baptized, together with the following servants; Tom, Carolina, Dereford, Friday, Chloe, Sally, Caty and Sylvia (svts of Col McIntosh), York & Adamy (svts of Thos Evans) Harry & Lucy (svts of Magnus Cargill) Sharper & Lucy (of Josiah James), Dick (to Abel Edwards, Harry belonging to Josiah James), Bill, to Jno Wilds, Will to Est of David Williams Puff, belonging to Martha Evans, Lawney belonging to Mr Hubbard. Jeffrey (to Charles Mason) Amey to Jno Hewstess, Hannah to Tho⁵ Ayer. Sue, to Capt Brown.[85]

"This shall be written for the generations; and the people that shall be created, shall praise the Lord."

This day died brother John Sutton.

" [illeg.][86]

Capt Tristram Thomas, John & Rebecca Hodges, Thomas Evans Junr with Elizabeth (his wife), Joel & Martha McNatt, and Anne Poland, were received to union and communion with the Church, and signed the Covenant; having been baptized before.

[28]

1779
Augt 20th
Ch^h constituted
William Luke and Josiah James were examined and baptized.
This day the negroes were constituted into a Church by themselves.
" *22nd*

This day William Luke, Josiah James, Anne Evans, Elizabeth Jarrel, Betsy Hicks and Sarah Mumford were received to union and communion with the Church, and signed the covenant, having been baptized before.
" "

Anne Peggy Ayer intending to reside in Charleston for some time received a Letter of dismission from this Church to the " [Charleston] Church.
" *23rd*
1 Baptized
Mary Harper was baptized.
" *29th*

Mary Harper was received to union and communion with the church, and signed the covenant, having been baptized before.
31 persons baptized
Robert Hodges, Evander McIver, Jemima Bruce, Feribe Lang, wife of William Lang, and Mary Ivy were baptized. Also <u>twenty six</u> negroes who were at the same time received into fellowship, with the others in their Church, and signed the Covenant. Therefore their names are not expressed here.

Septr 5th
Conclusion of Mr Winchester's record

---

[85] There are only thirty-seven people listed here.
[86] The missing date is presumably 14 August or 15 August.

Robert Hodges, Evander McIver, Feribe Lang, and Mary Ivy were received to union and communion with the Church, & signed the covenant having been baptized.

    N.B. With the above, Mr Winchester concluded his record. It is thought that he left this Church in the month of Septr of the present year. The following N.B. is in the hand writing of Mr Botsford who succeeded Mr Winchester and will furnish some evidence of the latter part of his life.[87]

    N.B. A great many of those baptized by Mr Winchester have been excommunicated, both white and black; but the greater number of blacks; many of the latter upon examination appeared to be very ignorant of the nature of true religion

    Soon after Mr. Winchester left Pee-Dee, he fell into the error of universal restoration, which he first published in Philadelphia, where after baptizing a great many, he was the means of dividing the Baptist Church in that city.[88]

Mr. Botsford invited to take the pastor in charge.
Mr. Botsford's absence
N.B. Revd Edmund Botsford[89] Pastor of a church in Georgia, being invited, visited this Church in October 1779 and preached several sermons among us: The Church then requested that he would come and settle at this place; accordingly he came with his family in November, and continued with us, till the 1st of June 1780: at which time, on the approach [of] the British Troops, he

---

    [87] According to Winchester, it was he who invited Botsford to take his place at Welsh Neck. In autumn 1779, Winchester left for a visit to New England, as he had done in past years. Botsford agreed to take Winchester's place during this visit and promised to take over permanently if Winchester failed to return. Winchester started back south again in early 1780, but en route was persuaded to stay in Philadelphia, and so never came back to Welsh Neck. Stone, *Winchester,* 28-29. The narrative in the Church Book makes Winchester's departure sound abrupt, and Botsford's comments on Winchester do not sound like those that a chosen successor would make. See the introduction for a more complete discussion of this issue.
    [88] These "N.B.s" are a good illustration of the multiple layers of commentary in the transcription of the Church Book. The transcriber added the first N.B. to make it clear that the handwriting changed from Winchester's to Botsford's at this point in the text. The second N.B. appears to have been the first entry made in the Church Book by Botsford, presumably looking back at Winchester's revival after he took over as pastor on a permanent basis in 1782. If Botsford originally wrote the notes for 1781, he must have relied on minutes made by other church members.
    [89] Edmund Botsford (1745-1819) served as interim pastor at Welsh Neck from 1779-1780 and then on a permanent basis from 1782-1797. For more detailed biographical information, see the introduction.

left us, and went into Virginia.[90] He returned to us again in 1782. During a portion of Mr Botsford's absence, the Church was supplied by Rev[d] Joshua Lewis.

[29]

1781
Aug[t] 4th
At a Church meeting,_ having no minister of our own, we called to our assistance the Rev[d] Joshua Lewis, and the Rev[d] John Thomas.
Appointed three deacons viz John David, Magnes Cargill & Thomas Lide.
Sundry members that have walked disorderly were sent to, and cited before the Church by different messengers.

Sept[r] 1st
Joseph Pledger appeared, and satisfied the Church relative to the crime of which he was accused.
Mary Evans (widow) was called on; she gave satisfaction to the church, and is restored to her place.
Mary Walsh was called on, She also gave satisfaction & was restored. Celete Luke the same.

1782
Janry 5th
A call prented to M[r] Botsford
The Church met for business. M[r] Botsford was received into this church, and a call presented to him, to him to take the charge of the same, which Call, he accepted.[91]
Constitution of the Church at Cheraw

---

[90] The British captured Charleston (and took one Welsh Neck Church member, Abel Kolb, prisoner) on 12 May 1780; on 29 May, after the British-Loyalist victory at Waxhaws, about fifty miles northwest of Welsh Neck, the Continental Army in the Carolinas had been utterly destroyed. It is possible that Botsford's departure was prompted or at least hastened by news of Waxhaws. The British set up an important backcountry post at Cheraw, about twelve miles north of Welsh Neck, and the Pee Dee became a region of intermittent guerrilla warfare in which several Welsh Neck members were involved, until U.S. forces won back control, during the summer and fall of 1781. As violence waned, church activity resumed.

[91] Botsford had only arrived back at Welsh Neck a few days earlier; he had left Virginia on 3 December 1781 and his journey south had taken 28 days. Mallary, *Botsford,* 59.

Application being made, for those members residing at and near the Cheraw Hill to be constituted into a distinct Church: appointed Edmund Botsford, Abel Edwards, and as many of the members as can conveniently attend, to meet Mr Lewis and those members on Saturday next, at the Hill, to confer with them, and if it should appear for the glory of God, for them to be constituted into a distinct Church, Mr. Botsford to assist in the Constitution.

Revd Joshua Lewis applied to the Church, for the loan of part of the Church's Library. The request was granted: Deacon Edwards was desired to take an account of the books lent, and a receipt for them.

" *19th*
Report
N.B. The members as above appointed, and the church was constituted. The Church [met] according to appointment;[92] and brethren Botsford and Edwards reported that, they with the Revd Messrs. Mulkey and Lewis, and some others of the members, did meet on Saturday last Jany 12th at the Cheraw Hill, with those members residing at and near the same, and after some consultation, assisted in constituting them into a church: and signed a letter of dismission in the name of this Church for the following persons George Hicks, Thomas Lide and James Croker.

[Febru]ary 2nd
Elizabeth Walsh appeared and gave satisfaction to the church.
Messengers were sent to Daniel McDaniel, John Pledger, Rhod Booth, Rebecca Scott, Sarah Stubbs, Welcome Hodges, and Sarah Lang.
Concluded to deal with any member who had been guilty of plundering.
Gideon Parish was accused of plundering, he confessed it & promised to make restoration.

[March] 2nd
No church meeting on account of high water.

[30]

1782
April 6th
The Church met, and proceeded to business as follows.__ Gideon Parish was dismissed to the Church at the Cheraw Hill.__ Welcome Hodges gave

---

[92] Presumably, "met" is missing here.

satisfaction. Daniel Sparks, Tristram Thomas and Owen Darby who were accused of disorderly walking, appeared and gave the church satisfaction.

Whereas our late beloved Pastor the Rev^d Mr Winchester in the year 1779 baptized a number of negroes, and constituted them into a distinct Church, and whereas, they have no officer in the Church, and as our present Pastor does not think it duty to take the superintendency of both churches; and as we believe there are many of them truly pious, we are desirous they should enjoy the privileges of saints; we therefore desire brother Botsford to invite such of them as he might judge were pious to join this church. Accordingly the negroes were informed of the intention of the church, and applied for admission: upon which the Church requested brethren Botsford, John Evans, Josiah Evans, John Wilds, Evander McIver, Enoch Evans, John David and Abel Edwards to examine them, in order for their admission into the Church. They were examined and 46 received.

N.B. Several more of them have been received since.

May 4th

The Church requested Edmund Botsford and deacon Edwards to favour them, with a catalogue of the Books belonging to the Church, and to examine how many are missing.

The Church requested brethren Thomas Evans, William Luke and Edward Jones to make application to Mrs Kolb, for titles for the Land, on which part of the Meeting-House Stands &c.[93]

The following persons living more convenient to the Church at the [in margin: Cheraw] Hill, petitioned for dismission, and accordingly were dismissed viz._ Elizabeth Hicks, Mahetabel Irby, Hall Hudson, Eleanor Hudson, Elizabeth Flanagan, Joseph Pledger, Elizabeth Pledger, Sarah Hewstess, and Elizabeth Medford.

June 1st

Mr. Botsford and Deacon Edwards reported that our examining the Church. Books, there are 12 volumes wanting of the catalogue given by the Revd Nicholas Bedggood.

Revd Edmund Botsford applied to the church, for the loan of the books, belonging to the church, now in the hands of the widow Wilds. The same was granted and Mr Botsford desired to give a receipt.

July 6th

---

[93] Abel Kolb was killed in partisan fighting on 28 August 1781; hence Mrs. Kolb would hold the titles to her late husband's land.

The covenant read. Messrs Botsford & James were appointed to visit Rebecca Scott; Mr James to visit Edward Gilman; Mr Downes to visit Rebecca Stubbs, and Mr Botsford to visit Stinson and __ Terrel, to cite the above to meet the church, and give satisfaction for offences committed.

[31]

1782
Augt 3rd
Messrs Terrel and Stinson appeared, and gave the Church satisfaction.
Mrs Anne Brown was received into the church by Letter from Charleston church.
   " 31st
The church covenant read. Whereas Rebecca Scott and Sarah Stubbs appear to be incorrigible, concluded to excommunicate them the next Lord's day publicly_ accordingly they were excommunicated Lord's day, Septr 8th.

Septr 5th
The Church appointed Edmund Botsford, William Terrel, John Evans, Thomas Evans, Tristram Thomas, Moses Pearson and Evander McIver, delegates to represent them in the Association, which by appointment is to meet here next month.
   " "
Brother Thomas was requested to speak to Owen Darby, Joseph Mason and Mr Stephens.
   " "
Sister Mary Cooper was dismissed to any Church of the same faith & order

October 5th
The church Covenant was read: Messengers were sent to Mary Hudson.

Novr 2nd
Brother Matthew Griffin died.__ Abel Evans died.

1783
February 8th
Mary Goodwin died.

March 1st
Church covenant was read.__ Mary Hudson was excommunicated.
   " "
Alice Lucas died.

April
Church met: and Jemima Bruce received: She had been baptized by Mr. Winchester but not received into the church before.

July
Church met as usual.__ Covenant was read.

August 11th
Brother John Wilds died.

September 6th
Ministers of other denominations allowed to preach in this Church
The Church met, and proceeded to business as follows._ Concluded to insert the names of the members present at church meetings for the future.___ Concluded that our minister have the privilege to invite any ministers to preach in our place of worship of other denomination of sound principles, agreeably to our confession of faith: and who has good credentials: and none but such. Neither shall any member introduce any minister for the purpose of preaching among us, knowing him to hold principles contrary to our confession of faith.
Concluded to have a monthly meeting on the 2nd Lord's day after next monthly meeting.
Twenty members were present at this meeting. It is unnecessary to copy the names, as they can be seen by referring to the original.[94]

[32]

<u>1783</u>
Septr 13th
Obediah Hudson died. (18th) Anne Baldee died.

Octr 4th
The Church met, and appointed Edmund Botsford, Thomas Evans Junr, and Evander McIver messengers to the Association.

Decr 1st
Died Sarah James. (4th) Sarah Evans died.

---

[94] It is not clear whether this last sentence is a comment inserted by the original transcriber, or whether it was written in the original copy of the Church Book by someone (probably the Rev. Botsford) who had access to the minutes of the church meeting, where the names of those present could be found.

" 6th

The Church met for business. Covenant was read: Messengers were sent to Eddy Stinson, George Trawicks, and Magnus Cargill.

Sixteen members were present at this meeting.

1784

Janry 29th

Thomas Evans Senr died. (18th) Mary Evans wife of Josiah Evans died.

Febry 28th

Died Sarah Lang

April 3rd

The Church met for business. 19 members were present.

May 24th

Died Celete Goodwin.

June 5th

The Church met for business: Twenty five members were present. Elizabeth Gennens late Raburn who had been guilty of disorderly conduct, confessed her fault, as also Eddy Stinson who was guilty of the same crime, but were desired to desist from communion, till the Church were better satisfied of their repentance.__ Daniel McDaniel was excommunic^d. Tristram Thomas was desired to acquaint O Darby that unless he appeared and gave the Church satisfaction, he would be excommunicated next month.

5 persons baptized

Enoch Evans son of Thomas E. was baptized.__ Also Moses belonging to Genl McIntosh's Estate. Prince servant of Thos Powr Esq. Hannah servant of Danl Sparks, Maria belonging to Mrs Kolb.

2 received

John Edmundson was received by experience, and Esther Brown by letter from Catfish.

July 3rd

1 received

The Church met. 20 members were present. Mrs Trawicks wife of George T gave an account of her conversion __ was accepted.

A resolution

The Church concluded that persons guilty of the following crimes viz murder, adultery, theft, swearing or, drunkenness, should be summoned to appear at the next church meeting, after they had been accused to the church, and if such did

not appear, or send a reasonable excuse for their non-appearance, and give satisfaction of their repentance, they should be excommunicated.[95]
Mrs. Sloane, and Elizabeth Walsh were sent to, and desired to show cause, why they should not be excommunicated, they both having been guilty of disorderly conduct.

" 31st
Members present at this meeting 19.__ M[rs] Sloane appeared & gave satisfaction. Elizabeth Walsh, not being able to attend, by information of her mother, her case postponed.
1 received
Celia Evans gave an account of the work of Grace on her soul __ accepted

[33]

1784
July 31st
Owen Darby having been guilty of drunkenness several times, and as he appears to continue in the practice of that vice: and as he has note made his appearance, though often cited, concluded to excommunicate and he was, accordingly

August 22nd
4 baptized
Pen[illeg] Traweeks, Hanibel a freeman, Bob belonging to the estate of Abel Wilds, and Peg belonging to the Est of Col Kolb were baptized.
" "
Paul Baldee died[96]

Sept[r] 4th
The Church met for business as usual. 28 members were present. The Covenant was read.___ Bro Shadrack Fuller was dismissed._ Eddy Stinson gave

---

[95] This is a far more draconian procedure than that employed during the early years of the Welsh Neck Church. In earlier cases, multiple messengers of care or letters were sent before any action was taken, and, once guilt was established, suspension, rather than full excommunication, was the usual step. Quarreling, attending dancing schools, and other lesser infractions are omitted from this list; perhaps these offenses were dealt with less summarily, or perhaps the list does intend to include all misconduct, since swearing is one of the behaviors listed.

[96] The Rev. Joshua Edwards, pastor of the Welsh Neck Church from 1751-1756, also died on this date. He was no longer a member of Welsh Neck, having been dismissed to Cashaway in 1756, but he was buried in the Welsh Neck churchyard. Rippon, *Baptist Register, 1794-1797*, 500.

satisfaction._ Bro John David was sent to Elizabeth Walsh to know the reason of her not appearing as desired.

" *5th*

4 baptized

This day, communion. Celia Evans, Bina svt. of Evander McIver, Betty svt of M Cargill, and Bob were baptized, who together with those baptized before, were received into the Church.

Died Mary Hollingsworth.

Oct' 2nd

Church met: 22 members were present.__ Covenant was read.

Elizabeth Walsh's case laid over.

" *12th*

1 Bapt'd

Peter Kolb was baptized.

" *14th*

Died William Terrel.

" *31st*

John Edmundson and Rebecca his wife, were dismissed to any church of the same faith and order.

Nov' 2nd

Joshua Terrel died.

" *6th*

Church met._ Elizabeth Walsh's case laid over.

Brethren Edmund Botsford, Aaron Pearson and Evander McIver were appointed delegates to the Association in Charleston, which by appointment is to be held on Monday after the 4th Lord's day in this month.

Twenty members were present at this meeting.

1785

Janry 1st

Twenty Two members met for business. William Cherry and Sarah his wife were dismissed to Cashaway Church. Died William James.

   Whereas Elizabeth Walsh has not appeared to show cause, why she should not be excommunicated: and as it appears by information from one of the members that she has not a proper regard for her crime, concluded to excommunicate her; which was done accordingly.

" *15th*

Died Walter Downes (27th) John Hughes died.

Febry 12th

Church met for business. Sixteen members were present. Nothing was transacted worthy of record.

" *13th*

Mary Winds died.

March 19th

Died Edward Jones.

[34]

1785

April 3rd

Members present at this meeting seventeen.

Messrs Abel Edwards, John David and Evander McIver were appointed a committee to revise the church covenant, which appears to the Church to be deficient in some things.

Whereas information was given to the church, that Mary Walsh has entered herself a scholar in a dancing school. Messrs John Evans, and John David were appointed to request her to appear and answer for the same.

Moses Pearson and his wife were dismissed to Cashaway Church.

Mr. Botsford visit to Charleston

Application being made our Pastor visited the Charleston Church in February, March and a part of April. That Church being now destitute of a Pastor: he remained eight weeks; in which time he baptized Eleven persons.[97] At his return, the Church in Charleston sent a letter of thanks to this Church.

May 9th

John Stinson departed this life.

June 4th

Twenty members were present at this meeting. The messengers sent to Mary Walsh reported, that she did not choose to appear, and desired that her name might be erased from church covenant. She was therefore excommunicated. Concluded to meet on Saturday 18th inst.

" *18th*

Met according to appointment. The committee appointed to revise the church covenant reported. The covenant was presented, and after some alterations was

---

[97] In his letter to Richard Furman of 4 April 1785, Botsford noted that he had baptized 2 whites and 5 blacks, with the hope of baptizing 1 or 2 further whites later that week. Botsford's visit to Charleston did not go altogether smoothly; he fell out with one of the Charleston church's preachers, Mr. Hill, who began preaching to his supporters in his own home.

adopted unanimously. Concluded to set apart Saturday 2nd July, as a day of solemn prayer to God for his blessing on this Church, and for signing the covenant. The following is the covenant.

In pursuance of an agreement made at a Church meeting the 18th of June 1785, the following covenant contains our solemn and explicit obligation as a church of christ to God and to each other.

Church covenant adopted 1785

Knowing that it is our happiness and duty to pay a solemn regard to the laws of love, and the ordinances of the gospel, which are commanded and instituted in God's holy word. We do for the better regulation of our conduct towards God and each other, renew our covenant and do solemnly promise the serious, conscientious regard to the following articles. And to this we desire to be the more induced, by a remembrance of our past neglects and for which we would be humbled before the Lord and one another.

We promise to walk in all holiness and humility with brotherly love, that our fellowship may be more acceptable to God, agreeable to the churches of Christ and comfortable to ourselves.

We promise to watch over the conversation of each other, & not willfully to suffer sin upon one another without a gentle reproof, & that we will endeavour to stir one another up to love and good works by mutual exhortation & a good example.

[35]

1785

June 18th

We promise to pray for one another, bearing each other's burdens and to fulfil the Law of Christ, and also to pray for God's presence & power in our Assemblies and that our Church may flourish and many be added to it who shall be saved.

We promise to endeavour to keep the unity of the Spirit in the bond of peace, to bear with one another's infirmities, putting on bowels of compassion as the elect of God; to forbear rash judging; evil surmises, and reproachful or censorious language. And also that we will not expose the weakness or faults of any to others either within or without the Church, without some special necessity and in point of duty, and always in conformity to the rule given us by own Saviour 18 chap Matthew.

We promise each for ourselves, that if God gives us children to bring up, whether our own or others, that we will use our utmost endeavours, to bring them up in the nurture and admonition of the Lord, setting good and wholesome examples before them, praying with and for them. That we will keep a strict watch over their conduct, and at all convenient seasons, give them such advice, admonition and correction as their cases shall appear to require and that we will take due care to have them taught to read and to learn the chatechism, and also that we will use our authority to keep them as much as possible from wicked company and vain pleasures such as playing at cards, dice and other unlawful games, and from going to dances, balls and sinful assemblies, and horse races, &c.-- and as we will not allow it in our children, neither will we practice such things ourselves, knowing that a companion of fools shall be destroyed, and that lovers of pleasure are not lovers of God. And we likewise promise, that if we should be remiss in the practice of these duties, that we will submit to, and thankfully receive the friendly reproof of a brother, or the Church.

We promise to meet together every Lord's day, and at all other opportunities as divine providence shall permit, for the public worship of God; likewise attend all the meetings of the Church for business, (of which public notice shall be given) keeping our places in the House of God as becometh Saints; not forsaking the assembling ourselves together, as the manner of some is.

We promise that if we should be possessed of negro or other slaves, that we will act a truly christian part by them; by giving them good advice, laying our commands on them to attend the worship of God in public on Lord's days & in private in our families when convenient & we also promise, that we will not treat them with cruelty, nor prevent their obtaining religious knowledge, & will endeavour to prevent their rambling: and will encourage those who can read, at proper times to instruct others; & in all things endeavour to act in our families, as to obtain the blessing of God.[98]

[36]

1785

June 18ᵗʰ

We promise to strive together for the truth of the gospel and the purity of gospel Institutions; desiring by the grace of God, to live and die in the faith of God's elect; constantly and steadily adhering to the glorious doctrines of free grace: __ Such as a Trinity of persons in the Godhead, particular and personal ~~redemption~~ election, the everlasting love of God: the covenant of grace; the fall of Adam: particular redemption through the incarnation; obedience, sufferings: death: resurrection, and intercession of the Son of God: pardon though his blood: justification by his righteousness: the efficacious grace of the Holy Spirit in

---

[98] The provisions regarding the encouragement of public worship and religious education among slaves and refraining from cruelty towards them were new additions to the Church Covenant; the former version of this Covenant, set out in the Church Book on 2 August 1760, said nothing about slaves (see WNCB, 5-6). The reference here to "negro and other slaves" may suggest that some members of the Church held Native American slaves.

regeneration; the perseverance of the Saints in grace to glory: the resurrection of the dead & eternal life: with all those doctrines connected with or dependant on them, as more fully set forth in our confession of faith, adopted by the Charleston Association: the administration of baptism by immersion to those persons professing their faith in Christ, and to them only, likewise the administration of the Lord's Supper as directed in the word of God.

We promise that with the ability, which God shall be pleased to give us, we will freely contribute to the support of the minister, whom the Lord shall be pleased to make our shepherd, and that we will endeavour daily to pray for a blessing upon his labours.

These and all other evangelical duties, we resolve and promise by the grace and strength of our Lord Jesus, honestly to perform, and for our being at last admitted into the Church triumphant in Heaven, we desire to trust entirely upon his precious blood and spotless righteousness.

The following no doubt was transacted about the same time.

Petition for an act of incorporation.

We the members of the Baptist Church at the Welch-Neck on Pee Dee River, in the State of South Carolina, desirous to be incorporated according to the Constitution and Laws of said State: Do therefore agree to and subscribe the following five articles as our belief viz[99]

First-That there is one eternal God, and a State of future rewards & punishment.

Second-That God is publicly to be worshipped.

Third-That the Christian religion is the true religion.

Fourth-That the Holy Scriptures of the old & new Testament are of divine inspiration, & are the rule of faith & practice.

Fifth-That it is lawful, and the duty of every man being thereunto called, by those that govern to bear witness to truth.

Incorporation

N.B. The Church was incorporated as per Act of Assembly 1785.

July 2ⁿᵈ

---

[99] It is interesting to reflect that in the early years of the United States, when church and state were in the process of becoming more separate at both state and federal level, a legal instrument such as an act of incorporation could be used to define church doctrine. One purpose of including beliefs in such an instrument was to clarify who got to keep the church building and other property in cases of schism within the congregation. Baptist churches in Charleston underwent protracted legal battles over control, between groups with different interpretations of doctrine. The Church Book referred above (WNCB, 28) to the division of Elhanan Winchester's church in Philadelphia over the doctrine of the Restoration; that division involved a bitter dispute over control of property. Stone, *Winchester*, 44-57.

After prayer, sermon &c., we proceeded to sign the covenant: about 52 members signed it: several were absent and it was concluded that at the next monthly meeting those who are absent be requested to sign it.

[37]

1785
August 6ᵗʰ
2 received for baptism
After reading the covenant, those who had not before, signed their names.__
Jesse Evans, and Rachel Evans were examined for baptism, and received. Rebecca Hodges was dismissed to Cashaway Church.
2 baptized
N.B. Jesse & Rachel Evans were baptized.

Octʳ 1ˢᵗ
At this Church meeting brethren Tristram Thomas and E. Botsford were appointed delegates to attend the Association at the High-Hills of Santee. N.B. This day a demand was made of the legacies left the Church by Thomas and Josiah James.

Decʳ 27ᵗʰ
Departed this life, Mʳˢ Sarah Wilds, daughter of Mʳ James James.

1786
March 31ˢᵗ
Church Meeting Members present Edmund Botsford, Abel Edwards, John David etc. The following brethren were chosen Trustees for the Church viz Edmund Botsford, Abel Edwards, John David, Enoch Evans, Evander McIver, Thomas Evans, Josiah Evans, Enoch Evans Junr, Jesse Evans and Abel Goodwin. Any Three of the above to transact business. Abel Edwards chosen acting Trustee. Several brethren were desired to speak to some of the members who had acted disorderly.

Septʳ 30ᵗʰ
2 excommunicated
4 dis by letter
Church Meeting. Present nineteen members. John Stephens and Charles Mason were excommunicated.__ Bʳ Tristam Thomas and wife, John Williams and S Bingham were dismissed by Letter.

Novʳ 4ᵗʰ

3 ex

Church meeting. Present Sixteen members.__ The following persons were excommunicated: viz William Luke, Edy Stinson, and Scipio a negro.

Decr 2nd

Church meeting. Present Ten members.__ John David and Evander McIver were appointed to settle with Josiah Evans and Thomas Evans for monies left to the church by Josiah James and Thomas James. Evander McIver was desired to assist the Deacons.

1787
Janry 7th
Church meeting. Nothing to record
Febry 3rd
Church meeting. No record

March 3rd

Church meeting. Concluded that agreeably to the word of God it is not right that one member should sue another.
    " *31st*
Church meeting.__ Requested Thomas Evans to have the Titles of Land given by Mr Kolb proven and recorded: and Edmund Botsford to speak to Rev^d Mr Lewis respecting the Books borrowed of our church.

[38]

1787
Decr 1st
Funds left to the Church
Church meeting__ John David and Evander McIver who were appointed to settle with Josiah Evans and Thomas Evans _ Reported as follows- amount of legacy left to the church by Thomas James in the month of February 1780 was 100 £ currency, when depreciated according to Law is 6/9 sterling. The amount left by Josiah James was 10,000 £ currency, when depreciated is 28 £ sterling.[100]

---

[100] During and after the Revolutionary War, South Carolina issued its own paper money. Economic problems in the state meant that South Carolina pounds or "currency" rapidly lost value against British sterling, a stable and safe form of money. After the war, trade with Britain resumed and sterling was again widely used. The state government set conversion rates between the two monetary systems. Once the new U.S. constitution

1788
Febry 2nd
Church meeting.__ Alexander Walden and wife dismissed by Letter. Appointed a day of Fasting, and Prayer for a revival of religion.

May 3rd
1 excom.
Church meeting.__ Welcome Hodge was excommunicated.
N.B. From the commencement of 1786 concluded to record in this Book only such things as are deemed necessary to be kept on record, out of the minutes taken at each Church meeting.[101]

Sept 27th
Appointed our brethren, Edmund Botsford, Josiah Evans & Thomas Evans messengers to the Association.

Nov 7th
1 died
Died Arnold Colvin
Decr 31st [102]
1 died
Died Nancy Gilman.

1789
July 11th
1 ex
2 negro baptism
Church meeting.__ Betsy Raburn excommunicated for adultery.
Two negroes were examined for baptism.

Augt 1st

1787 was ratified, the Federal government was able to replace weak state currencies with a single national currency.

[101] One aspect of this limit of information in the Church Book to what was "deemed necessary" is that the last baptisms recorded were those of these two African Americans on 11 July 1789; it is known that 30 were baptized during the revival of 1790 and 16 during Rev. Botsford's last year in 1796, but the names of these and any others were omitted. The Book continued to record excommunications, deaths, and property matters until the end.

[102] Botsford's letter to Richard Furman, dated 17 December 1788, shows that he spent part of this month in Georgetown.

Church meeting._ Appointed Messrs Abel Edwards, Abel Goodwin; Enoch Evans and Evander McIver to enquire of Capt. Dewitt the boundary of the Land on which the Meeting-House stands, and to report the next meeting.
1 dismissed
Comfort Hinley was dismissed.

Sept' 5th
Church meeting.
Oct' 3rd
Ditto
    " 31st
    " [Ditto]
Dec' 5th
Ditto
1790
Janry 2nd
Church meeting. nothing to record.
Febry 6th
Ditto " " ....
    " 8th
1 died
Died Josiah Evans
March 9th
1 died
Died Susanna Botsford[103]
May 1st
Church met _ nothing to record.[104]
June 1st
Church met.[105] Abel Edwards, Evander McIver, and Thomas Evans appointed by the Trustees a committee to settle the church's funds.

---

[103] This brief note refers to the death of Botsford's wife, Susanna. For a more personal statement of Botsford's grief at her passing, see his letter to Richard Furman, 15 March 1790, his letter to Oliver Hart of 6 April 1790 (Mallary, *Botsford*, 71), and his eulogy in Rippon, *Baptist Register, 1790-1793*, 104-105.

[104] In his letter to Rippon's *Baptist Register,* sent in the late summer or fall of 1790, Botsford looked back at the May meeting very differently. It was at this meeting that he proposed Monday evening prayer meetings, a practice that stimulated the revival of 1790-1791. The first of these meetings, on 10 May, was so successful that he immediately decided to suggest the practice to other churches in the local area. Rippon, *Baptist Register, 1790-1793,* 104-105.

Samuel Evans was appointed a Trustee in the place of Josiah Evans dec[d]

[39]

1790
July 31st
Church met. Agreed that a Bond given by Thomas Evans for the sum of [blank] the legacy left this church by Josiah James deceased, shall be considered as a fund for the church, not to be used for any purpose for a year to come.[106]
Committee to have meeting house repair[d] appointed.
Abel Edwards, John David, M McNatt, Enoch Evans and Evander McIver are appointed a committee to adopt a plan for the repair of the meeting-House, and enclosing the graveyard, and place the same before the Church at their next meeting.

Sept[r] 4th
Report of the above committee
1dis by letter
The Church met. The committee above mentioned, reported _That it will be necessary to have new sills, and the House raised on pillars of brick, and a new Pulpit: To have the stairs of the Gallery removed and a Shed the length of the House ___ feet wide for the use of the negroes and a good board and post fence around the burying ground. All of which they suppose will amount to 120 £ Sterling._ Daniel Sparks was dismiss[d]. Deacon Edwards was requested to procure a small Trunk to deposit the papers in, which belong to the Church.

Oct[r] 16th
Church met. Messrs Botsford, Edwards and McIver were chosen to represent the Church in the Association.

Dec[r] 25th
Church met. N.B. A great revival this year. Thirty were baptized.[107]

---

[105] This date cannot be correct, unless the church deviated from its usual practice of meeting on the first Saturday of each month. 1 June 1790 was a Tuesday; presumably, the meeting was on 5 June.

[106] The amount of the legacy was omitted in the original transcription, and a blank left instead; possibly the amount in the original document was illegible. The entry for 1 December 1787 above states that Josiah James left £10,000 currency, the equivalent of £28 sterling. In his letter to Richard Furman of 17 August 1791, Botsford reported that there was about £40 in the church's fund, and that he hoped to augment it annually. The Josiah James legacy seems to have been the beginning of an endowment for the Welsh Neck Church.

1791
March 5ᵗʰ
Plan for educating ministers adopted
Church met: Agreed to adopt the plan proposed by the Association for raising a fund, to support young men in their preparation for the ministry.[108]_ The following Brethren were appointed a committee to hear the experience of Negroes; and to settle any matters among them viz-- Edmund Botsford, Abel Edwards, John David, Enoch Evans Senr, Thomas Evans, Enoch Evans junr, and Evander McIver.
1 dis by letter
Mary Cochran was dismissed._ Monday next a day of prayer.[109]

April 2ⁿᵈ
Monday next a day of prayer
" 29ᵗʰ
Monday a day of prayer

June 4ᵗʰ
Church met. John Bennet was dismissed.

July 2ⁿᵈ
Church met. A charity Sermon to the preachers.[110]

---

[107] This revival was due in part to Botsford's decision to adopt the practice of holding special prayer meetings once a month on Monday evenings, a practice already in force among certain Baptist churches in England. These meetings, which began on 10 May 1790, attracted significant numbers and brought young people, especially, into the church. Botsford's different approach to the Church Book, compared to his predecessors', is evident in his failure to record the baptisms inspired by this revival or indeed to say very much about this important development at all; elsewhere, he waxes enthusiastic about the prayer meetings and conversions of 1790-1791. For example, we learn from his letter to the *Baptist Register* that eleven were baptized on Sunday, 22 August 1790. See Botsford, Letter to Richard Furman, 4 August 1790 and Rippon, *Baptist Register, 1790-1793*, 104-105, 108.

[108] The plan to create this fund was proposed at the Charleston Association meeting at Black Swamp in December 1789 and adopted at its November 1790 meeting. Rippon, *Baptist Register, 1790-1793*, 100-101, 112-114. Botsford had benefited from a similar fund that Oliver Hart had created during the pre-Revolutionary period. Mallary, *Botsford*, 36-38.

[109] These monthly Monday days of prayer, instituted by Botsford on 10 May 1790, were only recorded in the Church Book at this point. Rippon, *Baptist Register, 1790-1793*, 104-105.

August 6th
The committee appointed to wait on Capt Dewitt, reported that they had settled the business.[111]__ Brother Botsford was requested to cite Charles Lide to appear & to answer the accusation charged against him.

[40]

1791
Septr 3rd
1 excluded
Church met. Charles Lide was excommunicated. This had been a very promising youth.[112]__ Abel Edwards, Enoch Evans & Evander McIver were requested to lease a piece of Land of Mr. Benjamin Kolb adm^{er} of the Estate of Col Kolb.

Octr 8th
Association Convened at W.N.
Church met: Appointed Messrs A Edwards, J David, Thomas Evans Enoch Evans Jnr, Enoch Evans Junr and Edmund Botsford to represent the Church in the Association to be held here.[113]

---

[110] Per Botsford's letter to Richard Furman, 17 August 1791, the collection to support the Association's fund for educating prospective ministers raised only a few dollars in cash, but pledges amounted to £14.

[111] This committee had been appointed on 1 August 1789 and was supposed to report at the next church meeting. Clearly the issue took far longer to resolve than they had originally thought.

[112] Charles Lide had been baptized at the beginning of August, 1790. In his letter to Richard Furman of 4 August 1790, Botsford spoke of the 14-year-old Lide in glowing terms: "I almost fear to say all I might in justice say respecting him, however I must inform you he is a kind of prodigy." On 17 August 1791 Botsford wrote to Furman that Lide "has turned his Back on the good Way & appears much worse than before his Reformation..."

[113] Enoch Evans, Jr. is named twice; possibly Enoch Evans, Sr. is meant. The Association met at Welsh Neck from 5-9 November 1791. Nine churches sent representatives. The first two days were spent in worship. The business meeting began on Monday, 7 November. Correspondence from local churches and from churches in Virginia, Kentucky, Philadelphia, and England was read. Guidelines were laid down to ensure that unfit candidates were not ordained for the ministry, and Richard Furman announced a plan to apply for legal incorporation of the Association's education committee. Botsford was appointed to deliver the official sermon at this Association meeting, but he was too unwell, and Henry Holcombe preached instead. Rippon, *Baptist Register, 1790-1793,* 300-302; Furman, *Charleston Association,* 42. Botsford did deliver the opening sermon at the Bethel Association meeting in August 1793. Rippon, *Baptist Register, 1794-1797,* 193.

Decr 3rd
Church met. Monday next a day of prayer.

1792
Febry 4th
Church met. No record.
March 3rd
Ditto. "   "   "
" 17th

Agreed to raise Three pounds towards printing Mr. Holcombe's sermon preached at Association.[114]

May 12th
Rent of Pews
Church met: The price fixed for the Seats, are as follows._ The Two front Seats at £5 each. The next at £4.10s. The back ones at £3. Mr. McIntosh's at £6.

June 2nd
Church met. No Record.
June 30th
Ditto "   "   "
Augt 4th
Ditto "   "   "
Sept^r
Ditto "   "   "

Octr 6th
Church met: Appointed Messrs Botsford, McIver, Vining to represent the Church in the Association at Coosawhatchie. Botsford one of the committee as he was last year.[115]

1793
Janry 5th
2 dismissed 1 excluded

---

[114] Henry Holcombe (1762-1824) was pastor at Beaufort. His address at the Charleston Association's 1791 meeting at Welsh Neck, entitled *A Sermon, containing a brief illustration and defense of the Doctrine commonly called Calvinistic*, was printed in Charleston by Markland and McIver in 1793. Evans, *American Bibliography*, #25616.

[115] Botsford preached the opening sermon, on Psalm 138, at this Association meeting. Rippon, *Baptist Register, 1790-1793*, 539-540.

Church met. Eli Burdo & his wife Eve were dismissed. Moses a negro excommunicated. Monday a meeting for Prayer.

March 2nd
Church met. no record made.
March 22nd
State of the Church
When Mr Winchester left this church there were 220 white persons members which was in September 1779.[116] At this time there are but 48 of those left in the Church. The rest are dead, dismissed, excommunicᵉᵈ or gone to other parts.

April 6th
Several members were written to.
May 4th
Church met. No record made. Revd John Gano visited us this month.[117]
June 4th
Ditto " " " "
August 31st
Ditto " " " "
October 5th
Abel Goodwin was excommunicted.[118] Enoch Evans Junr & Joseph Cook were appointed to represent us in the Association, to meet at the High Hills.
" *12th*
Death of A Edwards
Abel Edwards died. 5th May 1777 he was chosen Deacon. He was much esteemed in life & his death much lamented.[119] In Novr our pastor extremely ill.

---

[116] This number is roughly confirmed by the addition of all long-standing members, plus those baptized by Pugh in 1774 and those baptized during 1776 and early 1777 to the incomplete list on WNCB, 17-18. Presumably, Botsford wrote this note, and its import is that declining numbers can be explained by Winchester's over-eagerness to baptize all comers, including many who were not truly called by God.

[117] For biographical information re. John Gano, see note 79 above (WNCB, 22).

[118] A later entry on 4 October 1794 (WNCB, 41) states that the excommunication was mistakenly entered here, during 1793, instead of 1794. This comment raises questions about how this transcription was compiled: was information being incorporated from other sources, written or oral?

[119] An obituary of Abel Edwards by Botsford appeared in Rippon, *Baptist Register, 1794-1797*, 500-502. He was born in Pennsylvania in 1739, moved with his father to South Carolina in 1749. His father, Joshua, was pastor of the Welsh Neck Church from 1751 to 1756, when he moved to Cashaway. Abel was baptized at Cashaway and in 1761 was received by letter into Welsh Neck. He became deacon in 1777. He married Sarah Douthy; they had three children. Abel was buried next to his father at Welsh Neck.

[41]

1794
Janry 4ᵗʰ
The Church met. A committee was appointed to inquire into the case of Mary Ann Baker, and report to the Church.

Febry 1ˢᵗ
Deacon chosen. Committee appointed to settle legacies &c.
Church meeting. Evander McIver was this day chosen Deacon. Evander McIver and Enoch Evans Junr were appointed to settle with Mʳˢ Wilson, and the Executors of Josiah Evans, the Legacies left to the Church by Doctor James P. Wilson and Josiah Evans.

  The Executors of Abel Edwards were requested to procure a Bond and Security of John MᶜIntosh for the sum of £ 100 in his hands left to the Church by Abel Edwards. Enoch Evans Junr was requested to assist the Deacons in their office.

March 1ˢᵗ
Church meeting: Deacon John David and Enoch Evans Junr were appointed to request of the Revᵈ Joshua Lewis, either to return the Books loaned him by the Church, or to pay for them.¹²⁰

April 5ᵗʰ
Church meeting: no record.

May 3̶1̶ˢ̶ᵗ̶ 3ʳᵈ
1 rec'd by letter
Robert Parsley was received by letter; from the Church on Deep Creek.¹²¹
  " *31ˢᵗ*
Church meeting: Deacons David & McIver and Enoch Evans Junr were requested to meet a committee from the Church at Cheraw Hill respecting the Books loaned the Revᵈ Mr. Lewis.

July 5ᵗʰ

---

  ¹²⁰ These books had been borrowed by the Rev. Lewis when the church at Cheraw Hill was established on 5 January 1782 (WNCB, 29). The church meeting of 31 March 1787 had asked Botsford to talk to Lewis about returning the books (WNCB, 37).
  ¹²¹ Deep Creek was located on the road between Cheraw and Camden between ten and twenty miles from Welsh Neck.

Church meeting: Some members were written to: and some were appointed to wait on others &c.

Aug^t
No meeting: There being a Freshet in the River.
Septr 6th
The church met: no record made.

Octr 4th
Committee appointed to receive Bond &c
Church met: The church unanimously agreed to receive a Bond of Messrs Drury Robertson & Morgan Brown, for One Hundred pounds Sterling: the legacy of Abel Edwards. The following is a copy of the receipt given by the Church for the same __ Rec^d this 4th October 1794 of Mrs Sarah Edwards Ex^x & Edward Edwards & Evander McIver Ex^ors of the Est of the late Abel Edwards a Bond for £100 on Drury Robertson & Morgan Brown rec^d by us, as full satisfaction, for the legacy left by the said Abel Edwards, to the incorporate Baptist Church at Welch-Neck, Pee-Dee. Done at our church meeting, 4th Octr 1794 and ordered by the Church, to be signed for & in behalf of the whole church. Edmund Botsford, John David, Enoch Evans Senr Trustees for said Church. Appointed E. Botsford, Deacon McIver, and Jno Killingsworth to the Association.
      " 4th
Abel Goodwin excomm^td for immorality and apostacy. See page 40 Octr 5th inserted this mistake.
Novr 6th
1 died
Enoch Evans Junr died.
December 6th
Church meeting: Some members were sent to. Martin Dewitt was appointed to assist Evander McIver in settling the legacies left to the Church

[42]

1795
Janry 10th
The Church: no record made.

March 6th
1 excluded
The Church met: Mary Ann Baker was excommunicated for marrying a man whose wife was living. The Church agreed to loan brother Botsford £100 sterling for one year, and give him the interest due on the Church's funds. John

David, Thomas Evans, Macky McNatt & Evander McIver are appointed a committee to settle this business. NB. The loan was not executed.

May 2ⁿᵈ
1 dismissed
The Church met: John Williams was dismissed.

Augᵗ 1ˢᵗ
1 dis
The Church met: Barbara Judith was dismissed. Concluded to have prayer meetings, on the days the Church meets for business.

Octʳ 6ᵗʰ
Appointed E. Botsford, John David & Evʳ McIver to represent the Church in the Association. E. Botsford to be on the Genl Committee.

Decʳ 5ᵗʰ
1dis
The Church met: Agnes Creel was dismissed.
1796
Janry 2ⁿᵈ
1ex
The Church met: Rachel David was excommunicated.

Febry 7ᵗʰ
1died
Caty Botsford died.[122]
April 2ⁿᵈ
The Church met: several members were sent to.
  " 7ᵗʰ
1died
Sealy Evans died.[123]
  " 30ᵗʰ

---

[122] Edmund Botsford was widowed twice while at Welsh Neck; see above, 9 March 1790, for the death of Susanna (WNCB, 38). His letter to Richard Furman of 10 March 1796 describes his grief and spiritual struggles after losing Caty. His letters to Furman on 10 April and 3 May 1796 indicate that Caty died "in child-bed." She had had many difficult pregnancies; her husband's letter of 27 April 1793 refers to six deliveries of still-born children.

[123] Sealy Evans may be the church member who, like Caty Botsford, died in childbirth at this time. Botsford to Furman, 10 April 1796.

The Church met: nothing to record.
June 4th
The Church met: Several members appeared & gave satisfaction. Bro.. Botsford informed the Church, that he should give up the pastoral charge of the Church, at the close of this year.
July 2nd
Macky McNat, Martin Dewitt & Joseph Jones appointed Trustees in the place of those who are dead. Ev^r McIver appointed acting Trustee. Agreed to give Mr Botsford the interest due on the Church's funds.
Augt 6th
1 dis. 1 ex
Church met: Elizabeth Mason was dismissed. Thomas Evans was excommunicated.
Octr 14th
1 ex
Church met: Thomas Mason was excommunicated.
Novr 5th
Church met:_ Ordered that Mr Botsford deliver the Church's Books to Evander McIver.
Decr 3rd
Botsford &c dismissed
11 in all
Church met: The following persons were dismissed; viz. Edmund Botsford, Aaron Pearson, & his wife, Burrel Huggins & his wife, John Killingsworth & his wife, Joseph Lister & his wife, & William Beasly & his wife.[124]
" 31st
Church met: Jno Bridges & wife dismissed; Concluded to write to several gentlemen in the ministry for their assistance, while we remain destitute of a pastor. There are at this time only 31 members of the Church.[125] The others dead, dismissed etc.
Conclusion of Mr Botsford's record
This is the last record made by Mr Botsford on the minutes.

---

[124] Botsford was dismissed so that he could become pastor of the church in Georgetown, whose members had called him while he was visiting there during the fall. Letter to Richard Furman, 12 October 1796.

[125] Presumably, this number refers to white members only. On 22 March 1793, the Church Book stated there were forty-eight [white] members; since that date, the deaths, excommunications, or dismissals of twenty-seven whites were recorded, with one new member received. If the record of the losses of membership is complete, that would suggest only nine whites had been baptized during Botsford's last four years as pastor.

Edmund Botsford was born in Old England Novr 1st 1745; Arrived in Charleston 28th Janry 1766; baptized march 13th 1767, ordained March 14th 1773;[126] married Susannah Nunn July 20th 1773; came to this place Octr 1779; went to Virginia June 1st 1780, returned Decr 11th 1781. Took the charge of this church Janry 5th 1782, married Caty Evans may 3rd 1791. He baptized 92 persons who joined this church, several in Charleston and [illeg.] since his residence in this place. Janry 1st 1797, members 63 whites, 64 blacks = 127. 16 baptized in 1796.[127]

[43]

1797

Febry 4th
What follows is in the handwriting of the late venerable Deacon Evander McIver
At a church meeting- it being Saturday—the following members were present viz. _ John David, Samuel Evans, Martin Dewitt, Enoch Evans, Joseph Jones & Evr McIver. Bro John Williams's case being considered, it is agreed that the brethren on the South-west side of the River, contribute to the relief of his wants.

March 4th
Saturday, Church met: present John David, Enoch Evans, Samuel Evans, Evander McIver & Martin Dewitt. Rec^d this day 20 minutes of the last Charleston Association.

April 1st
Church met. present_ John David, Mackey McNatt, Martin Dewitt, Josiah David Evander McIver, Enoch Evans, Samuel Evans, William Lang & John Williams. Also present with us, Revd David Lilly, to whom we had previously written, desiring that he would visit us: who at our request, consents to be with us, this day and tomorrow two weeks.

May 6th

---

[126] Most of these dates agree with Mallary's biography, which is based on Botsford's memoir. However, Mallary records Botsford's ordination as 24 March 1773 and his return to Welsh Neck as 31 December 1781. Mallary, 13, 27, 34, 45, 59.

[127] It is hard to reconcile this statement about numbers of members with the statement just above, that there were only 31 members in the church as of 31 December 1796. Botsford's correspondence with Furman does suggest that membership—along with financial support of the pastor—had fallen off significantly. Letter to Richard Furman, 3 May 1796.

The Church met and with us Revd Evan Pugh. Appointed Brethren Samuel Evans, Evander McIver, and Martin Dewitt to apply to the Revd David Cooper of Jeffries Creek, for a part of his time, to preach to us statedly.

June 10th
The Church met. Revd David Cooper attended: and agrees to attend us monthly, each second Saturday and Sunday in the month. As a compensation for which, we agree to make him up what we can conveniently by subscription. Communion tomorrow.
July
No church meeting.

August
4 baptized
Second Sunday Mr. Cooper baptized Phebe servant of Alexr McIntosh Esqr also Allen, Winney svts of DR Williams and Orange svt of J McIver.

<u>1798</u>
Jan'ry 6th
Church met: nothing to record.

February
2 bap
The 4th Sunday in this month, Rev^d Mr. Cooper baptized Raney & Delila svts of DR Williams.

March 25th
3bap
The 4th Sunday, Grace svt of DR Williams, & Amy and Marsh svts of the Estate of Joshua Edwards were baptized by
   " *25th*
1ex
Bill a negro man being charged with adultery & not giving satisfaction was excommuni^td
   " *31st*
Church met: Revd David Lilly was with us, and agreed to remain the ensuing week. Concluded to hold a prayer meeting on Tuesday next, according to the appointment of the Association.

April 21st
Mr Lilly Pastor

Church met: present with us, Revd David Lilly, who agreed to take the pastoral charge of the church during this year__ Resolved to continue to subscribe for 18 nos of the Baptist Register[128] __ also Resolved that a subscription be raised to build a Meeting House on Society Hill.__ The church agrees to board bro: Lilly & his family till the end of the year, or while expedient.

[44]

<u>1798</u>
June 2nd
Rec'd by Letter
Brother David Lilly having removed his family; presented his Letter of Dismission, and was received as a member of this church; and invited to take the pastoral charge thereof which he accepts during the present year.
" 30th
Church met: The minutes of a meeting of the subscribers for building a Meeting-House on Society Hill, were presented, read, and ordered to be filed with the Records of the Church. Agreed to examine the List of Church members. The church agreed to loan 100 £ sterling due by Mr Robertson to the church to Bro: Evander McIver, whose obligation with security, to be taken and executed this day.

Augt 4th
Church met: Requested bro: Lilly to write to Mrs Anne Goodwin of George-Town respecting a Letter of Dismission.__ Rec^d of bro: E McIver his Bond for the above mentioned 100 £, and his note for 14 £ which is delivered to the care of Bro: John David.__ ¶ The Title for Two acres of Land of Capt William Dewitt, on Society Hill, to the Church are now in the care of bro: E McIver, who is requested to have them proven and recorded. ¶ Church concluded to have preaching at the next meeting, so as to give those members an opportunity to sign the Church Covenant, who have not yet done so.

Septr 1st
Church met: nothing to record.

Octr 6th
Church met: Resolved _ That bro: Lilly be requested to preach a charity sermon, the Third Sunday in this month:- and that a collection be made afterwards, in support of the Funds of the Association.

---

[128] See the introduction for details about the purpose of the *Baptist Register* and its role in the Welsh Neck Church.

Novr 2nd
No Church meeting on account of unpleasant weather.

From this period to July 1803, there is no Record of any meeting: The presumption is, that the Records have been lost. We must therefore pass over in ignorance, a long period of useful and interesting matter. It will be perceived however, that during this time the Revd Mr Lilly supplied the Church, at least occasionally, if not constantly.

Part III

Selected Writings by Edmund Botsford

A. Letters from Edmund Botsford to the Rev. Richard Furman, 4 April 1785 – 24 March 1797[129]

Revd Richard Furman[130]

---

[129] The original letters transcribed here can be found in the Botsford Papers, Series I, Folders 1-5, Special Collections, Duke Library, Furman University. I have included only those letters that Botsford wrote during the years that he served as pastor of the Welsh Neck Church. Botsford and Furman first became acquainted when the latter accompanied John Gano to Georgia during the early years of the Revolutionary War; they met thereafter at Charleston Association meetings and formed a close friendship. When the correspondence transcribed in this volume opens, Furman had twice been called by the Charleston church to be its pastor, but had refused, in part because he felt committed to his congregation at the High Hills, and in part because Oliver Hart, Charleston's pre-1780 pastor, was still holding open the possibility of returning. Botsford served for short stretches in Charleston during this period of uncertainty. When Hart finally declared, in 1786, that he was going to stay in New Jersey, Furman accepted the call of the Charleston church, taking up residence in November of the following year. Rogers, *Furman,* 31, 52-54.

[130] Richard Furman (1755-1825) was converted to the Baptist faith in 1771 by Joseph Reese. He was a prodigy, earning a reputation for his preaching when he was only 16 years old. He was ordained in 1774 and preached at High Hills. During the Revolution he worked hard to end special privileges for the Church of England in South Carolina. He also preached for the patriot cause in the backcountry. From 1787 he served as pastor in Charleston, and played an active role in the Charleston Association. He was a strong advocate for creating central organizations for the Baptist Church, and he helped initiate national Triennial Conventions in 1814 and the South Carolina Convention in 1819. He was also a strong proponent of education: in 1790, at his urging, the Charleston Association created a permanent fund to help educate young men for the Baptist ministry. In 1817 Furman persuaded the Baptist Triennial Convention to create a national university in Washington, DC, along with preparatory institutions in each state: see William H. Brackney, *Congregation and Campus: North American Baptists in Higher Education* (Macon, GA: Mercer University Press, 2008), 105-108. These efforts led to the founding of Columbian College (today's George Washington University), Furman University, Mercer University, and Southern Baptist Theological Seminary. *Encyclopedia of Southern Baptists*, vol. 1, s.v. "Furman, Richard;" Brackney, *Dictionary*

Welsh Neck, South Carolina

High-hills of Santee

Rev^d & dear Sir   Charleston April 4, 1785

               Some time ago I sent you a few hasty lines I am
going to do the same now, to acquaint you I am desired it is the desire of friends
here that you will favour them with your company again as soon as you
conveniently can. Mr Hill has shut himself out of the meeting, & now [heavily
crossed out words, illeg.] preaches in his own house. It is not impossible but
you may blame me for it, unless I could relate the whole of the matter, & which
I cannot at this time do however I must give you a short acct of it. A Mr Cooly
came here from England as a Baptist Minister, but his papers were not approved
of however he was permitted to preach, his preaching was not approved on
either, when I came to Town he was gone to Edisto Island, & his wife & 2
Children at Mr Hills, for [?] about 2 weeks after I came Mr Cooly returned to
Town, Mr Hill sent a Note to me acquainting me M^r Co requesting me to lett Mr
Cooly preach that evening, as he himself was poorly (it being Mr Hill's turn to
preach) & he would wish to be excused from preaching, I returned for answer
that I did not know but I might give offence by Asking Mr Cooley as he was not
approved on before – He then wrote to me to ask the members & trustees leave –
I did – the answer was no – but before I had an opportunity to acquaint Mr Hill,
he sent another Note, as I was not at home Mrs Brown opened the note & sent
for Mr Hill and told him she thought he acted very imprudent, as he was the first
person who objected to Mr Cooly's papers – This I take it gave the first offence.
When I first came to Town before I preached, I went to Mr Hill & asked him to
preach with me on the morrow (this being Saturday night) [end of page 1] I have
baptised a twice 2 Whites & 5 Blacks & am in some expectation of 1 or 2 whites
this week, several are in a pritty way, I have preached at private houses several
times & God blesses the word – I leave town God willing this day week, I have
time to say no more but love to Mrs Furman & your Honoured Parent with other
friends & remain Dr Sir

                                 Your unworthy brother
                                 & fellow labourer
                                 in the Gospel of Jesus
                                 Edm^d Botsford

---

of the Baptists, 238-239; *Oxford Dictionary of American National Biography,* s.v.
"Furman, Richard." See G. William Foster, ed., *Life and Works of Richard Furman, DD.*
(Harrisonburg, VA: Sprinkle Publications, 2004); James A. Rogers, *Richard Furman:
Life and Legacy* (Mercer University, 1985).

Rev. Richard Furman
Honoured by Rev Mr Burton
Charleston

Rev & d^r Brother   Geo Town Decm 17 1788

      This will be handed to you by Rev John Burton from Nova Scotia, a
gentleman going through the States to collect for building a place of worship in
Halifax. Mr Staughton speaks of him as "a gracious man better calculated to
comfort Saints than collect dollars." In this place his preaching is acceptable to
the lovers of truth. We shall do but little for him, however every little helps.
We have lost another Member, Mr Jacob Dunam he died the 17th inst. By whom
shall Jacob arise? Our affairs put on a serious aspect, the righteous taken from
the evil to come & none to fill up their place. This morning I heard from my son
who has been at the Cheraws about 2 weeks. On the 14th he writes "I have
missed the fever two days." I am much concerned lest he never fully recover his
health. The rest of my family well, except my self troubled with a cold. I rec'd
your favour by Mr Waldo, thank you for the information it contained. Friends in
general pritty well, tho some complaining. I send you by M^r B a 2 [...] bill & 1
dol rec'd of Mr Cooper for the fund will thank you to mention in your next the
rec^t of it & of the money rec^d by Mr Hutchinson for this church. I wish also for
my Acc^t with you. I am at this instant by my self, my daughter having gone to
Mr Blackwell's. With love to Mrs Furman & Children, I remain in much
affection yours &c

                          Edm^d Botsford

Reverend Richard Furman
Charleston

Reverend & dear Sir   Bethel Jan 11th 1789

                I was in hopes by this time to have been able
to write something which might have afforded you some satisfaction, but my
mind is in such a state of perturbation that I am not myself – Do you say what is
the cause? I can hardly tell you – A mixture of many things, & no one thing
worth mentioning. I would wish to give you my reasons for not mentioning to
you when in Town the little piece I intended to have printed, & I am at a loss
how to do it. I could say many things that perhaps might appear plausible, but

the truth is what should be told, if I tell any thing – Well then, before you left Town I thought to have read it to you, but I thought again I would not. Why? because I concluded you would think it a triffling thing & perhaps say some thing which would prevent my publishing of it, & I was determined to publish[131] – Well when you returned, I was in truth ashamed to mention it, as I had not done it before – now there is the plain truth – I really wished a thousand times I had ~~have~~ made a friend of you, & requested your advice & assistance to have finished it—& there is another plain truth. And a third plain truth is, upon the whole I have acted very childish, as I have done all my days; [on separate fragment] Will you permit me to mention a fourth plain truth, which is without flattery, That I really have a more sincere regard for you than ever I had in my life, as a Minister of Christ, As a Master of a family, as a Christian & Gentleman &c&c Dont view this as fulsome flatterings but as the effusion of an honest weak mind.

I hardly remember what I wrote to you by M^r McIver respecting the piece he was to print, however he was requested to deliver it to you when done, if you will be so kind as to receive it. If Mr Simmons Mr Mc Donald & Mr Brown applies to you for any [end page 1] of the copies you will be so obliging to let them have as many as they chuse to take, perhaps my Brother could dispose ~~well~~ of a few & when a convenient opportunity presents send the remainder to Mr Cuttino directed for me. You will excuse this freedom, and if it is inconvenient or disagreeable to you to receive them &c you will be so kind as to request Mr McIver to send them to Mrs Brown's. Our friend M^r B is now restored to health and is very busy – but not in the preaching line, though I am infom'd he considers himself as an ordained Minister by virtue of the call received from the Church. He has agreed to take a plantation & 9 or 10 hands which is situated contiguous to him on this side of the river, at least I am informed so, & says if Mr Hart does not conclude to come to Pee dee, he will take Mr McIvers land and some hands, as the land joins his place on the other side of the river, & all this to enable him to spare ~~tim~~ more time to attend to the ministry – so says my informer*– see what it is to be industrious – I feel ashamed of myself when I look round my pine barren spot of a few acres & have but 2 hands (one not my own) & complain that this poor dirty affair ties me down at home so much – how ever I wish his dirty acres may not bedaub his mind in such a manner that his sermons will not be very clean. Well but a thought has just struck my mind – which is to request you will candidly give me your opinion on the Letter. I dont ask this favour on the foot of merit, as I rather deserve your censure; I mean in not being more open & plain with you – but what is past cannot be recalled. We will try & do better for the future, in the mean time

---

[131] If Botsford did publish the work he refers to in his letter, it does not seem to have survived; Evans, *American Bibliography* contains no reference to it.

excuse this scribble & believe me
your friend brother
& fellow labourer
in the gospel
Edm^d Botsford

*He embarked in his
own boat laden with
corn, yesterday (Saturday)
for Georgetown.

Revd Richard Furman
To the care of Mr John McIver, Printer in Charleston

Rev^d & Dr Sir   Bethel August 31, 1789

It is long since I received a Line from you or
any of my Friends in Charleston, however I will not impute it to Disrespect; yet
I must acknowledge it is a little mortification, as I have written to several of my
acquaintance more than once since I received a line from them. I should esteem
it a favour if you will send the Pamphlets to Georgetown as soon as you can, if
they are not already sent, if they had been sent to me as soon as finished, I could
have disposed of them before now. I have lately received a letter from my
Father Hart in answer to one I wrote to him on the subject of Incorporation, and
now I despair of ever being convinced of the propriety of it; though I do not
intend to oppose it, yet I must still say I hope it will not take place in my day. It
appears to me upon the same principle of reasoning (if that is a proper
expression) almost any thing may be introduced among us, even Infants baptism
and I really think the reasoning for the one & the other ~~are~~ is much alike; I am
much more confirm'd in my opinion of the unlawfulness of it, since I received
my Father Hart's letter than I was before, & am pleased I bore my testimony
against it. I hope my writing thus free will not offend my Brother, I wish not to
offend any one.[132] I suppose before this you have heard Doctor Harts eldest son

---

[132] Botsford refers here to the plan to create a legal corporation to administer the
education fund. He opposed the idea because he felt such an act would strengthen the
authority of the Association over individual churches, in contravention of Baptist
principles. Botsford had similarly opposed a plan put forward in 1787 to incorporate the
Charleston Association as a whole. Hart and Furman approved of both incorporation
plans. In the end, Botsford gave way on incorporating the education fund (see his letter of
14 February 1791 below), but his opposition had helped to ensure that the education fund
would be a distinct body from the Association, and under the control of the individual
churches that contributed to it and appointed members to its board. Mallary, *Botsford,* 67-

was killed by the kick of a Horse, he died the 1̶7̶-8 Inst. on the 15th a child about 1½ years of age was taken in the time of service with a fit & expired in a few hours, on Lords day 16th a Mrs Paisley returning from Worship at the Hill was killed by her horse taking fright & throwing her against a tree; I think it was on the 14th Mr Gaven Witherspoon's child was shot, by the accidental going off of a gun & expired in a few minutes, these are alarming calls to be in readiness. I must beg the favour of you to send the enclosed by first opportunity; through mercy we are all well Mrs Botsford joins me in love to Mrs Furman & yourself and I remain Rev^{d} & Dr Sir with every sentiment of respect you unworthy Brother in best bonds.

Edm^{d} Botsford

Revd Richard Furman
to be left with Mr John McIver
Printer
Charleston

Bethel March 15 1790

Rev^{d} & dear Sir

Difficult as the Task is I must inform you, my dear Companion is no more – To describe my feelings on the Occasion I shall not attempt, neither is there any call for it, to command pity from one who has experienced the same, & who has professed regard – O my Brother pray for me write to me, advise me,—My Soul is too full to explain my self.[133] I have written to Mrs Brown as fully as I can at this time, tho' very short,

---

70; Furman, *Charleston Association,* 21-24. Botsford was not alone in his concern about the growing power of the Association over individual churches. Townsend, *South Carolina Baptists,* 293-294.

[133] Botsford later expressed his feelings about his wife, Susanna in a published letter that appeared in Rippon, *Baptist Register, 1790-1793,* 104-105: "On the 9th ult. I closed the eyes of my dear Mrs. ------ ; such a trial I never before experienced. In the course of the war, I lost a pretty library, a fine interest, and also four children; but this loss exceeds all expression—My consolation is, I doubt not she is gone to glory. She died as she had lived -- a saint. Two days before her death, when we thought her better, as I was conversing with her about her soul concerns, she said to me, "I am near eternity, but quite calm and resigned—my only dependence is on the blood and merits of my precious Redeemer, and they are sufficient, quite sufficient for *me,* and for *you* too, my dear— don't grieve for me." She was remarkably attached to her children, above most women. "I give my dear children up to the Lord and you—death is hard work, but it will soon be

I refer you to her, excuse me to M^{rs} McDonald, my love to your dearer Self & all my friends as tho mentioned by name & believe me   your friend Brother
& distressed fellow labourer
Edm^{d} Botsford

[No address]

Rev^{d} & dear Sir   Bethel Apl 20. 1790

Your Favour by Capt Brown I rec^{d} on Lords day, the minutes have not yet arrived. I am much obliged to you for that Sympathy you so tenderly express, & also for the Hints given, the good Lord grant I [illeg] improve by them. I have been very poorly since my return from George Town, while there I enjoyed little satisfaction, but through mercy since my return my Mind is in a more tranquil state than I expected it would be in six months. Before this ~~this~~ you have been inform'd of the manner of M^{rs} B's death, which afforded me such consolation as I cannot express: I doubt not but my Brother will remember me at the Throne of Grace could I always be exercised as I now am, there would be no ~~danger~~er from difficulties or temptations, but alass we are changeable creatures. I cannot answer for one hour to come, however I hope & trust that God who called me when a graceless wanderer, & who has hither ~~too~~ supported me under a variety of scenes will not now forsake me, I am sensible my Brother, at least in some measure, of the justness of your observation, that it will require much Prudence & fortitude to conduct with propriety in my situation. Will my dear [end p 1] Brother favour me with some general (or even particular advice) I assure him it will be kindly accepted, & I will promise, that I will endeavour to improve by it. The situation of my Family at present is as follows. I have an aged & honourable Matron, Mrs Martha Evans a member of the Chh, of long standing, who manages the concerns of my House, which I am informed is pleasing to all our members & my acquaintance.[134] My eldest daughter Polly is nurse to the youngest, Sally &

---

over." Being asked whether she was happy in her soul, she replied, "Yes, O yes!" These were the last words we could understand from her. A few hours after she breathed out her precious soul into the arms of the adored Redeemer, whom she sincerely loved. She was in the 39th year of her age. We had lived together between 16 and 17 years in great affection."

[134] Martha Evans was not always quite so respectable. On 2 January 1762 she and her husband David were suspended for "criminal conversation before marriage," perhaps

Jerry go to School, my two Negro men are put into a Crop with M^r McIver my very good friend; I have a little Negro Boy, & a Wench about House, I have no boarder, nor do I intend to take any. I am pleased with ye acct you have favoured me of the State of the Baptists, hope you'll not forget the publication. As you have had such an inundation of country Preachers, I am glad I return'd home from G T without visiting Ch'ton: However I intend as soon as I can make it convenient to visit Ch'ton, as I dont believe what you wrote was with a view to prevent my coming. I suppose you dont open the pulpit to all, & I hope private lectures will not be productive of much hurt.

Apl 24. This day I rec'd the minutes & a valuable parcel from England consisting of several Pham Pamphlets, minutes of Associations, some of Mr Jonathan Edwards's Works &c &cc & a letter from a valuable correspondent at Olney Bucks viz Revd John Sutcliff, who has cut me out work for a month or two [end p. 2] I will give you one Paragraph " After many enquiries respecting the State of the Baptist Churches among us & giving me a general acct of the State of the Baptists in England he adds "I have on my desk Manuscrips Minutes of the Welch Association for the present year. (89) I find that 45 churches met, & only 2 but had additions. The number of the Baptised in all amounted to 603 [?] a fine number. Blessed be God!"

I thought when I sat down I had much to write but I find I must break off abruptly adieu my dear Brother & fellow labourer

Your E Botsford

Lords day morning – 25 I cannot seal up this without informing you of some sweet experiences of last night. I was very poorly in the evening with a pain in my head[135] & went to bed about eight o clock, I soon fell a sleep & awoke I believe about 10 perfectly easy. As I could not get to sleep again I set myself to wrestle with God, first for my own Soul & soon began to find a very great earnestness [?] & familiarity with God, my [illeg] desires were soon extended to my children, my Neighbour, my acquaintance, our Church the Churches in General the cause of God universal^{ly} O how sweetly was I employ'd for an hour or two. I then ran through the transactions of my whole life, particularly my Christian life, ministerial life, conjugal life, widowed life &c &cc And I think I never found such a sweet submission to to the will of God in my whole life,

---

manifested by an advanced pregnancy too soon after they had wed. She was reminded of her need to repent on 3 April, and then appeared before the church and satisfied them of her repentance on 1 May. Her husband was not reconciled to the church until February 1763, and he was later suspended again, this time for drinking to excess, on 16 April 1768. WNCB, 10, 11, 14.

[135] This affliction might well have been the *tic douloureux* or trigeminal neuralgia, a nervous disorder that causes excruciating and sometimes incapacitating pain on one side of the face. Botsford suffered from this periodically through much of his life. Townsend, *South Carolina Baptists,* 70.

such desires for the conversion of souls, for the revi ~~ing~~ val of my Christian Brethren & all with such soul humbling views & submission to God as I cannot describe. My dear Brother was not forgotten in this (what shall I call it) restoration. I cheerfully gave up my once dear ~~Mrs~~ B nay I gave up my children, myself, my all to my God. O my Brother this last night has been a time of love, a time of light, a night never to be forgotten by your unworthy Brother & fellow labourer in our

Masters vineyard,
E Botsford

Rev. Richard Furman
Charleston

Rev$^{d\,\&}$ dear Brother   Bethel August 4. 1790

I return you many Thanks for your last Favour, & the Abstract of the Minutes. God has been at work among us, which now begins to appear; last Lords-day I baptized Charles Lide the 4th son of the late Col^n Lide, a lad just turned of fourteen I almost fear to say all I might in justice say respecting him, however I must inform you he is a kind of prodigy. I expect several more to baptise shortly, 4 experiences I have heard, & a great number of our youth of both Sexes are under serious impressions & some aged. On Monday being the first Monday in the month to unite with our English Friends we held the their monthly time of Prayer; it was a solemn time, more attended than I ever saw in our M H on a Week day except the Saturday preceedings.[136] I rejoice but I can truly say with fear & trembling. I have but just time to give you this information, I'll write more particularly shortly, in the mean time pray for us, for me, my Children the Chh &c May the best of blessings attend you & yours – love to Mrs Furman in which my dear Children join me & I remain in haste your

unworthy Brother &
fellow labourer in the Gospel
of Jesus Edm^d Botsford

---

[136] Botsford described these Monday prayer meetings in Rippon, *Baptist Register, 1790-1793*, 105: "May 13 [1790]. I lately proposed to the members a meeting to join with you and the rest of the churches in England, who keep a *Monday evening meeting in prayer to God* FOR A REVIVAL OF RELIGION. It was agreed to; accordingly we met, and I trust God was with us. All our members were much roused, and some young people arc under very serious impressions."

Rev'd Rich:^d Furman
Charleston
Honoured by
Mr Chambers

Rev^d & dear Sir   Mr Blackwell's feb 14. 91

          I have been disappointed in going to Pee dee till today. When I arrived at Colⁿ Screven's I was so fatigued I had thoughts of staying a day or two there, but I proceeded next morning on my journey & reached Georgetown by dusk, could not get my Horse over the River. I was now so very weary & sore I could not ride the next day which was Thursday, hence concluded to stay Sabath over – I preached 5 times with some degree of freedom, I hope they were not lost opportunities -- Though Bishop Asbury was in Town & preached, & the day unfavourable, we had a good number of hearers.[137] Friends are very desirous of seeing you in Town – in general well. I greatly fear it will take me almost the week to get home, I really am good for nothing – I have had our last Assoⁿ minutes & thought on them much, & approve of the plan for raising a fund, so you may depend on my best exertions.[138] Please to present my love to your Honoured Parent Mrs Furman, children Mrs Brown & McIver & all friends & believe me your real friend

                                 & fellow labourer
                                 Edmund Botsford

Revd Richard Furman
Charleston
Hon^dby M^r J Brown

---

[137] Botsford refers to the famous Methodist itinerant preacher and bishop, Francis Asbury (1745-1816). Botsford need not have worried about competition from Asbury; Asbury wrote with disappointment about the impact of his preaching during this visit to Georgetown. "I preached a plain, searching sermon; and some felt the word: but it is a day of small things. In the afternoon...the wicked youth were playing without and inattention prevailed amongst those within. I was, and continued to be, under great dejection during my stay." *The Journal and Letters of Francis Asbury*, ed. Elmer T. Clark et al. (London: Epworth Press, 1958), Vol. I, 667.

[138] The Welsh Neck Church agreed to support the fund at its 5 March 1791 meeting. WNCB, 39.

Rev^d & dear Sir   Bethel August 17. 1791

Your Favour of 27 Ult was rec^d the other Day, I return you many Thanks for it. I am much pleased with the Account you give me of Mr Holcombe, I pray God make him very successful. Mr Hart's Letter came safe. He writes to me also in Raptures respecting Mr Holcombe's Sermon.[139] I think you acted a truly brotherly part in acquainting Mr Richards respecting Mr Bainbridge's conduct, I have done the same & have written to M^r B what I call a very plain faithful Letter. Well we have had our Collection, & how much do you suppose we collected? A few Dollars only, in cash, we have about 14£ on Paper, I believe the greatest part will be paid by the meeting of the Association, if so, it will do pritty well.[140] I am of your Way of thinking respecting our old Friend Pugh, especially since I conversed with him last. I received a Letter the other Day from our good little Brother Mosely, who has lately made a Tour in N^o Carolina, where he met with a young Mr Gilbert, whom he heard preach, was pleased with Him, & conversed with him respecting Education, found him desirous to obtain it, hence advised him to come & see me, the young Man promised; if He comes I shall write you more concerning him. I am afraid several of the Churches will not chuse & send P+ Persons for the Committee; I will write to four respecting the Matter. A few days after our Collection I received an anonymous Letter addressed to the Association, which I scarcely think deserves the Honour of being read before that Body; it appears to have been written by a serious Person of some reading; He argues against our Mode of raising a Fund, the term Charity-Sermon, & Learning in general, otherwise than promoting Schools in our Neighbourhoods & educating our Children. I cannot conceive who is the Author, except Mr Boykin or Mr Mickill, & it is only from one single circumstance I guess at one of them. [end p. 1] Respecting our Church. We have had no Additions since I wrote you last. Some two or three I trust have experienced a Change, but have not yet offered for Baptism. One of those I baptised last year has turned his Back on the good

---

[139] Henry Holcombe (1762-1824) was a rising star in the Baptist community in South Carolina. The sermon referred to here was probably *A Discourse on the Sovereignty and Unchangeableness of the Deity*, which Holcombe had delivered in 1790. It was possibly a preview of Holcombe's *A Sermon, containing a brief illustration and defense of the Doctrine commonly called Calvinistic*, which he preached at the Charleston Association meeting in November 1791. Evans, *American Bibliography*, #s 25615 and 25616. Holcombe was ordained in 1785; he served as pastor at Beaufort, at Savannah, and then, from 1811, at Philadelphia.

[140] The collection referred to here was probably taken up after the preaching of the charity sermon on 2 July 1791, in support of the Charleston Association's fund for supporting the education of promising young men for the ministry. *WNCB*, 39.

Way, & appears much worse than before his Reformation, it is one whom we all
thought the most of, vis Coll^n Lide's Son Charles, a Lad of a very extraordinary
turn. We have as yet the most pleasing prospect of large crops of corn; but as I
plant but little, little must be my share, may I be content with my little.

My family are not all well, our little Daughter is very unwell, the rest of us are
troubled with Colds, Mrs Botsford but just keeps on her feet, through mercy. I
am pritty well at present, have been very poorly lately, my Sight has failed me
so much that it is with difficulty I read in a large quarto Bible by day-light
without glasses, I am obliged to use them when I write, & can read nothing by
candle-light without them.

So Mr Simmons is returned to Town! Well we must have trouble from several
Quarters, I do verrily believe the poor Baptists bring on themselves the most
trouble of any Society. If they would but behave with common Prudence they
would go through the World with much more reputation than they generally do;
Doctor Gifford of London used to call them the Lord's Simpletons, if they were
only such it would not be so bad, but the Worlds cunning Fellows creep in
among them & defile them, & poor things many of them who are simple
enough, try to immitate in too many things particulars the wise men of the world
& so hurt themselves & the Cause. ------ I think very strange I cannot hear from
Ireland, if I could get that Affair properly settled it would enable me to settle all
my debts & bring me square with the World once more, & if ever that should
take place I now think I will endeavour to keep clear of debt if possible, in the
mean time I shall be on my guard. [end p. 2]

I believe We have forty pounds towards a Fund for our Chh. which I shall
endeavour to augment annually while I live with these People.[141] Mr Jarrel has
been with us, & proposes teaching Psalmody; He is now gone to the Bethel
Association; Mr Pugh wishes to procure him for Muddy-Creek Church. Suppose
I advise that Church to try & raise some thing against the Association, & chuse a
Committee Man, they intend to join the Association & I make no doubt of their
being received. I think it would be a good beggining, even suppose it was only
two or three Dollars, I think it would be very pleasing to those among us who
approve of the Scheme. I am glad you intend drawing up some Rules, I shall
turn my Thoughts on the Subject, but dare say shall offer nothing. I wish you
would write to Mr Holcombe to come prepared to preach the Association
Sermon. I shall prepare for it but as it is at our Meeting-House, if M^r H comes
shall wish him to preach. The Cheraw Church have built a very handsome
Meeting-house for Mr Lewis at Pledger Saw-Mills. Some of his People continue
so prejudiced against him respecting Masonry that they do not yet hear him.
When he came to perform the ceremony of Marriage for me, I had a little

---

[141] The money to institute this fund was a legacy from a church member, Josiah
James. *WNCB*, 39, 31 July 1790.

conversation with him, but he was so very short with me that I found I could not keep my Temper so dropt it. He must certainly attend this Year to be sure as it is so near to him, yet I have my doubts, as some of his People I have been informed intend proposing some query respecting Masonry, & some of our People could not sit down with him. May He, may they & us be enabled to act aright.

> With every sentiment of respect I remain Rev^d & dear Brother yours in best bonds Edmund Botsford

PS. Many Thanks for the Philadelphia Minutes

On outer flap:
Sep 18. Since I wrote the within I have baptised one person. The week before last a Negro belonging to Mr Josiah Evans's Estate, died at my House, one of mine was very ill at same time, but is now better.
So the very amiable & very useful Doctor Manning is no more. What a loss! Pray have you heard who succeeds him as President?

> EB

Rev. Richard Furman
Charleston

Rev. and dear Brother   Bethel Decem 12 1791

> Mr Gilbert (the young man

Mr Mosely mentioned to me) has been here, I heard him preach once, I think he has a ministerial Gift, appears modest & diffident of his Abilities, I think he may make a usefull Man. Our People seem willing to do something for him. We wish for your advice respecting the Matter, I suppose with the Assistance of 10£ we could school, board & cloath Him, he is willing to devote two Years and a half to study, it is more than probable before that Time is expired he may be convinced of it will be Duty to devote more of his time to Education. He has a Letter of Recommendation & Dismission from the Church to which he belongs, & means to join our Church. I wish to be informed respecting the mode of application, is the Candidate to apply to the President, to the Committee or to who? And at what Time? My bad memory is the cause of these Questions I suppose, as the Rules you presented no doubt pointed out the mode of Applications.

You will be pleased to make our Church a Subscriber for three dozen of the Baptist Annual Register's, we will procure more subscriptions if we can; we wish for as many of the first part if they can be had, the money shall be sent at or before receiving the Books just as you please.[142]
A few days since M^r __ Vineing [?] Brother to Jeptha the Preacher gave into the Church his experience of the work of the Lord on his Soul, & is to be baptised, He has been a steady opposer all his life till lately, a man of good morral character, but looked on Religion as a delusion. The Winter is very severe, we have had snow several times, this day it has snowed & sleeted all day, I think we have had more cold than I ever remember so early; through Mercy very healthy. Mrs Botsford joins me in love to your Self & family x I remain yours &cc Edm^d Botsford

Rev. Richd Furman
Charleston

Rev & dear Brother   Bethel Apl 23. 1792

I am just returned from Jeffers's Creek where I have had a very comfortable meeting with B Moseley & his People, and where I was informed that Mr Reese was about to leave his congregation; my Information was from Captn Turner who is acquainted with Mr Reese & I think he said either M^r R himself or Mr Hunter related the matter to him.[143] If Mr Reese should move M^{r}McCullen [?] & Master Cook may both be accomodated at Pee-dee if you think proper to send them. As I have heard

---

[142] Botsford refers here to John Rippon's *Baptist Annual Register,* instituted in 1790 in order to promote "a more comprehensive knowledge" by Baptists in Europe, America, and elsewhere of "each others religious circumstances." The Register would make the history of the Baptists better known, and provide a means of "relieving each others wants, of praying for each other...and of praising God." Rippon promised up to two issues per year, with all but the first costing 1shilling. Both Botsford and Furman were contributors. The work proved popular enough to be reissued in three compilations, covering 1790-1793, 1793-1797, and 1798-1801. Rippon, *Baptist Annual Register, 1790-1793,* i-vi. See the introduction for further information about the Register and its role in the life of the Welsh Neck Church.

[143] Joseph Reese (1732-1795), originally from Pennsylvania, emigrated to South Carolina c. 1745 and was converted by Philip Mulkey. He was ordained by Oliver Hart and Evan Pugh and became pastor of the High Hills Baptist Church. Reese converted Richard Furman in 1771 and joined with Pugh in ordaining him in 1774. *Encyclopedia of Southern Baptists,* vol. 4, s.v. "Reese, Joseph."

nothing of Mr Gilbert, I suppose he has laid aside all Thoughts of procuring Education, except he has gone to Rev Burket; which B Moseley hopes may be the case.

We have had ~~one of~~ the highest Freshes every known in Peedee, the May & September Freshes only excepted. In some Places the Land is much damaged, but through mercy no lives lost, nor much of our Stock, except Hogs. There has been a great mortality among the Cattle this Spring. Capt McIntosh has lost 60 hdd Mr Jno Pagget 44 & most of those who live back of us have lost, some more, some less; in this particular I have been favoured, not having lost any kind of Stock. Should be glad to be informed if you have received & sent a Packet of Letters for England & 2 Letters for Ireland. I must again trouble you with the charge of Letter for d^r[?] Rogers. Through Mercy Self & Family are in Health, hope this may find you & yours in the enjoyment of the same desirable Blessings. With love to you Mrs Furman & the Children, in which Mrs Botsford & my children join

I remain Rev & d^r Brother yours in best
Bonds Edmund Botsford

Rev Richd Furman
Charleston
Honoured by Mr Marshall

[handwriting looks very hurried]

Rev^d & d^r Sir:

I have just time to thank you for the Packet in which was enclosed several Letters, one from your Self, which I rec'd yesterday on my coming to the Bluff where I now am Mr Marshall I found preparing to set off for C Town. My Family well & Neighbours in general. never was there so gloomy a prospect of crops as at present in general, however mine is an exception, if we should ever be favoured with rain from this time I may make a good one. M^r & Mrs Johnson with us, he I believe is going to set up a Distillery near us.

In the greatest haste I remain d^r Sir

Yours &c EBotsford

Monday July 9 – 92

Welsh Neck, South Carolina

Rev & dear Sir   [in pencil, Dec 1792]

Your favour by M^r McIver was very acceptable, as
are even the shortest epistles you write to me. You will permit me to say (as I
say it without flattery) every time I am so happy as to be favoured with your
company & every letter I receive from you endears you more to me, your letters
breath friendship, your company is always [illeg. – torn], I wish I could
consistent with duty enjoy more of it. Well my dear Brother I trust we shall
meet in those happy regions where we shall [sic] each other in a far more
exalted manner than we can now, then poor Botsford will have got over his
blunders &c which I doubt not cause a friend like to you to feel while in this
imperfect State. What you write respecting the honours of the College¹⁴⁴ pleases
me much, because I believe you write your real Sentiments; no doubt some may
sensure you, what wont some do, especially to a Baptist? You see my friend
that others have a better opinion of you than you have of yourself; you may
perhaps think those concerned were not sufficiently acquainted with you & did
not as you would have wished them to maturely consider the cause of God; will
you permit me to say I hope they did right, I trust it will be an in induce my
Brother to continue his dilligence that the Chh & World may see the honour was
confered on a proper object.
Mr Hart has given me account in detail of his complaint & though he has got
over it for the present, I fear his valuable life will not be lent to us much
longer.¹⁴⁵
I hope my Brother has put no wrong construction on what I wrote respecting the
Register; I by no means wish him to have all his trouble &cc & be a looser in the
bargain. [note up side of page: hence what you write entirely satisfies me] I
have charged 5s each, will send or bring the money as soon as possible. [end p.
1] Your advice respecting the materials I wish to take, but I hope my Brother
dont think I am so vain as to think of publishing, no Sir I wish to preserve those
things that probably may otherways be lost, & which may be of service in some
future day to some person who may have the inclination & ability to write a
History of the Baptists in this State; if what I collect may never be wanted no
harm will be done. Master Cook came here last Thursday the 6 inst as he

---

¹⁴⁴ Botsford refers to Furman's receipt of an honorary Master of Arts degree from
the College of Rhode Island (later Brown University) on Wednesday, 5 September 1792.
Rippon, *Baptist Register,1790-1793*, 393.
¹⁴⁵ Oliver Hart survived three more years, until 31 December 1795. Rippon, *Baptist
Register, 1794-1797,* 513.

understood it was your desire; I have concluded to let him board with us, as yet we are all fond of him; his behaviour is truly pleasing. He informs me M^r McCullen [?] wishes (he believes) to go to Pipe-Creek as there is a Tutor, & the Chh in that place wishes him for a Pastor; Joseph says this he partly conjectures from hints dropt, & I suppose wishes that what he says might not be mentioned; however I fear there is a woman in the way, tho my reasons or rather conjectures I must confess are trifling. If he should come you may be assured I will with pleasure do all in my power to have him agreeably accomodated &c.

I have just heard something respecting Mr Roberts which affords me a great deal of pleasure, 1st that he is clear with respect to baptism by immersion being his duty 2^d that God has met with him in a very remarkable manner within these few days. 3^d that he thinks it duty to devote himself to the ministry. I am glad you are on your guard respecting Rev Mr Johnson, you know not yet what he is, he is not however a Baptist, but much opposed to our denomination when it suits, as indeed most are who are not of it.

What you write respecting Mr Waldo corresponds with Mr Parks acct of him, I shall be truly sorry if he should not suit the People whom he has come to serve. We are building an addition to our school & have engaged a respectable young gentleman as Usher or rather as English Tutor [end p. 2] and we expect shall be obliged to procure a Latin-Usher; Several Schollars are promised & some are come already to be here at the opening of the # Schooll 1st Jan. I have had 19th I have had Mr Goodwin with me, the same person who was to have been at our Asso^n two years ago; another hint has droped respecting McCullen viz. Goodwin was preae speaking of his returning to Jeffers's Creek, round by Euhaw [?] &c, & remarked M^r McCullen [Cullers?] had a notion of traveling with him if he return'd as by that time his year would be up, these are Goodwin's words, I have written to Mr Moseley to speak to M [torn] & represent to him the advantages now to be obtained, which could can not be hereafter; the discouragement of the Committee for their first object to disappoint them, the obligations he laid himself under when taken under their Patronage, the uneasiness it must cause Mr Holcombe who recommended him, the hurt it must be to you who was so intent on his education & who had been at so much trouble to provide for this, together with the uneasiness it must cause in the minds of all concerned.

I have also written to Capt A Ellison on the same subject. Yesterday I married Mr Willm Stuart to Miss Wilmina Poelnitz if I have spelt it right, however you know I dare say that it is I mean Barron Poelnitz' daughter.

Mrs Botsford & Children unite in love to your Self Mrs Furman & Children & I remain Rev & dr Brother

yours in best bonds
Edm^d Botsford

PS The other day I had appointed to marry two couple, on my way I met one couple in the woods about 2 miles from any house, as it was a wet day & I had to ride 5 miles farther & return that day I did not chuse to return to the house 2 miles back & the couple did not chuse to return 2 miles to the house they had passed, as they were to celebrate the wedding at a distance – so we dismounted & I joined them in the woods by a very remarkable Pond called the Dish [end p. 3]

Decem 30 I have been informed M^r the Church at Jeffers's Creek have suspended Mr Moseley from preaching; do you ask "for what?" I answer I do not know; however I am inform'd it is [illeg. crossed out letters] not for any thing immoral but respecting a Society of which he was a member, it is truly a shocking affair; there are a few very ignorant overbearing [torn – possibly meddlesome or troublesome] men that have ever been endeavouring to turn things [up]side down; & now they have obtained their ends; it is thought they will excom Capt Ellison, as he is a great Advocate for this same Society. Do ask what Society this is; I am informed it is a very useful institution, I wish, sincerely wish we had such an one among us, I rec'd my information from one of the members, he said they had also suspended 2 other members, from what I can learn they have acted not to say worse very foolishly, in haste once more

farewell

[on last page is written Nov or Dec 1793]

April 27. 1793
Rev Rich Furman
Charleston

Rev & very dr Sir   Bethel Apl 27. 1793

It is now long since I rec'd a line from you, I heard of you in Georgetown, but ^not^ from ~~not~~ you: I also hear of your success there ~~with~~ respecting additions to the Church, such good News is very agreeable. I wish I had as good to acquaint you of, but as I have not must send you such as I have. Mrs Botsford has been very weak & low a great while though I cant say very dangerous; on L d Apl 7th she gave me a daughter, which is the first live born child she has had of 7.[146] Both Mother & Child I hope will do well, the child indeed has not been sick, the Mother is but just able to sit up a little.

I wish to hear respecting Capt B & Lady; his brother has left these parts & is gone to little Peedee.

We have been in some dangour of the Smallpox among us, hope the dangour is over.

Pray what is the general opinion respecting the War between Great Briton & France, as to America. I received a line from Mr Waldo who informed me of the sentiments of the Chh respecting himself, he seems much at a loss what to do. Mrs Botsford & family join me in love to Mrs Furman & family & remain d^r Sir with every sentiment

of real esteem your Servant & fellow-
labourer in the gospel
Edm^d Botsford

Rev. Richd Furman
Charleston

Rev. & dear Sir   Bethel Augt 29: 1793

                   I returned from the Bethel Association on the 19th Inst. very much fatigued, am scarcely yet recovered; found all my Family well but my eldest daughter, who continues poorly.[147] I had a very agreeable journey, except the last two days in which I rode too far. I am much pleased with the part of the Country where the Asso^n was held; the Asso^n was full & 6 Churches joined, it was supposed that on the lowest computation there were upwards of four thousand people present, & above 40 Preachers; I never saw better order observed or greater harmony; Asplund was with us, I hard him preach, he went on to Georgia, left with me the enclosed.[148] At this time our

---

[146] Botsford refers to the birth of their daughter, Caty. His wife died while giving birth some three years later. See his letter to Furman, 10 April 1796.

[147] The Bethel Association's annual meeting for 1793 was held at Jamey's Creek Baptist Church, Spartanburg, from Saturday, 10 August to Tuesday, 13 August. On the Monday, Botsford preached the introductory discourse on Col. i. 28. He was asked to furnish a copy of his discourse for publication, though he does not mention that request here. The Bethel Association minute in the *Baptist Register* records seven new churches joining the Association, rather than the six Botsford states in this letter. Rippon, *Baptist Register, 1794-1797*, 193.

[148] John Asplund (1750-1807) was originally from Sweden. He migrated to England, and then to America, where he was converted to the Baptist faith. He dedicated himself to collecting data on North American Baptists, undertaking an eighteen-month

Neighbourhood is very sickly, several children have died, some of the Croup, our little one was very bad with it but through mercy is recovered. Our Chh wishes for 50 ^copies^ of Mr Holcomb sermons I have since my return received a Letter from Rev: Morgan Edwards relative to the Affair you mentioned in your last; I suppose the best method we can persue will be to get Mr Edwards & Capt Evans's depositions &c with the State seal annexed. Elisha James's Wife was Mr Edwards's Sister Capt Evans's Mother was her Sister also, & Elisha James's last surviving child left his Estate to Capt Evans. I have made ^public^ proclamation respecting the matter. I wish for your advice, as Mr Edwards is desirous of proper information Mrs Botsford & the Children join me in love to your Self, Mrs Furman & family & I remain Rev & dr Sir

your Brother & fellow
labourer in the Gospel
Edm^d Botsford

Rev: Richard Furman
Charleston

Rev: & dear Sir,   Bethel Nov 18 1793

            I have been confined upwards of five Weeks & am yet very weak & low can just walk about the House have not been able to ride.[149] I really thought I was going to enter the joy of my Lord, but I am detained a little longer what for I know not; more trials no doubt, I fear not much more usefulness, many things to me appear very gloomy, however if I am but upheld by an Almighty Power, I trust all will be finally well. I wish I had strength to communicate some of the experience I was favoured with in the near

---

journey of 7,000 miles in 1790-1791 and visiting 250 churches. On a second journey between 1792 and 1794 he covered 10.000 miles and visited 550 churches. The information he gathered was published in three editions of his *Register of the Baptist Denomination in North America*, (Richmond, VA: 1792; Boston, MA: 1794; and Hanover, NH: 1796). *Encyclopedia of Southern Baptists*, vol. 3, s.v. "Asplund, John"; Brackney, *Dictionary of the Baptists*, 36-37.

[149] Botsford's illness prevented him from preparing the Circular Letter for the Charleston Association annual meeting in November, 1793, as he had been charged to do; he was requested to have it ready for the 1794 meeting instead. Rippon, *Baptist Register, 1794-1797*, 73. Botsford's 1794 Letter was entitled "On the Duty of Christians in Matters of Controversy." Furman, *Charleston Association*, 98-104.

views I had of death. I can at present only say I never before had such a view of sin & Christ, pray for me my Brother that this sore Affliction may be sanctified to me.

Mr Adams has the following paragraph in his Letter to me "I beg you will send an order down to any of your friends for my sons board & schooling & it shall be paid as soon as it comes to hand." He does not mention who is to pay it, perhaps you are acquainted with his factor. I have however enclosed the Acct & order & beg you if you know who to apply to to receive the money & apply it as follows. vis to the payment of the two accts you sent me, & at a convenient time send me a rec^t I am quite fatigued. Mrs Botsford joins me in love to Mrs Furman your Self & children & I remain Rev & dear Sir in much Affection

yours in best Bonds
Edm^d Botsford

PS Excuse no notice being taken of your last letter to me

Revd E. B. April 14th 1795
Rev: Richard Furman
Charleston

Rev & d^r Sir   George Town Apl 14. 1795

I came here on the 2^d Inst on a visit to my old friends & to Mr Staughton and as usual was kindly received, found them in general well in health, but Religion at a low ebb, as is the case every where to my knowledge. Mr Staughton intends to remove, so that our friends will probably be left destitute, I am sorry for them as they are a worthy People. as a Church they soon begin to experience trials. I am truly sorry to perceive the distance which is kept up between the Minister & the people, but am convinced it can never be otherwise while M^r S is among them; what a pity that so aimiable a Man such a good preacher, such an agreeable companion which every one allows M^r S ~~is~~ to be should be so unhappy.[150] I have rec'd nothing from you since the Association

---

[150] William Staughton (1770-1829) was born in Coventry, England. He was recommended by John Rippon, editor of the *Baptist Register,* to Richard Furman, who proposed him as pastor to the Georgetown Church in 1793. As Botsford indicates here, Staughton did leave Georgetown in 1795 and moved to New Jersey. His later career was far more successful than his unhappy eighteen months in Georgetown. He was awarded a

but as the minister &c are not here I suppose they are sent by Mr Morgan to Jeffers's Creek. You will excuse this short epistle as my mind is not composed for writing. You will be so good as to accept the will for the deed. Mr Cuttino's family joins in best love to

Mrs Furman & family & I remain dr &

Rev'd Sir with sincere affection yours &c

Edm^d Botsford

Mr Botsford. July 20th 1795
Revd Richd Furman
Charleston

Honoured by
Capt McIntosh

Rev & dear Sir

Bethel July 20. 1795

Enclosed I send you the Acct of Mr Edwards; you will easily perceive I have been assisted in the language, ~~but~~ it is but Justice to say the Ideas are my own; much more might in justice be said of him, but what is said is strictly true and I think from the acct given any of his acquaintance ~~would~~ even, if his name had not been added, ^would^ have known for whom it was designed. Now my Brother I send it you, & beg you to peruse it & if you see proper, make any alterations, either to add or diminish or send it as it is, or not send it at all, just as you think it may be best, for which you have my entire approbation, & shall have my thanks.[151]
I have also finished all the writing respecting the commission & shall close the whole tomorrow. Blessed be God we had a large congregation yesterday, & I

DD by Princeton in 1798, became Minister of the First Baptist Church in Philadelphia, the first President of Columbian College, now The George Washington University, from 1822-1827, and the first president appointed to Georgetown College in Kentucky. He died en route to Kentucky before taking up his responsibilities as president. *Encyclopedia of Southern Baptists*, s.v. "Staughton, William"; Brackney, *Dictionary of the Baptists*, 540-541; *Oxford Dictionary of American National Biography*, s.v. "Staughton, William."

[151] It is likely that Botsford here refers to an obituary for Deacon Abel Edwards (1739-1793) of the Welsh Neck Church. An obituary for Edwards appeared in Rippon, *Baptist Register, 1794-1797*, 500-502 and Furman was a regular contributor to the *Register*.

trust something more like the power of religion among us than I have seen lately. It has been a comfortable quarterly meeting.[152]

July 28 I am now waiting for an opportunity to send the packet. I have as directed by Mr Falconer fastened to & sealed up with the commission, the depotitions & ~~Capt M^eIntoshes~~ our certificate & directed it to the Judge, under cover to Rev Ustick.

I have heard that two others have applied for baptism at Jeffers's Creek, the Church have applied to Rev Pugh & myself to ordain Mr Cooper, I have not seen M^r P on the occasion, but expect shortly. As I forgot to write a few lines to Mr Ustick in the cover of the commission you will be so obliging a[illeg.]nd the one directed for him Last night we had the heaviest rain which fell this year & small rain & thick cloud all this day, ~~as~~ my sight has failed so much I can with difficulty write, every stroke of my pen appears to me at the ^small^ distance I am obliged to keep my eyes from the paper, as three or four, so that in a great measure I write by guess. Mrs Botsfords & children join in respects to Mrs Furman & family & I remain

Rev: & d^r Sir with real affection
your Edmund Botsford

PS You will be kind enough to
excuse the scant paper; as I
had written on the other half sheet,
& did not discover it till
I had finished the above

Rev: Richard Furman
Charleston
Honoured by M^r J Brown

Rev & dear Sir   Bethel Octr 7. 1795

For some days past I have been quite poorly, yet keep about. I shall enclose in this a long Letter which will tire you to read it, it will however shew I think of you sometimes.

We have had a nother very high fresh, which has hurt us a little more. We are in such a wretched hardned [?] situation that nothing seems to move us; even the sudden death of young Mr Edwards who we all were fond of, makes no impression, except on the poor distressed Mother. The news reached her at a

---

[152] Botsford wrote that eight or nine churches in the Pee Dee district met quarterly to confer and preach. Rippon, *Baptist Register, 1790-1793,* 105.

time when his ^only^ Brother lay as we all thought in a dangerous situation, poor Woman! He however is almost recovered. My Negro Fellow is now cleared even of the s suspicion of the robbery alluded to in the enclosed. It proved to be a fellow belonging to a Mr Furnice. He was tried for the fact by 5 freeholders & 2 magistrates 3 of whom gave their opinion it was Burglary, so that he very narrowly escaped death, for the robbery he was punished with 100 stripes & the loss of an ear. I have gathered my River Crop, I believe there may be in the whole 50 bushels of good corn. I have 2 other Horses sick which I expect will die. Well, I will try to be resigned, the Lord gave & the Lord takes away, I will add, Blessed be the name of the Lord. All will be right at the last I hope, all my fear is I shall not improve these trials as I ought. I hope to have the pleasure of seeing you at the Association,[153] in the mean time I remain Rev & d^r Sir your unworthy Brother

&c Edmund Botsford.

12 March 1796. Mr Botsford Answered
Rev Richard Furman
Charleston

Honoured by
Mr Ja^s Brown

Rev & d^r Brother   Bethel Mar 10 1796

Your very consolatory epistle of the 29 ult came to hand yesterday. I return you many thanks for it, I hope I shall profit by it; at present I am in a very distracted state of mind & my health some what impaired; I am not fit for business of any kind, yet have begun to force myself to it. In the midst of a busy world I am like one in a waste howling Wilderness. O my Brother if I was in darkness & in a backsliding state before the loss of my Earthly treasure, as I certainly was, how much more so now, yet I have no right to complain, I do not charge God foolishly, I do believe the trial is designed for my good, but O wretched man that I am, I do not wisely improve it. O my Brother it is now above a month since I consigned my once dear M^{ra} B to the

---

[153] Botsford was chosen, along with John David and Evander McIver, to represent Welsh Neck at the Charleston Association meeting for 1795. Botsford was to serve on the Association's General Committee. *WNCB*, 42, 6 October 1795.

silent tomb, & not one gleam of light hath been afforded, not one word from that best of Beings has been spoken to my poor distressed Soul, & perhaps never may in this world.[154] I see the propriety of what you have written, but O my hard, hard heart I cannot O I cannot return to my God. O my Brother all the darkness & distress I ever experienced before this, is in ^no^ way to be compared to the present, surely if Jesus should condesend to speak to my poor Soul once more It will be the sweetest voice I ever heard. I have heard some of the d[r] people of God speak of their distress in such times which I thought bordered on exaggeration but now O my poor Soul is plunged into a dismal gulph indeed. I feel like a sparrow alone on the house top; can it be that ever I shall have reason to say either in time or eternity, this affliction was good for me! O blessed Jesus what didst though suffer in the garden, on the Cross!

Since I wrote the above these words slipt into my mind, & I fear only slipt in, however they are the first that have even slipt in as I remember. I will lead thee by a way which though knowest not. & also the following What I do now thou knowest not but shall know hereafter. O if God will lead me all will be well, it must be well, & tho I am so blind as not to see the reason of his conduct towards me now, yet I shall see in a coming day. 12th These two last days my mind has been more composed than at any time since the 7th of feb, for which I desire to be thankful.[155] Those four Worthies you mention as dead, must be a great stroke to the Church of God. Romain was the last preacher I heard in England
Lords day evening 13th This day I was enabled to say some thing from those comfortable words of the Prophet Isaiah 51:11 [?] The Reedeemed of the Lord shall return &c. I think I felt some assistance from above, some of the hearers I thought gave more attention than usual. This morning a poor Negro belonging to Mr. D[?] Williams related his experience to me, I hope God is at work with him, & I heard of another Negro under soul trouble; believe me my dr Brother I think it affords me more satisfaction to find the Lord is at work upon those 2 poor creatures, than I should be to call the globe my own. As M[r] Ja[s]-Brown sets off tomorrow for town must finish this to Night. I have not had an opportunity of enquiring who will take any of the sermons; I fear but few. All M[r] Hart's acquaint- are gone but 2 or 3, and times with us are bad, very bad I assure you,_ I rec[d] the Register N[o] 9 & 10 some time ago & have disposed of them all, the minutes are not yet come to hand, but have heard of them, expect them this week. Have sent M[r] Woods. I am obliged to you for your kindness in sending

---

[154] Botsford is referring here to the death of his second wife, Caty, on 7 February 1796. See WNCB, 42.

[155] Botsford went through a similar period of despair followed by religious consolation after the death of his first wife, Susanna. See his letter to Furman, above, 20 April 1790.

the pieces you mention, I hope to receive them safe, & shall introduce them among my acquaintance, but I rather think they will not sell, you can hardly conceive the situation we are in, a few & but very few in ~~hor~~ our neighbourhood have made any thing for market & they that have will not buy books.

I sincerely request you to write a few lines by Mr Brown, if you knew how much I prize your letters in general & your last in particular, you would steal an hour from your numerous avocations to favour me. I hope my mind will be more composed, indeed I cannot long continue as I have been lately, but I <u>will hope</u> God will send releif [sic], as I trust since I began this, He has begun. I think you had better not send but a dozen of the sermons. Could I afford it I would order 50 copies, but I cannot, it is a question if I shall not have to pay for half what I have mentioned, I do not know if you will be able to read this as I am obliged to use a pair of spectacles which are too old for my eyes, & they magnify very much, so that I have just observed when I look on the writing without them I cannot read a word.

Do my d^r Brother lay my case before the Lord, O pray that I may return to him with my whole heart. Wishing you every blessing

I remain d^r Brother in distress yours & c

E Botsford

PS My d^r little Caty has been very ill of the croup, but is nearly recovered thanks be to God.

I requested Mr McIver to insert in the papers the death of Mrs Botsford, I do not know if he has done it as I seldom see the Charleston papers lately. I would thank you for information by Mr Brown

Revd Richard Furman
Charleston
Honored by
Mr Ja^s Brown

Dr Brother   Bethel April 10 1796

I feel my self obliged to you for your good wishes for me; I am still much in the dark & very uncomfortable; in many respects my Way seems hedged up; most appearances are very gloomy, I am more & more satisfied my work is done in this place, and the Lord only knows how I am to be disposed of, I feel desirous to be found in the path of duty when I know it. On Tuesday last we met for worship, I found a little liberty to tell the few who met the situation we are in, I conclude this place will not be long before it will be deprived of the gospel; when a people get light by the Word it surely will be taken from them; I was in hopes some time ago it was midnight with us, but I now begin to fear I was mistaken, however in cold winter nights, it often seems a long time from midnight to morning; especially to those who are upon watch. I must confess I feel almost at liberty to go if a door was to open for me any where else.[156]

Time has been when it was very agreeable to me to visit Charleston, but I have some time past given up the Idea of ever preaching there again, (unless on some particular occasion, such as for instance as the present,) not from any dislike to any person, or any usage I received, for I have nowhere been treated kinder than in Charleston: And I believe my unworthy labours have in some measure been blest there, for which I hope I feel thankful. But the truth is Pride is in the way; till within these few years I did not see & feel my self as I ought; I frequently blush at the remembrance of my past headlong forward conduct; now I am rather afraid I err on the other hand, I really feel my self a poor empty worthless trifleing old man, at least almost an old man.

I am however really sorry that I cannot oblige my dear Friend, for such I esteem Brother Furman. My temporal affairs are in such a situation that I do not see how I can leave them, I have not a Horse will carry me to Town, my provision just out except bread, almost all my work before me, no overseer, over head & ears in debt, my people conceive themselves not able to help me, the present & next month 2 very busy ones. I really feel very desirous to oblige you, I wish you to visit Savannah & G Town, because I think it would be for the glory of God; but to promise my Brother assistance when it is more [than?] probable I cannot comply would be wrong. I have talked of visiting G [Town but?] scarcely think I can. If I can make out that it will be as much. If however I can go to GT I will come to Chton, & if I do it will be late in May. Would not Mr Cooper be acceptable? if so I could supply for him. I am truly sorry at the discription you give of the situation of the Charleston Church. Surely my Brother some great evil is coming upon us & those pious souls who have lately taken their flight, are take from the evil to come. Since my d^r M^{rs} B died, two other Women have died in child-bed, one a member with us. My daughter Polly is expected shortly to lie in.

My d^r Children unite with me in a kind rembrance to you M^{rs} F & Children
        & remain d^r Brother yours in Jesus,
                Edm Botsford

PS. I am much pleased at the information

---

[156] Botsford did indeed find an opportunity to leave Welsh Neck and move to Georgetown at the end of this very year.

of Doctor Keith's preaching for you, & of your preaching at the Scotch Church, this looks like Brethren, I hope a liberal spirit will continue to be cultivated especially among Xtians.

May 3^d 1796 from Mr Botsford
Rev Mr Richd Furman
Charleston

Honored by Mr E King
Daughter Polly a child (dr) [note written sideways on front]

Dr Brother   Bethel May 3^d 1796

      Your fav[our by] Mr Brown together with the other articles all came safe, & for which [I than]k you. I am truly sorry I cannot oblige you, by supplying your place, I find it is not in my power, be assured my dr Sir it is no small mortification to me, as I wish much to see you, if it were only for two or three hours conversation, & I sincerely wish you to go to Savannah. O how sorry I am at what you mention respecting your pecuniary difficulties, I hope however you have resources in some measure adequate thereto. I suppose 300£ would clear me, but that sum sued for & property sold as usual in such cases would take all I have. I am in a great strait respecting leaving Pee Dee, I wish not to do it if I can avoid it, but I have been sinking money these three years and my people seem to act as if they thought I could live on the air, several who used to be good subscribers have fallen off, & for what I know not, I do not know or hear of any thing alledged against my Character, or preaching Infidelity increases, & hence a neglect of attendence on the Word. And for three years past but little made, even those who have made pritty good corps [sic], plead the same excuse as those who have made none. And what adds to my uneasiness I have not the regard for the people at large I once had & which I think a Minister ought to have for a people with whom he is connected, it is true there are a few for whom I have the highest regard, but I speak of the Whole taken together, & this has been the case for some time, I had some serious thoughts of leaving this place before my d^r M^{rs} B died, & she had consented to it, if I thought it duty. As for G Town, I think a person of superior abilities to mine should be there, true my poor labours have been in some measure owned there & in Cha'ton, but there is a great deal of difference between visiting a people & residing among them, however I must confess I have had some thoughts of G Town, but I would do nothing in haste, nor without the advice of some of my Brethren, yourself in particular, & I should take it as a favour for your candid opinion on the matter. They are a people I love, I feel myself as it were at home among them, but after all I rather feel diffident respecting my suiting them. I trust I shall continue to pray for your son, I am glad to hear such an acct of him, I hope he will be a comfort to you; I sincerely congratulate you on the marriage of your daughter, please present my sincere compliments to them & tell them I wish them happiness. I believe you have made a small mistake or two in the dates, in your acct of my venerable Father Hart[?] I have the following in a letter from him dated Nov 30 1785:__ I was baptized Apl 3^d 1741.-- ordained Oct 18, 1759 -- arrived at Chton the 2^d of december following -- you say August 3^d -- Oct 10 -- early in November – I think the Account very Just, O may I be found more worthy of such a Father!^{157} I confess I do not so well approve the detracting from a good character, we all know every one has imperfections, but they need not be published, it gives a handle to some, especially if their own failings are of the same nature. I now refer to your account of your honoured parent – if she was hasty, I did not know it, no body ~~knew it~~ but her acquaintance knew it, why then publish it^{158} You will excuse this freedom, I am not alone in the opinion, my paper is full & it is the last half sheet I have

yours in best bonds Edm^d Botsford

[on the back, a separate note]
I am glad to hear Mr Staughton is likely to be so well provided for, I wish he may be useful. The Acct of the Missionary Society in London is truly surprising. Surely My Brother God is fast preparing the way for the accomplishing those great things he has promised to his Church, O when shall we see the outpouring of his spirit among us? I think every American ought to read the Spirit of despotism, it pleases me much, I am obliged to you for sending it, I have one bespoke, & hope for more, as I wish many to read it. I preached on Lords day from "The Kingdom of Heaven is at hand", but I fear, greatly fear it is at a distance from this place, however the residue of the spirit is with the Lord. I can with pleasure inform you that 2 or 3 or 4 Negros are under serious concern; but not one white person that I know of. Not less than 4 Women have died in child-bed since my dr Mrs B. My daughter Polly was safely delivered of a daughter on Saturday 23 last and is quite brave. We are now suffering a great drought, & cold nights, very hurtful to small grain & to forward corn. I have

---

^{157} Furman used the dates supplied by Botsford in the obituary he wrote for Hart in the *Baptist Register*. Botsford refers to Hart as his "Father" because Hart converted him to the Baptist faith and later assisted at his ordination. Rippon, *Baptist Register, 1794-1797*, 507-508.

^{158} Botsford is presumably referring here to Furman's obituary for his mother, Rachel, who had died on 15 October 1794. Published in the *Baptist Register,* it described Rachel as having a "warmth of temper [that] sometimes caused her to be imprudent..." Rippon, *Baptist Register, 1794-1797*, 281-283.

been labouring under more violent temptations lately than I remember ever to have been assaulted with, however Glory to God I have been in some measure I trust supported under them, & please my self the friend of sinners will enable me to overcome them. With love to Mrs Furman & Children in which mine join I remain

> dr Brother yours in best bonds,
> Edmund Botsford

Mr Botsford July 18th 1796
Revd Mr Richard Furman
        Charleston

Honoured by
M^{r} U Coggeshall

Rev & d^{r} Brother   Bethel July 18. 1796

        I have only time by this opportunity to write a few hasty lines, which will inform you that through Mercy my self & Family are well, at least we are all about. We have had two swells in the River present one being about 3 feet higher has destroyed nearly a third of the crops in those Plantations which are low; however I suppose if we should escape at this, very little complaint will be heard.

In Payn's paper of 11th inst. I perceive in the list of letters in post office one directed to Rev E Botsford which I suppose to be mine, I should therefore take it as a favour if you will be so kind as to take it out, if it is not returned to the General Post Office in Philadelphia, if so I would thank you to inform me by post, as it may be from Ireland & if it is I suppose the contents are of importance to me, & wish to send for it, which I can easily do, if I am inform'd in time to prevent its destruction.[159]

Yesterday was quarterly meeting with us, only Mr Rob Thomas attended, he delivered the best discourse I ever heard him, or I was in the best situation to hear; the subject was important "For ye are bought with a price, therefore &c"

Is the 12 N° of the Register arrived?   In consequence of a letter from Mr Cuttins I informed him of the resolution I had taken of leaving this place & the

---

[159] Presumably, this letter from Ireland was connected with the financial matter that Botsford mentioned in his 17 August 1791 letter—news of some property that would allow him to settle his debts.

steps I had taken relative to it. The more I think on the subject the more I am convinced of my duty to leave this, yet I cannot say but I feel a considerable struggle, here are some few & but very few friends & Children who lie near me. Will you favour me (if you can steal so much time) with your oppinion on the subject, I mean what those things are (in a general way) which may determine a Minister to leave a place.

But I must conclude with my best wishes to your self
Mrs Furman & family & remain Rev & d^r Brother
yours in best bonds
Edm^d Botsford

PS. Please present my love to your son
if he could find freedom, I should be
fond of a line from him.
I beg leave to add my mind was much exercised yesterday in prayer for two
discriptions of persons viz. Missionaries & those in distress, I hope the exercise
was from the Lord.

Cheraw Ch
14 Oct 1796 Mr Botsford Paid 15

Rev. Richard Furman
Church-Street
Charleston

by[?] Post

Rev & dear Brother Bethel October 12, 1796

It seems a little age since I heard from you, indeed when in George Town I heard your son Richard had been sick with the Fever prevailing in Chaston & saw an advertisement in a late paper respecting your appointment to deliver an oration in the Orphan House or something of the kind, but have rec'd no line from you a great while. I wrote to you some time ago by M^r U Coggeshall to request you would be so obliging as to take out of the post office a letter I saw advertised, as directed to me, & to send it by the post; as I did not receive it I was in hopes of meeting it in George Town, but when there found there had been little or no communication between the two

Towns a great while, I suspect you have not rec'd my letter by Mr Coggeshall, however I would now thank you to enquire for it, & be so kind as to inform me by post if it is sent on to Philadelphia. I said I have been to George Town, but I did not write to you from thence, as I was inform'd it was not probable that there would be any opportunity of conveyance by land for some time, & to send by Water it was said was very uncertain as to your receiving. I had acquainted my friends of my intention ~~respecting~~ to leave the Cheraws, & in answer to a letter of theirs, had given them some intimations they might expect me to George Town. While I was in Town the Chh gave me a call, & it appeared to me to be the voice of the Town in general for me to settle there. I have therefore concluded to go. I am really sorry for these People, but still think I am in my duty to leave them.

In a very candid manner I informed our Church before I went to Town, of all that had passed between me & G T friends & also my views & difficulties &c &c. nothing has as yet presented to cause any quarrel & I hope nothing may. Not many Months since I thought scarce any thing but sickness in my Family or person should prevent my attendance on the Association, but however I am disapointed in my intention, for which I am truly sorry. I am so ~~very~~ particularly circumstanced at this time that I cannot think it duty to leave home; my Affairs are so deranged & must ~~be~~ in some measure be arranged before I leave this that I have not time. My little crop to get in, many things to settle & sell &c &c that I really have not a moment to loose. I believe Mr Cooper will attend & if so, by him shall find our letter, & what little money we have collected for the fund. Some of Mr David Williams's Negroes appear to be enquiring the way to Zion, two or three have given their experiences & are accepted but not Baptized, as M^r W is not returned. Also two or three of those Negroes which did belong to Capt Brown, gave in & rec'd but now they are sold & shortly to go off. It is probable you have heard that Capt Brown sold his Negroes to Doctor Mason, He (doctor Mason) has sold them to a Charles Brown who is going to send them to Cat Island (a little distance from George Town) Doctor Mason it is said made 300£ by the bargain. Now I am upon the raids [?], it is said Mr Brown prior to the sale of the Negroes by Capt Brown to Doctor Mason, sold them to David Williams, what gives the Report some credit among us, is, that Capt Brown offered the Negroes to David for 500£ & he refused them; Doctor Mason sold them for 900 £ & reserved a likely boy to himself. So much for the news of the day among us. I wish I had better to communicate. I have heard by way of M^r McIver you have had an addition to your Church of several Members, I sincerely congratulate you on the occasion & wish you many more seals to your ministry; thus you have mercies amid Judgments.

Some of Gods Children have their severest trials in their early days, others in the close of their lives; I seem to be of the latter class; well if I am but a Child of

God, all will be well in the end, but I wish to be a dutiful one, for my heavenly Father has been kind to me, to me who have been one of the unworthiest. As I am now about to enter on a new scene of life, I wish to close my Peedee life in such a way as (at least) no dishonour may be justly cast on the cause of Religion. When at Jeffers's Creek some time ago, Mr Dawson [?] asked me if I had not a half bound volume of the Register, which I rec'd by the way of Mr Morgan, I told him I had, he said was designed for him. I rec'd but the one & for which I accounted with you. it is true I did not send for it, but you have charged me with it & I wish to keep it. Nevertheless if you wish me to deliver it to Mr Dawson [?], I shall, at same time I wish for one.

I shall endeavour to settle a plan on some certainty respecting the Register before I leave the Cheraws.

Our Neighbourhood as yet has been very healthy in general among the exceptions, Capt McIntosh is one who has been on the very verge of Eternity. I had not returned from Town before he was on the recovery, but have reason to believe his principles were staggered in the view of death, & no wonder for they were the reverse of those derived from the Scriptures. What a mercy my dear & Honored Sir it is that you & I were not left to embrace such, which at this time are so fashionable. Not unto us, but to thy name O God be the Glory. May we be so happy to hold fast what we already have, & daily feel the sweet influences of the Holy Spirit enabling us to reduce to practice those truths we profess to believe, then my d^r Sir we shall not be afraid even in the valley of the shadow of death.

My children unite with me in love to yourself Mrs Furman & family & with every sentiment of affection

I remain Rev^d & d^r Brother
yours in a dear Redeemer
Edmund Botsford.

Rev Richard Furman
Charleston

Honoured by
Capt J Brown

Dear Brother   George Town Mar 24. 1797

Your favour of the 8th inst & the Packets I received & have forwarded all of them. I am much obliged to you for your kind wishes & prayers for the Church & my self, the good Lord grant your request. O my Brother I feel for you with respect to your temporal affairs. I hope you may not meet with ill treatment; & that you may settle the whole better than your present fears may suggest. My mind has been a good deal soured already in my settlement & I have but made a beginning; I have however met with kindness also. I am in hopes to close the whole in a few months or nearly so. I think I shall have 4 Servants left when all is finished, if in the mean time no accident happens & my creditors do not sue me. I am now on a bargain of importance, if it takes place I shall not have much more trouble. O what a world we live in! Yet I must think all things considered it is best it should be so; not that I mean to excuse any neglect or bad conduct of mine, for that I must suffer. Shall we be favoured with your company this spring? If you can make it convenient it will be esteemed a singular favour by us all, but by none more than my self. My dear Children unite with me in an affectionate remembrance to Mrs Furman, your Children & all friends & I remain

d^r Brother yours in best bonds

Edm^d Botsford

B. A Spiritual Voyage

A Spiritual Voyage
performed between
the years 1766
and 1813

By

Edmund Botsford AM

Presented to Mrs Maryann
McIver
a sincere friend to the Author
George Town
1813[160]

Dear Madam,

Your honoured parents Mr. David & Mrs Anne Williams were
~~very~~ particularly kind to me at a time when I was in need of friendship. They
gave me a home when I was destitute; your Father instructed me when I was
ignorant & your Mother paid every attention to my wants. Since your
remembrance, you know, I was always esteemed by your Mother, as one of her
friends, for whom she ever expressed a singular regard; you also Madam have
honoured me with your friendship. As a token of gratitude & as a keep-sake [2]
keep-sake[161] to remember one who considers himself under peculiar obligations
to your family, I have taken the liberty to present you with an Allegory which I
call a spiritual voyage.[162] It is possible some of the sea terms used may not be

---

[160] The original ms. is in the Special Collections of the Duke Library at Furman
University. It is part of the Botsford Family Collection, Box 2, Ser. III, Folder 46.

[161] At the bottom of each odd-numbered page, Botsford usually wrote the first word
of the next page, in order to facilitate uninterrupted reading, in imitation of many printed
works of the period. The numbers in square brackets represent the start of a new page in
the manuscript.

[162] Botsford's allegory is likely inspired by John Bunyan's *Pilgrim's Progress*
(1678), one of the most widely printed works in the English language. (As it happens,
Botsford came from Bedfordshire, the county where Bunyan had lived and preached for
most of his life.) *Pilgrim's Progress* was one of Botsford's favorite books as a boy, and
several parts of it he "committed to memory." Mallary, *Botsford*, 14.

Although Botsford refers to this work as a "Spiritual Autobiography," he refers to
few actual events of his life; the only two identifiable events in this tale are his departure

quite familiar to you, but as you have in the course of your reading perused voyages of another nature I presume you will be at little loss for my meaning. As I have lived several years in a sea-port I was led to ~~adopt~~ prefer a voyage, to a journey by land, for my subject.[163]

[3] The Ship Convert was launched from Conviction Dock, in the port of Repentance-unto-life, in the Island of Regeneration, where she was fitted for a voyage to the Port of Felicity, on the Continent of Glory.

    This was in the year of our Lord 1766.[164] I took my passage a few days before she sailed. As I never intended to return, I took leave of all my friends & the place of my nativity. The place in which I was born was called Dark-Island, which I left without the least regret as I was informed by Mr Tell-true that the place would certainly be destroyed; and at the same time he advised me to [4] to undertake this voyage. I soon fell in with his opinion, took his advice and engaged a passage. Our Ship as I said was named the Convert, she was commanded by Capt Godly-fear; carried sixty six guns, & was every way equiped [sic] for a long voyage and for defence. The 1st Leiut [sic] was Mr Serious-consideration. 2d Leiut Mr Spiritual-man – The sailing Master Mr Experience, Master Mate Mr True-peace; the Ships Clerk Mr [illeg.] Notice-everything, the Steward, Mr Careful, the Boatswain Mr Fortitude. There were several midshipmen, as Mr Hate-sin, Mr Love-holiness & Mr pray-for-all. The Chaplain Mr Watchful, the chief [5] chief gunner, Mr Resist-the-Devil & some as brave men as ever trod the deck of a ship, such as Jack Honesty, Tom Trusty, Bob Industry, Ned Hope-well & the very Cabin Boys were smart lads, Dick Ready-mind & Joe Swift-to-obey. We also had a Company of Marines commanded by Capt: Resist-unto-blood, Leiut [sic] Courage, Sergeant Fear-nought & corporal Feignt-not, & among the rank & file some as brave fellows as ever handled a fire-lock, as John Patience, Wm Piety, Joseph Virtue, Charles Hardy & Ben Love-truth. We were well supplied with all sorts of armour, ammunition & small arms. Our ship was victualed with a never failing [6] failing supply of the Bread of life, the water of consolation & the wine of the

---

from his homeland, England ("Dark-Island"), and his baptism. Most of the narrative concerns the typical struggles, temptations, and triumphs of a Christian. Botsford wrote another memoir that provided more conventional autobiographical details; though lost, much of it was incorporated into Charles Mallary's *Memoir of Elder Edmund Botsford* (Charlestown: W. Riley, 1832), though Mallary added additional material from Botsford's letters and from information provided by family and acquaintances.

   [163] Botsford lived in Charleston when he first arrived in America and he had lived in Georgetown since leaving Welsh Neck in 1797. His use of a sea voyage distinguishes his work from Bunyan's tale of a journey by land.

   [164] Botsford actually left England on 18 November 1765 and arrived in Charleston on 28 January 1766. Mallary, *Botsford,* 26-27.

Spirit. Were you going [on] a voyage would you not be pleased to sail in such a
Ship, with such a commander & such a crew? I sailed in this same vessel
upwards of forty years. Well all things being in readiness we sailed out of the
Harbour with a fine wind, & had for several days pleasant weather. You might
hear from stem to stern of the ship the sailors singing "The Lord is my
Shepherd;" to the tune of, "I shall not want," all day long. However after a
while, the wind shifted & a storm came on, in the Night too, & as we had [7]
had been favoured with such fine weather & most of us young sailors, the storm
appeared dreadful. The sea run high, most of us were seasick, much of our fresh
provisions were washed overboard, & our songs were turned to mourning. O it
was a dreadful night. As soon as day appeared, we discovered Land; we found
by our maps, this must be the Island of Spiritual-pride, near to which are
dangerous rocks and quick-sands. There we saw the Rock Selfsufficiency on
which Capt Peter had nearly been lost, there is also the Rock Highmind, &
several others among which we found ourselves entangled. It was our [8] mercy
the storm abated or what the consequence might have been who can tell. This
Island is laid down in the latitude of, Off-guard, in the chart it was thus
recorded,"Let him that thinketh he standeth take heed lest he fall;"[165] and also
this note [drawing of a hand with pointing finger] "The Lord knoweth the proud
afar off." The Capt now called all hands on deck & represented to the crew that
they had not behaved as the [sic] should have done during the storm; that it was
more owing to their misconduct than to the badness of the weather that they had
suffered so much, but he hoped however that for the future they would behave
better, [9] that it was a mercy they had not been lost among the Rocks.
  The weather now cleared up & the wind came fair & we got into a pretty good
way again. We had not sailed far however, before we perceived a large ship
bearing down upon us, & was soon along side us. I do not know how it
happened, but before we were aware of it she poured a whole broadside upon us,
& killed & wounded several of our men, & threw us into great confusion, &
before we recovered from the confusion she boarded us fore & aft; and now we
had dreadful work of it, for by this time it was dark. This ship was [10] a large
man of war, belonging to Lucifer, commanded by Capt Temptation & was full
of men, most of whom was now on board of us, & you may be sure we had
dreadful work of it, as these fellows fight best in the dark. Although some of
our men behaved cowardly, yet the greater part behaved manfully, especially
considering this was the first engagement. After a long struggle our Capt came
at swords point with Capt Temptation & wounded him sorely, crying out in the

[165] Botsford's memoir states that on the voyage over he became convinced he was
saved, though he later decided that this was a false conviction, due to spiritual pride.
Mallary, *Botsford,* 27. It is possible that he is representing this experience allegorically in
this segment of the *Spiritual Voyage.*

full strength of his soul, "Rejoice not against me O mine enemy, when I fall I shall arise." The other officers seeing the spirited [11] spirited behaviour of the Captain, all at once rushed upon the enemy with such fury that they soon cleared the decks of them; & now being able to use the great guns, they soon made the villan [sic] glad to sheer off. However we suffered much in the action, many were killed & more wounded; although most of the Officers were wounded; as God would have it, none were slain. And what was very remarkable, those which were killed were mostly such as could be best spared. I remember the names of two or three of them. There were Tom Live-on-flames __ Harry Fair-speech __ Jac Rest-on-prayer—& Will Scruple-truth. We set too, to put [12] put things to rights. We had scarcely trimmed our sails & got under a good sailing way, before we saw another vessel. But now, we not ~~only~~ knowing what vessel it was were soon prepared to defend ourselves. However it proved to be the Formality, commanded by Capt Blind-to-truth. When they came up with us, the Capt said we were a parcel of inthusiasts [sic] & knew not to where we were going. One of his Officers held out a purse of gold to invite some of our men to leave our Ship & enter with them. Another Officer told us we were a company of poor mean scoundrels & would be treated as such at every port we put in at.[166] [13] But we paid little attention to them & kept on our course, & soon observed another Sail, she proved to be ship Please-flesh, commanded by Captain Love-ease. This ship kept us company some time, indeed too long, for by often speaking her & some of our officers going on board, some of the men got no good by it. I perceived for some time after we had been in company with this Ship, our officers were not so strict in keeping order as they had been. The next Ship we discovered was one which shewed the colours of our nation & we took for a friend. Her Capt invited the Capt on board & several of his officers. [14] These were such company as pleased us for they praised every thing they saw; I observed the Master Mr Experience was very fond of them & shewed them every thing, he thought worth their notice. Even the Chaplain, Mr Watchful was pleased with their company, indeed the Captain himself shewed them much civility. I thought the clerk, Mr Notice-everything seemed a little uneasy at the freedom that was used. However they continued with us the whole day. In the evening they went on board their own ship, and as she tacked &

---

[166] It seems very possible that the *Formality* refers to the Church of England, which had been the established church in South Carolina when Botsford arrived in the colonies, as well as in his birthplace of England. The language of Captain Blind-to-Truth sounds very similar to comments made about the Baptists and other evangelical denominations by Anglican churchmen such as Charles Woodmason (c. 1720-1789). Baptists in many of the Thirteen Colonies had taken advantage of the Revolution to campaign for the end of church establishments. Botsford's predecessor at Welsh Neck, Elhanan Winchester, had taken a leading role in lobbying the revolutionary government of South Carolina to disestablish the Church of England. (See WNCB, 20).

stood from us I saw very plainly the word Vanity written in capital letters on her stern, this I [15] observed to our Capt, who told me (I thot [sic] with some concern) that one on board had informed him it was the Ship Vanity, commanded by Capt Flattery; & truly they flattered us almost out of our senses. We had scarcely lost sight of her before a sudden squal [sic] had like to have split all our sails, & as our ports were not secured we were soon half full of water, & the Squall ~~was~~ issued in a hard gale of wind; & I should have observed that just before dark, land was discovered & land too that we did not expect or know any thing of; however we had small hopes but of being wrecked on it before morning; & to add to our misfortune there was a disturbance among the officers. [16] The Clerk Mr Notice-every-thing quarilled [sic] with every one. I did not know till now that he was a person of such consequence, or that his office was of such importance. As for Mr. Experience, all blamed him. So that what with the storm without & the disturbance among the Officers & crew it was a dreadful night; nor were our fears lessened but with the day light; we then saw the emminent [sic] danger we had been in, & the storm still continuing, most of us gave up all for lost. We saw several vessels wrecked on the beach, & we expected our Ship would be added to the number. However about Noon the sky became clear [17] so that we were able to take an observation; & by the Latitude we found ourselves in, we concluded the Island we now saw & on which we were nearly cast away, was the Island of forgetfulness, a very dangerous place. Here Capt Look-back was cast away. It was very remarkable, that while we were near this Island, our minds were strangely bewildered. We had scarcely got clear from this Island before we saw a large Ship in chase of us, & it proved a Man of war belonging to Lucifer, called the Unbelief, commanded by Capt Doubting, she was very large, she soon came up with us, & fired away at a dreadful rate & soon took us [18] they treated us very roughly & put a number of hands on board to navigate the Ship, but as providence ordered it they took only a few of our hands out of the Ship; but they plundered us of almost everything that was valuable. Thus we were in a bad situation; we were going we knew not where. Although they thought they were sure of us, it happened otherwise. In the night it blowed hard, & seperated [sic] us from our Captors; & now finding we were by our selves, we plucked up heart and rose on the hands & after a desperate struggle we recovered our Ship. It was true we recovered our Ship but we were in a shattered condition; but [19] but to our great Joy, in the morning we made point comfort on the Island of deliverance, which was one of the places we were to touch at, & here we met with several Ships of our Country. Some of which had sailed long before us, & others who had left port after we had sailed. We soon found we was not the only ship that had suffered. Some that sailed from our port were totally lost; as the Ship Received-with-Joy; commanded by Capt Pleased –awhile. Also the Snow Good-intentions, commanded by Capt Soon-weary. One ship in particular was shattered in a most terrible manner, & the greater part of her men [20] men were killed, indeed it was a wonder she ever got into port. Her name was the R Resistance commanded by Capt Vallian, & truly a valliant officer he was, he had the courage of a Lion; he fought his way through a whole fleet of the Enemy, & finally arrived safe in this Island.

  This same Island is a charming place, the language spoken by the inhabitants is a very peculiar dialect, it a good deal resembles the language spoken on the Continent to which we were bound. Here are several semenaries [sic] of learning in which the several branches of spiritual Navigation are taught. Here we met with [21] some of our old Companions, who had undertakeng the same voyaged [sic] we had. & with whom we now had much satisfaction. We were entertained at this Island with every thing we could wish for. Here we got acquainted with an old gentleman by the name of Mr Prophesy who gave us much information; we were also introduced to another worthy man, Mr Record-mercy. We also engaged some new hands to supply the place of those we had lost as Ned Needful, Joe Watch-well, Nick Pray-often & Paul Humble-mind. We now having been refreshed & put our Ship into good sailing order, we again set sail [22] sail & directed our course to the Island of Ordinance. We now kept a clear Ship & exercised our men at the great guns, & the Marines at the small arms. We soon reached the Island of Ordinance, & cast our anchor in the midst of the harbor which is called the harbor of fellowship. Here also we had fine times. We were invited to a banquet which we understood was prepared at the expence [sic] of the Prince Emanuel Governor of the place to which we were bound, & who it is said frequently pays a visit to this Island; & it happened very lucky for us that He was now on the Island. [23] There is one peculiarity attending the invitation to this feast, all who are invited must, before they are permitted to his table, ŧ give an account of themselves, how they came to engage in the voyage, & also what kind of a voyage they have had since they left the port of Repentance-unto-life; then if those to whom they relate these things, approve of them, they are led into a bath in that part of the Island called Enon, after they are washed they have change of raiment given them at the cost of the Prince, & then are admitted to the feast _ and such a feast, I never before saw _ there was the [24] the Prince at the head of the Table, & you would have thought you had got among Kings – they were all cloathed in a garment that shone brighter than gold, even the garment of Humility.[167] The feast was of fat things

---

[167] The requirements for being included in Prince Emanuel's feast correspond exactly to the requirements for membership in most Baptist Churches, including Welsh Neck: candidates for membership had to make a confession of the work of God's grace on their soul that met with the approval of the congregation, and then undergo full immersion baptism. Botsford was baptized on 13 March 1767 after relating his experience of God's saving grace to Reverend Oliver Hart. Mallary, *Botsford*, 27-34.

& full of Marrow and wine on the lees well refined. I never saw such substantial joy in my life, & all the time the Prince smiling on every one of the guests in such a pleasing manner, that every one felt himself welcome, & at the close we all united in singing a song of praise to Him who had thus favoured us, & so we parted – for my part I was so delighted I could have [25] taken up my abode at this Island; but as I had engaged my passage for the continent I was compelled to leave the good company to pursue my voyage. Before we sailed our Capt engaged a Pilot one Mr Scripturish a very worthy gentleman & who understood his business well. All things being ready we again launched out into the deep, not knowing what was to befall us, but we had plenty of the very best provisions, maps charts & every thing necessary for such a voyage, & a good Pilot to steer our course, & who was well acquainted with every league of the way. Nothing material happened till we made [26] the group of Islands which lie in the latitude of difficulty & which form a strait called the narrows or narrow way which lead into the great Sea of trial, over which we had to sail in which Sea many a vessel had foundered, & many taken by the enemy. If we had not been favoured with a good Pilot we never should have hit on the right strait. At this place many a ship has been lost, owing to a mistake in taking the right way. At this time there were several vessels hovering about these Islands & at a loss which strait to enter; among them all there was but one that [27] would terminate right. There was the strait Morality, & the strait profession, & the strait Orthodox and many others – The right strait could be distinguished, by those who had a good spy=glass, by an Island on the right called Holiness & one on the left called Godliness _. Now if you steer right in the middle of the channel, you will keep clear of a little rock called depend=on=duty & a little further on you will have to guard against a spit of sand, on which many a ship has been wreck'd the sand bank is called formality, & just at the end of the strait you will meet with a quick sand which [28] has been the grave of many a vessel. this is called the quick sand of Hypocrisy. If you are careful you will observe about this dangerous place, the water bubbles up & seems to be much disturbed, some times it makes a roaring noise, at other times it is quite calm when the other parts of the strait are agitated. Haveing [sic] passed these you get into the open sea & now we thought the most of our dangers were at an end. But we were greatly mistaken, seldom a day past [sic] but we met with some difficulty or another, some times we were sickly on board, at other times storms & calms at length [29] however we made the Island of great grace; & now we got groundings on the coast of the continent of glory. But even here we sometimes we had hard times of it, our ship was crazy; the sails much worn, the masts much decayed & her upper works beginning to rot; in the best things belonging to the ship was the anchor & cable. Although we were so nigh the end of our Voyage, we found the coast a very dangerous one to some vessels. One day while we were tossing about in a hollow Sea, we saw a fine looking Ship cast a way on the Island of presumption & every soul perished. Her name was the Vain=hope commanded by Capt Not=right. [30] Another day we saw a fine new Brig cast away on the Island of Desperation; her name was, the Thoughtless, commanded by Capt Profane. She seemed to have not been long out of Port. But of all the misfortunes we were eye wittness to, the loss of the Foolish=Virgin, seemed the most to distress & alarm us. We had been in Company with her frequently on the Voyage & always understood, she was from the same port from which we came. It seems she was commanded by one Capt Deceive=self, a very clever kind of a man, but he did not understand his business, for at the very time the express came out of the harbour of felicity to order him [31] & some others over the Bar, under the direction of one of the branch Pilots, Behold this same Capt was ashore on the Island of commerce to purchase some necessaries. So the Pilot carried those who were ready over the Bar, & they soon landed safe _ But Deceiveself when he found he was left, attempted to Pilot himself in, & his Vessel was lost & every soul perished, for it was mid night when he attempted to cross the bar. We now came to the Island of Endure to the end, & here the Convert was to wait for a Pilot. While we lay here, we had an opportunity of visiting & being visited almost every day by the officers of the Ships which were waiting to be piloted over the bar. [32] This was the pleasantest time of the while voyage, as in the first place we were out of danger & almost in sight of the mouth of the harbour of felicity & then we had such good company. There was old Capt Contemplation & Comodour Stand=fast & Capt Rjoice=in=hope [sic] & many other old veterans who had long been in the service & who were now waiting for orders & a Pilot to conduct them over the Bar. Now to hear these old warriers relate their adventures, the battles they had fought, the danger they had escaped, & how finally they arrived safe, was very entertaining & instructive. [33]

At length a Pilot came to conduct the vessels into port, with orders for some of the passengers to be put on board a vessel called Wait=longer commanded by Capt Patience. I was of this number; however we had the opportunity to see the Convert go over the Bar, & by the help of our glasses could see all the way up the river to the City. As the Convert passed over the bar, we saw the Capt & most of the officers on the quarter deck shouting & singing, the last words I distinctly heard from the Catp [sic] were Glory Glory Glory!!!

O how I longed to be on board. As they sailed up the River with a fine breeze [34] they were met by vast numbers of boats & barges with colours flying & music playing. The guns also from all the forts fired salutes to welcome the Convert on her safe arrival at the port of endless Joy.

Finis

C. On Slavery

by Edmund Botsford[168]

[1] A Slave is one who is deprived of his freedom. If this definition is just, there are many kinds of slaves. But of all the different kinds, the Africans or Negro Slave is generally considered as in the worst kind of slavery. Of this however I am not a proper Judge, as I know not the usage of slaves in any country but the country in which I live, viz. S° Carolina. With slavery in this State I am well acquainted. Bad as their situation is, it is often represented much worse than it really is. I grant it was forty or fifty years ago much worse than at the present time. [2] I do not mean in this Essay to vindicate Slavery: All I aim at is to give a just description of the treatment of slaves in this State. S° Carolina is divided into the Upper & lower country. The lower country comprehends that part in which Rice is planted. The upper country, is where Corn, Cotton, Wheat &c is planted. Generally speaking on rice plantations are the greatest number of Negroes. But few Planters work less than twenty hands; many work from fifty to upward, of a hundred. There are but few plantations on which the owners do not reside a part of the year; & several on which the owners reside altogether. As I have lived a number of years [3] both in the upper & lower country and have been considerably conversant with the Negroes I am capable of giving a general description of their labour & of their treatment.[169]

And I shall first treat of the labour of the Negroes on a rice plantation. In this place it may not be improper to observe, that pounding or beating of rice, which is the hardest labour on a plantation, is now performed by Machinery, generally speaking throughout the whole State.

The plough is never used, except in some places, in breaking up the ground in the spring. The working of the land is performed with the hoe. The rice field is laid off in small portions called tasks. In some cases two Negroes are required to work one task in the day, but such is the variety, that in some parts of the work one Negro can work two tasks in one day. However except in very bad seasons & in harvest, the Negroes perform their daily labour & leave the feild [sic] from ten O clock in the morning to two in the afternoon. It is true the

---

[168] The original ms. is in the Special Collections of the Duke Library at Furman University. It is part of the Botsford Family Collection, Box 3, Folder 54.

[169] Edmund Botsford came to know slavery in the "Upper country" during his years as pastor of the Welsh Neck Baptist Church on the Pee Dee River (1779-1780 and 1782-1796). He became familiar with the different conditions of Low Country slavery during his years as pastor of the church at Georgetown (1797-1819).

labour is performed in the hot sun. But I never saw a Negro who would not prefer working in the rice field in the hotest [sic] day in Summer, to almost any kind of work in cold weather. The Negro does not love cold, nor does he complain of the heat.

[5] In every kind of work on a rice plantation the Negro has his task and generally speaking he performs it in the time above mentioned.

Few things have been more misrepresented than the labour of the Slave on a rice plantation in S° Carolina. Their labour is by no means excessive. Harvest is hard labour all the world over, so it is on a rice plantation; but the Negroes do not labour harder than the poor man in England, nor does he perform so much. With respect to their treatment. If the Negro performs his work well, as he may do, he meets with no ill treatment; why should he? [6] But if he is idle and does not perform his task, or does not perform it properly he is at the mercy of the Overseer; at least in a great measure. Most owners of slaves, now, employ, or wish to employ humane men. An Overseer who is attentive to his business, very seldom has to punish a Negro on account of his work. An Overseer on a large plantation must be a man of experience & activity, as he has the care & the management of the whole plantation on his hands.

With respect to the food for the Negroes, It is plain, but wholesome, & they have as much as they can eate. viz when fed with corn a peck per week, when [7] with small rice, the same, when with sweet potatoes a bushel per week. This I believe is the general stated allowance. Some Masters now & then give a Beeve, & some give now & then salt fish. I believe on most plantations the Negroes have some land to plant for themselves. When their daily task is performed, some employ themselves in fishing, others in making Matts, Baskets, Brooms, Piggins, pails &c for sale.[170] The plantations near Geo Town, many have the surpluss [sic] rice straw, for which they find a ready market at the 16th of a dollar per Bundle, and from April to harvest, they bring Bundles of crab grass, & wild oats by which many get more than a dollar in the week.

[8] With respect to their cloathing. [sic] The least given them is five yards of white or blue plains & a pair of shoes annually.[171] In this there is variety. Some Masters give woolen caps, & some osnabrugs &c.[172] However The honest industrious Negro & his wife & children will appear on a Sabath [sic] day neat & clean. And as he has considerable time to work for himself, & as some raise

---

[170] A "piggin" is a small pail with one stave made longer than the rest for use as a handle.

[171] By "plains" Botsford probably means plain-weave cloth, the simplest form of woven material, where warp and weft cross over each other in an alternating pattern.

[172] Osnaburg was plain-weave fabric made of flax or tow. Originally from Germany, it was manufactured widely in Scotland and exported to British America and the United States during the eighteenth century.

poultry, some a pig &c their living is by no means so wretched as persons who are unaquainted [sic] with them imagine.

I have seen many families in England among the labouring poor much more wretched than hundreds of the Negro Slaves with whom I [9] have been acquainted.

That which appears the most horrid to a stranger is the loss of freedom, & the thought of never obtaining it. I am fully convinced from a long experience that the Negro does not view freedom in the same light as most considerate white men do. Many Negroes were born slaves in Africa & America. And many in Africa who were not born slaves, their lives were miserable, & to my knowledge many prefer their present to their former state._____

With respect to the Negroes in the upper Country, generally speaking they fare better, in each of the particulars mentioned. [10] A great many live nearly as well as their masters. This is the case generally in families where there are not more then [sic] ten or a dozen. But in all the up country they generally are better fed & cloathed by their owners than on rice plantations; and yet a Negro on a rice plantation is not willing to go up the country; nor are the up country Negroes willing to go to a rice field. In large gangs there are always some who are ill disposed & frequently make disturbances on a plantation by their idleness, theivery [sic] & debauchery. In general, the Negroes are a very proud people. A Negro [11] Slave who has a good Master & is industrious, looks down with contempt or pity on a poor white man, he considers himself a degree above him. The treatment of the Negroes in our Towns varies according to the temper of the Master & the conduct of the slave. Some have good Masters & are well served; others are cruel & use their servants ill. I have remarked in general that the native Carolinians use their slaves better than forigners [sic] of any description. Of late years a great number of the slaves have become serious & are united with religious Societies; & many of them are to all appearance truly pious, these [12] are a restraint on some of a bad character. One of the greatest planters in the State told me, before some of his Negroes became religious, he could scarcely keep a Turkey or any kind of fowl on the plantation; but now Sir said he, those who are truly religious will not only not steal themselves but they prevent others from stealing. However there are a few Masters who will not suffer any thing on the plantation that has the appearance of worship; while others encourage it & give their Slaves permission to join the Methodists, Baptists or what Society they choose. [13] Upon the whole, slavery is attended with many evils & I wish not to defend it. At the same time it is pleasing to a generous mind to view the state of the slave so much better than it was before the American Revolution. There are some persons, either through ignorance of their usage or through prejudice or design shamefully misrepresent to the World their situation.

I really believe that thousands of the Slaves enjoy life with more satisfaction than millions in the world. From my own knowledge I can truly say, many even in England my native Land [14] of the lowest class, work harder, & are not so well fed & cloathed as a field slave in Carolina, who has a good master & is himself honest and industrious.

The punishment inflicted on the Negro is often severe. This is at the discretion of the Master, & therefore varies much.

After all, this kind of Slavery in its best state is a very great evil. It is to be hoped that their condition will continue to meliorate, till some way & means shall be fallen on for their emancipation, which however as matters are circumstanced must be a work of time.

Bibliography

Published Primary Sources

Asbury, Francis. *The Journal and Letters of Francis Asbury*, ed. Elmer T. Clark et al. London: Epworth Press, 1958.

Chanler, Isaac. *New Converts Exhorted to Cleave to the Lord. A Sermon on Acts xi.23. Preach'd July 30, 1740 at a Wednesday Evening-Lecture in Charlestown. Set up at the Motion and by the Desire of the Rev. Mr. Whitefield; with a brief Introduction relating to the Character of that excellent Man.* Boston, MA: D. Fowle, 1740.

DeBenneville, George. *A True and Remarkable Account of Some Passages in the Life of Mr. George DeBenneville, of an Ancient and Noble Protestant Family in Normandy.* Transl. Elhanan Winchester. London, 1791.

Equiano, Olaudah. *The Interesting Narrative of the Life of Olaudah Equiano.* Ed. Robert J. Allison. Boston, MA: Bedford/St. Martin's, 2007.

Furman, Richard. *Life and Works of Richard Furman, DD.* Ed. G. William Foster. Harrisonburg, VA: Sprinkle Publications, 2004.

Furman, Wood. *A History of the Charleston Association of Baptist Churches in the State of South Carolina; with an Appendix containing the principal circular letters to the churches.* Charleston, SC: J. Hoff, 1811.

Garden, Alexander. *Regeneration and the Testimony of the Spirit. Being the Substance of Two Sermons lately Preached in the Parish Church of St. Philip's, Charles-Town, in South-Carolina. Occasioned by some erroneous Notions of certain Men who call themselves Methodists.* Charles-Town, SC: Peter Timothy, 1740; Boston, MA: Thomas Fleet, 1741.

----, ----. *Six Letters to the Reverend Mr. Whitefield. With Mr. Whitefield's Answer to the First Letter.* 2d. ed. Boston, MA: T. Fleet, 1740.

----, ----. *Take Heed How Ye Hear. A Sermon Preached in the Parish Church of St. Philip, Charles-Town, in South Carolina, on Sunday the 13th of July, 1740. With a Preface, containing some Remarks on Mr. Whitefield's Journals.* Charles-Town, SC: Peter Timothy, 1741.

Holcombe, Henry. *A Discourse on the Sovereignty and Unchangeableness of the Deity, 1790.* Charleston, SC: Markland and McIver, 1793.

----, ----. *A Sermon, containing a brief illustration and defense of the Doctrine commonly called Calvinistic, Preached before the Charleston Association of Baptist Churches, 1791.* Charleston, SC: Markland and McIver, 1793.

Lee, Henry. *Memoirs of the War in the Southern Department of the United States.* New York, NY: University Publishing Company, 1869.

Mallary, Charles D. *Memoirs of Edmund Botsford.* Charleston, SC: W. Riley, 1832.

Pugh, Evan. *Diaries, 1762-1801.* Florence, SC: St. David's Society, 1993.

Purry, Jean Pierre. *A Brief Description of the Current State of South Carolina, New Edition, With Clarifications, and Acts of Concession on this subject to the author and for all who desire to join him. And finally, Instructions on necessary conditions to be met by those accompanying him to South Carolina.* Neuchatel: Jacob Boyve, 1732. In *Lands of True and Certain Bounty: the Geographical Theories and Colonization Strategies of Jean Pierre Purry.* Arlin C. Migliazzo, ed. Pierrette C. Christianne-Lovrien and 'Bio-Dun J. Ogundayo, transls. Selinsgrove, PA: Susquehanna University, 2002. 130-163.

Records of the Welsh Tract Baptist Meeting, 1701-1828. Wilmington, DE: The Historical Society of Delaware, 1904.

Rippon, John, ed., *The Baptist Annual Register For 1790, 1791, 1792, and Part of 1793. Including Sketches of the State of Religion among Different Denominations of Good Men at Home and Abroad.* London: Dilly, Button, and Thomas, [1793]; Gale, Eighteenth-Century Collections Online.

----, ----, ed. *The Baptist Annual Register For 1794, 1795, 1796-7. Including Sketches of the State of Religion among Different Denominations of Good Men at Home and Abroad.* London: Dilly, Button, and Thomas, [1797]; Gale, Eighteenth-Century Collections Online.

Siegvolck, Georg Paul. *The Everlasting Gospel commanded to be preached by Jesus Christ unto all creatures concerning the eternal Redemption found out by Him. Being a Testimony against the present Antichristian World.* London, 1795.

South-Carolina Gazette. Charleston, SC, 1732-1777.

Statutes at Large of South Carolina. Vols. 1-5. Ed. Thomas Cooper. Columbia, SC: A.S. Johnston, 1836-1898.

Winchester, Elhanan. *Dialogues on Universal Restoration.* London, 1788.

----, ----. *The Mystics Plea for Universal Redemption.* Philadelphia, PA, 1781.

----, ----. *An Oration on the Discovery of America, Oct. 12, 1792.* London: Keeble & Acutts, 1792.

----, ----. *The Outcasts Comforted; A Sermon Delivered at the University of Philadelphia, January 4th, 1782.* Philadelphia, PA, 1782.

----, ----, *Ten Letters to Mr. Paine, in answer to his pamphlet entitled* The Age of Reason. New York, NY: Samuel Campbell, 1795.

----, ----. *The Three Woe Trumpets.* London: Samuel Reece, 1793.

----, ----. *The Universal Restoration Exhibited in Four Dialogues between a Minister and his Friend Comprehending the Substance of Several Real Conversations which the Author had with various Persons, both in America and Europe, on that Interesting Subject.* Philadelphia, PA: T. Dobson, 1792.

Whitefield, George. *Journals.* Iain Murray, ed. Edinburgh: The Banner of Truth Trust, 1960.

----, ----. *A Letter From the Reverend Mr. Whitefield from Georgia, to a Friend in London, showing the Fundamental Error of a Book, Entituled The Whole Duty of Man.* Charles-Town, SC: Peter Timothy, 1740.

----, ----. *Three Letters from the Reverend Mr. G. Whitefield: Viz. Letter I: To a Friend in London, concerning Archbishop Tillotson. Letter II: To the same, on the same Subject. Letter III: To the Inhabitants of Maryland, Virginia, North- and South-Carolina, concerning their Negroes.* Philadelphia, PA: B. Franklin, 1740.

Woodmason, Charles. *The Carolina Backcountry on the Eve of the Revolution.* Chapel Hill, NC: University of North Carolina, 1953.

Universalism in America: A Documentary History. Ed. Ernest Cassara. Boston, MA:
 Beacon Press, 1971.

Unpublished Primary Sources

Botsford, Edmund. Letters from Edmund Botsford to the Rev. Richard Furman. 4 April
 1785; 17 December 1788; 11 January 1789; 31 August 1789; 15 March 1790; 20
 April 1790; 4 August 1790; 14 February 1791; 17 August 1791; 12 December
 1791; 23 April 1792; 9 July 1792; December 1792; 27 April 1793; 29 August 1793;
 18 November 1793; 14 April 1795; 20 July 1795; 7 October 1795; 10 March 1796;
 10 April 1796; 3 May 1796; 18 July 1796; 12 October 1796; 24 March 1797.
 Botsford Papers, Series I, Folders 1-5, Special Collections, Duke Library, Furman
 University.

----, ----. On Slavery. Botsford Family Collection, Box 3, Folder 54, Special Collections,
 Duke Library, Furman University.

----, ----. A Spiritual Voyage performed between the years 1766 and 1813. Presented to
 Mrs Maryann McIver, a sincere friend to the Author, George Town, 1813. Botsford
 Family Collection, Box 2, Ser. III, Folder 46, Special Collections, Duke Library,
 Furman University.

Cashaway Church Book. Microfilm copy at Furman University, Duke Library, Special
 Collections and Archives.

Edwards, Morgan. "Materials towards a History of the Baptists in the Province of South-
 Carolina." Furman University, Duke Library, Special Collections and Archives.

Hart, Oliver. Diary. Transcribed by Loulie Latimer Owens. Furman University, Duke
 Library, Special Collections and Archives.

Welsh Neck Church Book. Original ms. at Welsh Neck Baptist Church, Society Hill,
 South Carolina. Microfilm copy at Furman University, Duke Library, Special
 Collections and Archives.

Secondary and Reference Sources

Allen, William Cox. *History of the Pee Dee Baptist Association.* Dillon, SC: Pee Dee
 Baptist Association, 1924.

American National Biography. John A. Garraty, Mark C. Carnes, eds. New York, NY:
 Oxford University Press, 1999.

Anderson, Benedict. *Imagined Communities: Reflections on the Origin and Spread of
 Nationalism,* Revised Ed. London: Verso, 1991.

Andrews, Dee E. *The Methodists and Revolutionary America, 1760-1800: The Shaping of
 an Evangelical Culture.* Princeton, NJ: Princeton University, 2000.

Axtell, James. "The Invasion Within: The Contest of Cultures in Colonial North
 America," in *The European and the Indian,* New York, NY: Oxford University
 Press, 1981. 39-86.

Backus, Isaac. *A History of New England with Particular Reference to the Denomination
 of Christians called Baptists.* 2 Vols. Newton, MA: Backus Historical Society,
 1871.

Baker, Robert A. and Paul J. Craven, Jr. *History of the First Baptist Church of
 Charleston, South Carolina, 1682-2007.* Springfield, MO: The Particular Baptist
 Press, 2007.

Barnhill, Andrew Tower. *Reconstituting the Pulpit, establishing the South: the political and religious rhetoric of Richard Furman.* Unpublished thesis, Furman University, 2009.

Barrington, John. "Suppressing the Great Awakening: Alexander Garden's Use of Anti-Popery Against George Whitefield" *Proceedings of the South Carolina Historical Association* (2003): 1-14.

Bassett, T.M. *The Welsh Baptists.* Swansea, Wales: Ilston House, 1977.

Benedict, David. *A General History of the Baptist Denomination in America, and Other Parts of the World.* Boston, MA: Lincoln and Edmands, 1813.

Berlin, Ira. *Many Thousands Gone: The First Two Centuries of Slavery in North America.* Cambridge, MA: Harvard University Press, 1998.

Bonomi, Patricia. *Under the Cope of Heaven: Religion, Society, and Politics in Colonial America.* New York, NY: Oxford University Press, 1986.

Bourguignon, Erica. *Possession.* San Francisco, CA: Changler & Sharp, 1976.

Brackney, William H. *Baptists in North America.* Oxford: Blackwell, 2006.

----, ----. *Congregation and Campus: North American Baptists in Higher Education .* Macon, GA: Mercer University Press, 2008.

----, ----. *Historical Dictionary of the Baptists.* Lanham, MD: Scarecrow Press, 2009.

----, ----. with Charles K. Hartman. "From Ilston to Swansea: A Historical Introduction," in *Baptists in Early North America*, vol. 1: Swansea, Massachusetts. Macon, GA: Mercer University Press, 2013. xiii-cii.

Bradley, Patricia. *Slavery, Propaganda, and the American Revolution.* Oxford, MS: University of Mississippi, 1998.

Bressler, Ann Lee. *The Universalist Movement in America, 1770-1880.* Oxford Scholarship Online, 2001.

Brooks, Walter H. "The Priority of the Silver Bluff Church and its Promoters," *Journal of Negro History*, 7/ 2 (April 1922): 172-183.

Brown, Richard Maxwell. *The South Carolina Regulators.* Cambridge, MA: Harvard University Press, 1963.

Buchanan, John. *The Road to Guilford Courthouse: The American Revolution in the Carolinas.* New York, NY: John Wiley, 1997.

Butler, Jon. *Awash in a Sea of Faith: Christianizing the American People.* Cambridge, MA: Harvard University, 1990.

----, ----. "Power, Authority, and the Origins of American Denominational Order: The English Churches in the Delaware Valley, 1680-1730" *Transactions of the American Philosophical Society*, 68/ 2 (1978): 1-85.

Cashin, Edward J. *Beloved Bethesda: A History of George Whitefield's Home for Boys, 1740-2000.* Macon, GA: Mercer University Press, 2001.

Chase, Malcolm. "From Millennium to Anniversary: The Concept of Jubilee in Late Eighteenth- and Nineteenth-Century England" *Past and Present,* 129 (November 1990): 132-147.

Clayton, J. Glen. "South Carolina Baptist Records," *The South Carolina Historical Magazine*, 85/4 (October 1984): 319-327.

Colley, Linda. *Britons: Forging the Nation, 1707-1837.* New Haven, CT: Yale University Press, 1992.

Bibliography

Cook, Harvey Toliver. *Rambles in the Pee Dee Basin, South Carolina.* Columbia, SC: The State Company, 1926.

Conway, Stephen. "War and National Identity in the Eighteenth-Century British Isles" *The English Historical Review,* 116/468 (September 2001): 863-893.

Creel, Margaret Washington. *"A Peculiar People": Slave Religion and Community Culture among the Gullahs.* New York, NY: New York University Press, 1998.

Davidson, James. *The Logic of Millennial Thought: Eighteenth-Century New England.* New Haven, CT: Yale University Press, 1977.

Davies, Hywel M., "Transatlantic Brethren: Rev. Samuel Jones (1735-1814) and his Friends: Baptists in Wales, Pennsylvania, and Beyond." *Baptist Quarterly* 36 (1995): 132-149.

Davis, David Brion. *The Problem of Slavery in an Age of Revolution, 1770-1823.* Ithaca, NY: Cornell University Press, 1975.

Dowd, Gregory Evans. "The Panic of 1751: The Significance of Rumor on the South Carolina-Cherokee Frontier" in *The William and Mary Quarterly*, 3d. Ser., LIII/3 (July 1996): 527-560.

Drescher, Seymour, "History's Engines: British Mobilization in the Age of Revolution," in *The William and Mary Quarterly*, 3rd. Ser., LXVI/4 (Oct. 2009): 737-756.

Dunaway, W.F. "Early Welsh Settlers of Pennsylvania" *Pennsylvania History: A Journal of Mid-Atlantic Studies,* 12/4 (October 1945): 251-269.

Edgar, Walter. *Partisans and Redcoats: The Southern Conflict that Turned the Tide of the American Revolution.* New York, NY: HarperCollins, 2001.

Encyclopedia of Southern Baptists. Nashville, TN: Broadmen Press, 1958-1962.

Encyclopedia of Southern History, eds. David C. Rollen and Robert W. Twyman. Baton Rouge, LA: Louisiana State University, 1979.

Evans, Charles. *American Bibliography.* New York, NY: Peter Smith, 1941-1959.

Fliegelman, Jay. *Prodigals and Pilgrims: The American Revolution against Patriarchal Authority, 1750-1800.* Cambridge: Cambridge University Press, 1982.

Flinchum, Jessica Lee. "Reluctant Revolutionaries: The Philadelphia Baptist Association and the American Revolution" *Pennsylvania History: A Journal of Mid-Atlantic Studies*, 74/2 (Spring 2007): 173-193.

Frazier, E. Franklin, *The Negro Church in America.* New York, NY: Schocken Books, 1963.

Frey, Sylvia R. and Betty Wood. *Come Shouting to Zion: African American Protestantism in the American South and British Caribbean to 1830.* Chapel Hill, NC: University of North Carolina Press, 1998.

Frey, Sylvia R. *Water from the Rock: Black Resistance in a Revolutionary Age.* Princeton, NJ: Princeton University Press, 1991.

Friedlander, Amy Ellen. "Carolina Huguenots: A Study in Cultural Pluralism in the Low Country, 1679-1768." Ann Arbor, MI: University Microfilms International, 1979.

Gamble, Thomas. *Bethesda: An Historical Sketch of Whitefield's House of Mercy in Georgia.* Savannah, GA: Morning News Print, 1902; Spartanburg, SC: Reprint Co., 1972.

Gardner, Robert G. *Baptists of Early America: A Statistical History, 1639-1790.* Atlanta, GA: Georgia Baptist Historical Society, 1983.

Garrett, Clarke. "Joseph Priestley, the Millennium, and the French Revolution" *Journal of the History of Ideas,* 34/1 (January – March 1973): 51-66.

Genovese, Eugene. *Roll, Jordan, Roll: The World the Slaves Made.* New York, NY: Vintage Books, 1975.

Gilbert, Alan. *Black Patriots and Loyalists: Fighting for Emancipation in the War for Independence.* Chicago, IL: University of Chicago Press, 2015.

Gomez, Michael A. "Muslims in Early America," *Journal of Southern History,* 60 (1994): 671-700.

Gregg, Alexander. *History of the old Cheraws; containing an account of the aborigines of the Pedee...*Columbia, SC: The State Company, 1925.

Griffin, Patrick. "The People with No Name: Ulster's Migrants and Identity-Formation in Eighteenth-Century Pennsylvania," *The William and Mary Quarterly,* 3d Ser., LVIII/3 (July 2001): 587-614.

Groth, Michael E. "Black Loyalists and African American Allegiance in the Mid-Hudson Valley," in *The Other Loyalists: Ordinary People, Royalism, and the Revolution in the Middle Colonies, 163-1787,* Joseph S. Tiedemann, Eugene R. Fingerhut, and Robert W. Venables, eds. Albany, NY: SUNY Press, 2009. 81-104.

Hartmann, Edward George. *Americans from Wales.* Boston, MA: Christopher Publishing, 1967.

Hatch, Nathan. *The Sacred Cause of Liberty: Republican Thought and the Millennium in Revolutionary New England.* New Haven, CT: Yale University Press, 1977.

Hawkins, James Barney, IV. *Alexander Garden: The Commissary in Church and State.* Durham, NC: Duke University, Ph.D. Dissertation, 1981.

Heimert, Alan. *Religion and the American Mind: From the Great Awakening to the Revolution.* Cambridge, MA: Harvard University Press, 1986.

Herskovits, Melville J. *The Myth of the Negro Past.* New York, NY: Harper Brothers, 1941.

Horton, Robin. "African Conversion," *Africa,* XLI (1971): 85-108.

----, ----. *Patterns of Thought in Africa and the West: Essays on Magic, Religion, and Science.* Cambridge: Cambridge University Press, 1993.

Hoyt and Keys, *Historical Sketch of the Welsh Neck Baptist Church, Society Hill, SC.* Columbia, SC: State Printing Co., 1963.

Isaac, Rhys. "Evangelical Revolt: the Nature of the Baptists' Challenge to the Traditional Order in Virginia, 1765 to 1775," *The William and Mary Quarterly,* 3d Ser., XXXI (1974), 345-368.

----, ----. *The Transformation of Virginia, 1740-1790.* Chapel Hill, NC: University of North Carolina Press, 1982.

Jackson, Harvey H. "Hugh Bryan and the Evangelical Movement in Colonial South Carolina" *William and Mary Quarterly,* 3rd Ser., XLIII/4 (October 1986): 594-614.

Jenkins, Geraint H. *The Foundations of Modern Wales, 1642-1780.* Oxford: Oxford University Press, 1993.

Johnson, George Lloyd, Jr. *The Frontier in the Colonial South: South Carolina Backcountry, 1736-1800.* Westport, CT: Greenwood Press, 1997.

Kenney, William Howland III. "Alexander Garden and George Whitefield: the Significance of Revivalism in South Carolina, 1738-1741" *The South Carolina Historical Magazine*, 71 (1970): 1-16.

King, Joe M. *A History of South Carolina Baptists.* Columbia, SC: R.L. Bryan, 1964.

Klein, Rachel. *Unification of a Slave State: the Rise of the Planter Class in the South Carolina Backcountry, 1760-1808.* Chapel Hill, NC: University of North Carolina Press, 1990.

Kolchin, Peter. "Variations of Slavery in the Atlantic World" *The William and Mary Quarterly*, 3rd. Ser., LIX/3 (July 2002): 551-554.

Lambert, Frank. *"Pedlar in Divinity": George Whitefield and the Transatlantic Revivals, 1737-1770.* Princeton, NJ: Princeton University Press, 1994.

----, ----. "Subscribing for Profits and Piety: The Friendship of Benjamin Franklin and George Whitefield," *The William and Mary Quarterly,* 3d Ser., L/3 (July 1993): 529-554.

Linder, Suzanne C., "Pioneer Physicians in Marlboro County," *The South Carolina Historical Magazine*, 81/3 (July 1980): 232-244.

Lindman, Janet Moore. "'Bad Men and Angels from Hell: The Discourse of Universalism in Early National Philadelphia" *Journal of the Early Republic*, 31/2 (Summer 2011): 259-282.

Little, Thomas J.,"The Origins of Southern Evangelicalism: Revivalism in South Carolina, 1700-1740," *Church History*, 75/4 (Dec. 2006): 768-808.

Livingston, Helen E. "Thomas Morritt, Schoolmaster of the Charleston Free School, 1723-1728," *Historical Magazine of the Protestant Episcopal Church,* 14 (June 1945): 151-167.

Massey, Gregory D. "The Limits of Antislavery Thought in the Revolutionary Lower South: John Laurens and Henry Laurens," *The Journal of Southern History*, 63/3 (1997): 495-530.

McCrady, Edward, *The History of South Carolina in the Revolution, 1775-1780.* New York, NY: Russell & Russell, 1969.

McLoughlin, William. *New England Dissent, 1630-1833: The Baptists and the Separation of Church and State.* Cambridge, MA: Harvard University Press, 1971.

Milling, Chapman J. *Exile Without an End*. Columbia, S.C.: Bostick and Thornley, 1943.

Morgan, Philip D. *Slave Counterpoint: Black Culture in the Eighteenth-Century Chesapeake & Lowcountry.* Chapel Hill, NC: University of North Carolina Press, 1998.

Morrill, Dan L. *Southern Campaigns of the American Revolution.* Baltimore, MD: National Aviation and Publishing, n.d.

Mulder, Philip N. *A Controversial Spirit: Evangelical Awakenings in the South.* Oxford: Oxford University Press, 2002.

Mulkey, Floyd, "Rev. Philip Mulkey, Pioneer Baptist Preacher in Upper South Carolina," *South Carolina Historical Association Proceedings* (1945): 3-13.

Mullin, Michael. *Africa in America: Slave Acculturation and Resistance in the American South and the British Caribbean, 1736-1831.* Urbana, IL: University of Illinois Press, 1992.

Nadelhaft, Jerome J. *The Disorders of War: The Revolution in South Carolina.* Orono, ME: University of Maine, 1981.

Noll, Mark. *Christians in the American Revolution.* Grand Rapids, MI: Christian University Press, 1977.

Okoye, F. Nwabueze. "Chattel Slavery as the Nightmare of the American Revolutionaries" in *The William and Mary Quarterly,* 3rd. Ser., XXXVII/1 (January 1980): 3-28.

Owens, Loulie Latimer. *Oliver Hart, 1723-1795: a biography.* Greenville, SC: South Carolina Baptist Historical Society, 1966.

Pancake, John S. *This Destructive War: The British Campaign in the Carolinas, 1780-1782.* Tuscaloosa, AL: University of Alabama Press, 1985.

Prescott, Sarah. "'What Foes more dang'rous than too strong Allies?': Anglo-Welsh Relations in Eighteenth-Century London" *Huntington Library Quarterly,* 69/4 (December 2006): 535-554.

Quarles, Benjamin. "The Revolutionary War as a Black Declaration of Independence," in Ira Berlin and Ronald Hoffman, eds., *Slavery and Freedom in the Age of the American Revolution.* Charlottesville, VA: University of Virginia Press, 1983. 283-304.

Raboteau, Albert J. *Slave Religion: The 'Invisible Institution' in the Antebellum South.* Oxford: Oxford University Press, 1978.

Rogers, James A. *Richard Furman: Life and Legacy.* Macon, GA: Mercer University Press, 1985.

Rucker, Walter. "Conjure, Magic, and Power: The Influence of Afro-Atlantic Religious Practices on Slave Resistance and Rebellion," *Journal of Black Studies,* 32 (Sept. 2001): 84-103.

Russell, Charles D. "Islam as a Danger to Republican Virtue: Broadening Religious Liberty in Revolutionary Pennsylvania" *Pennsylvania History: A Journal of Mid-Atlantic Studies,* 76/ 3 (Summer 2009): 250-275.

Ryan, William R. *The World of Thomas Jeremiah: Charles-Town on the Eve of the American Revolution.* Oxford: Oxford University Press, 2010.

Schama, Simon. *Rough Crossings: Britain, the Slaves, and the American Revolution* Schama, Simon. *Rough Crossings: Britain, the Slaves, and the American Revolution.* New York, NY: Ecco, 2006.

Scherer, Lester B. *Afro-American Baptists: A Guide to Materials in the American Baptist Historical Society.* Rochester, NY: American Baptist Historical Society, 1985.

Schlenther, Boyd Stanley. "'The English is Swallowing Up Their Language: Welsh Ethnic Ambivalence in Colonial Pennsylvania and the Experience of David Evans" *Pennsylvania Magazine of History and Biography,* 114/2 (April 1990): 201-228.

Schmidt, Leigh Eric. "'A Second & Glorious Reformation': The New Light Extremism of Andrew Croswell" in *The William and Mary Quarterly,* 3d. Ser., 43/2 (April 1986): 214-244.

Shields, David. *Oracles of Empire: Poetry, Politics, and Commerce in British America, 1690-1750.* Chicago, IL: University of Chicago, 1990.

Sirmans, M. Eugene. *Colonial South Carolina, a Political History, 1663-1763.* Chapel Hill, NC: University of North Carolina, 1966.

Bibliography

Sobel, Michel. *Trabelin' On: The Slave Journey to an Afro-Baptist Faith.* Westport, CT: Greenwood Press, 1979.

Spradlin, Derrick. "'God ne'er brings to pass such things for nought': Empire and Prince Madoc of Wales in Eighteenth-Century America" *Early American Literature*, 44/1 (2009): 39-70.

Spangler, Jewel. *Virginians Reborn: Anglican Monopoly, Evangelical Dissent, and the Rise of Baptists in the Late Eighteenth Century.* Charlottesville, VA: University of Virginia Press, 2008.

Stokes, Durward T. "The Baptist and Methodist Clergy in South Carolina and the American Revolution" *The South Carolina Historical Magazine,* 73/2 (April 1972): 87-96.

Stone, Edwin Martin. *Biography of Rev. Elhanan Winchester.* Boston, MA: E.B. Brewster, 1836; reprint New York, NY: Arno Press, 1972.

Stout, Harry. "Religion, Communications, and the Ideological Origin of the American Revolution," *The William and Mary Quarterly,* 3d Ser., 34/4 (Oct. 1977), 519-541.

Strickland, John Scott. "Across Space and Time: Conversion, Community, and Cultural Change among South Carolina Slaves" Chapel Hill, NC: University of North Carolina, Ph.D. Dissertation, 1985.

Thomas, Hugh. *The Slave Trade: The History of the Atlantic Slave Trade, 1440-1870.* New York, NY: Simon & Schuster, 1997.

Thornton, John K. "African Dimensions of the Stono Rebellion," *American Historical Review,* 96/4 (Oct. 1991): 1101-1113.

Tolles, Frederick B. "The Culture of Early Pennsylvania," *The Pennsylvania Magazine of History and Biography*, 81/ 2 (April 1957): 119-137.

Townsend, Leah. "Discipline in Early Baptist Churches," in *The South Carolina Historical Magazine,* 54/3 (July 1953): 129-134.

----, ----. *South Carolina Baptists, 1670-1805.* Florence, SC: Florence Printing, 1935.

Tuveson, Ernest. *Redeemer Nation: the Ideology of America's Millennial Role.* Chicago, IL: University of Chicago, 1968.

Tyler, Lyon G. "The Gnostic Trap: Richard Clarke and his Proclamation of the Millennium and Universal Restoration in South Carolina and England," *Anglican and Episcopal History*, 58/ 2 (June 1989): 146-168.

Wallace, David Duncan. *South Carolina: A Short History, 1520-1948.* Chapel Hill, NC: University of North Carolina Press, 1951.

Williams, Gwyn A. *Madoc: The Legend of the Welsh Discovery of America.* Oxford: Oxford University Press, 1987.

Wood, Betty. *Slavery in Colonial America, 1619-1776.* Lanham, MD: Rowman & Littlefield, 2005.

Wood, Peter. *Black Majority: Negroes in South Carolina from 1670 through the Stono Rebellion.* New York, NY: W.W. Norton, 1974.

Woolverton, John Frederick. *Colonial Anglicanism in North America.* Detroit, MI: Wayne State University Press, 1984.

Wright, Donald R. "Recent Literature on Slavery in Colonial North America," *Organization of American Historians Magazine of History,* 17/3 (April. 2003): 5-9.

Wright, Louis B. *South Carolina: A Bicentennial History*. New York, NY: W.W. Norton, 1976.

Yewlett, Hilary Lloyd, "Early Modern Migration from the Mid-Wales County of Radnorshire to Southeastern Pennsylvania, with Special Reference to Three Meredith Families," *Pennsylvania History: A Journal of Mid-Atlantic Studies*, 79/1 (Winter 2012): 1-32.

Index

PERSONS

Index

Luke, Elizabeth (second of this name on
 1775-1779 list) 28
Luke, Joseph 27, 34, 37, 39
Luke, Sarah (see Winchester, Sarah, third
 wife of Elhanan)
Luke, William 27, 44, 48, 59
Lyon, Rev. Ebenezer xliii
Madoc, Prince vii
Magee, Martha (wife of Rev. Pugh) xxxvii
Manning, Dr. 87
Maria (baptized June 5, 1784) 51
Marsh (baptized March 1798) 72
Marshall, Rev. Daniel lxxx
Martin, Martha 12, 19, 23, 24
Mason, Charles 27, 42, 43, 44, 58
Mason, Elizabeth (wife of Joseph) 28, 41, 70
Mason, Joseph (husband of Elizabeth) 27,
 41, 49
Mason, Thomas 70
Mason, William 27, 34, 35, 37
Massy (or Massey), Elizabeth 33, 37
McCullen, Mr. 88, 91
McDaniel, Daniel 27, 40, 47, 51
McDaniel, Sarah 4
McDonald, Mr. 78
McDonald, Mrs. 81
McIntosh, Alexander xxiii, xxiv, xxxvi, 12;
 owner of baptized slaves lv, lvi, lxix,
 41, 42, 43, 51, 72; and Regulators
 xxxix-xlii
McIntosh, Jane (née Jones, wife of
 Alexander) xxxv, 5, 17
McIntosh, John civ, 65, 89, 107
McIver, Catharine (see Botsford, Caty)
McIver, Evander (deacon) civ, 27, 72, 73;
 and African American members 48, 63;
 baptized 44, 45; and church property
 59, 61, 62, 64, 67; keeps Church Book
 cv, 71; messenger to Charleston
 Association 49, 53, 65, 68, 69, 98n;
 revises church covenant 54; trustee 58,
 70
McIver, John 77, 79, 80, 84, 90, 106
McIver, Maryann, 109
McIver, Roderick xxiii, xxiv, 12
McIver, Sarah 28
McNatt, Dinah 26, 37
McNatt, Joel (husband of Martha) 27, 43,
 44, 62
McNatt, Macky 37, 69, 70, 71
McNatt, Martha (baptized June 1779) 28, 40
McNatt, Martha (baptized August 1779,
 wife of Joel) 28, 43, 44
Medford, Elizabeth 29, 42, 48

Mickill, Mr. 85
Mingo (baptized June 27, 1779) 41
Mingo (baptized July 25, 1779) 42
M'Lemore, Agnes 23
Monaghon (or Monochon), Barbara 3, 13
Monahon (or Monochon), Daniel 4, 11
Moore, Rev. 42
Morgan, Rev. Abel ix
Morgan, Celete 28, 40
Morphy, Mary (wife of Rev. Bedgegood)
 xxxii
Morris (baptized August 1, 1779) 43
Mosely, Mr. 85, 87, 88, 89, 91, 92
Moses (baptized June 5, 1784) 51, 66
Mulkey, Philip xxxvn, xlv, lix, lxviii, lxxxi,
 26, 47; conversion, xvn
Mumford, Sarah 28, 43, 44
Murray, John lxxvi
Nancy (baptized July 25, 1779) 42
Ned (baptized August 1, 1779) 43
Newbery, Sarah xviii
Nun, Susanna (see Susanna Botsford)
Orange (baptized August 1797) 72
Owen, Jeremy vi
Paine, Thomas lxxvii
Paisley, Mrs. 80
Parish, Gideon lxxxiv, 27, 39, 40, 47
Parsley, Robert 67
Patty (baptized August 1, 1779) 43
Pearce, Josiah (husband of Mary) 27, 40, 42
Pearce, Martha (see Sparks, Martha)
Pearce, Mary (wife of Josiah) 40
Pearce, Mary (see Thomas, Mary)
Pearson, Aaron (husband of Winiford) 27,
 34, 37, 53, 70
Pearson, Comfort 28, 42
Pearson, Moses (husband of Rachel) 27, 34,
 37, 49, 54
Pearson, Rachel (wife of Moses) 27, 34, 37,
 54
Pearson, Winiford (wife of Aaron) 28, 34,
 37, 70
Peck, Sarah (see Winchester, Sarah)
Peg (baptized August 22, 1784) 52
Peggy (baptized August 1, 1779) 43
Pelot, Rev. Francis xxxiv, lxxx
Penn, William iv, v, vii
Perkins, John 4, 6, 36
Phebe (baptized August 1797) 72
Pickering, Timothy lxxvii
Pilgrim, Amos 27, 34, 36
Pilgrim, Elizabeth 27, 34, 36
Pinckney, Roger xli
Plato (baptized June 27, 1779) 41

Places

Index

SUBJECTS

Index